Walking Targets:

How Our Psychologized Classrooms are Producing a Nation of Sitting Ducks

"I'm afraid you won't ever have the luxury of throwing in the towel. You are a leader, Beverly. A leader must consider how what they do will affect the people watching them. An old saying is 'Noblesse oblige.' You may not technically be nobility, but figuratively, you are. Thank you for all the great books, articles."

Charlene Sanders
Hot Springs, Arkansas

Walking Targets:

How our Psychologized Classrooms are Producing a Nation of Sitting Ducks

An examination of how educators and provocateurs
drive a wedge between parents and their children
B. K. EAKMAN

Midnight Whistler Publishers – Since 1979

Library of Congress Control Number: 2007941951

ISBN 978-0-6151-8122-6

First Edition

Cover Design by
Eileen Batson

.

Special Thanks to: K. Winfield
for her expertise in proofreading the manuscript.

Midnight Whistler Publishers
PO Box 91161
Raleigh, NC 27675-1161
midnightwhistler@gmail.com

Table of Contents

Articles--Subdivided by Category

ACKNOWLEDGMENTS

Among the fascinating aspects of having such a varied professional background—education, the space program, a presidential commission, the Voice of America, the U.S. Department of Justice and more—is exposure to a vast assortment of perspectives. My colleagues over the years have brought with them widely differing experiences relative to the issues of the day. In the process, they underscored the importance of anticipating in one's writings the reactions of individuals across the spectrum of any particular topic. For this reason, I am probably a better feature writer than an op-ed writer. The constraints of a 700-word op-ed format do not allow for a reasoned response to counter-arguments. There are those, of course, who excel in a short-and-pithy format, and do so admirably. But in working for so many years alongside people who are all over the place politically, I am more comfortable responding to what I imagine to be their comebacks even as I am penning the piece.

I am especially grateful to Jon Batson—songwriter, performer and novelist—and, more importantly, my good friend going back some 40 years. It was he who coaxed me (kicking and screaming) back into the writing mood by offering to take on the task of formatting my articles and speeches to accommodate a new kind of medium. To him fell the daunting task of comprehending and applying—then explaining to me (a slow learner)—the technical aspects of online communication mediums such as "MySpace," "YouTube" and "Lulu." As the concept of a literary agent and editor (in the form most of us once knew them) becomes passé, and as every word uttered or written down by a known entity is picked up and translated into multiple languages almost instantaneously, it becomes increasingly critical to keep up with the fast-growing, ever-changing, brave new world of Googles, Yahoos, blogs and "e-zines." So, to Jon, and to his wife, Eileen, go the kudos for bringing me up to speed—even if he had to do the job himself to get me onboard. Eileen Batson, for her part, has been

B. K. Eakman

invaluable in dealing with press and promotional issues. Her skill and diplomacy has turned what many authors think of as a "ritual of authorship" into a pleasurable experience.

I must thank Paul Walter, editor of what has become an online news/op-ed/commentary giant, NewsWithViews, for getting me involved with this new medium and forum, for putting loyalty to his writers above profit, and for being a refreshing representative of American journalistic tradition. Paul doesn't shy away from controversy, even within the conservative framework, recognizing that even authors usually in political agreement often see an issue from an angle that winds up placing the whole topic in a different light. Too many conservative organizations today have lost sight of what it means to have a true debate, or discussion, and thankfully, Paul has seen to it that his online service is not one of them.

Mark Salser, Executive Director of Halcyon House Publishers, has, since publishing my first book in 1991, been a person I could run an idea by. I thank Mark for forwarding to me research that comes his way, just to be sure I didn't miss it. He and other editors of my previous works, such as Scott Richert, executive editor of *Chronicles: A Magazine of the American Culture*, have been very thoughtful in passing along information in my areas of expertise and interest. Numerous state legislators around the nation have done the same, and I try to accommodate them, on my own time, by looking over legislative proposals they send me for loopholes.

And finally, acknowledgments would not be complete without mentioning my husband, David, whose patience and attention to business details has been invaluable. He has unfailingly looked out for my interests and supported me in the long hours that the writing life entails.

FOREWORD

The Road To Psychopolitics

This book is an anthology of my most popular columns, feature articles, speeches and lectures over the past 15 years. The book responds to scores of requests to create a compilation of my less widely disseminated lectures and printed works.

My primary focus, at least initially, was education and childrearing. Home and family necessarily became tangential issues—all reflected in my first book, *Educating for the New World Order* (Halcyon House, 1991). As government progressively inserted itself into the schools and impinged upon parental prerogatives, preventive psychology and privacy got incorporated into the mix—especially something called "predictive behavioral assessment." The result was a second book, *Microchipped: How the Education Establishment Took Us Beyond Big Brother* (Halcyon House, 1994). It was a collection of my speeches up to that time detailing an emerging capability to collect, assess and predict behavior patterns. The book exposed the first large-scale assessment projects, most of which were piloted in educational institutions. One side-effect was that schools became less about substantive knowledge and more about profiling and political correctness. This formed the basis of what would later come to be known as *data-mining*.

I was right on target—more than I knew. Rapid advances in computer technology since 1994, coupled to an alarmingly aggressive psychopharmaceutical industry, capitalized on data collection, behavioral analysis and sharing of heretofore personal information, bringing new meaning to the term "p.c."—an acronym that has come to symbolize the imposition of **p**olitical **c**orrectness by means of a **p**ersonal **c**omputer.

I was also among the first to warn in 1994 of a surgically implanted human ID chip—then in the offing—that included GPS tracking capability. By 2002, such devices were selling for big bucks under names like "the Babysitter," "the Constant Companion," "the Invisible Bodyguard," and "the Micro-

3

B. K. Eakman

Manager"—and some parents were buying them. In a 2002 piece included in this anthology, "The Slippery Slope of Safety" (for *Chronicles: A Magazine of American Culture*), I predicted that the next step would involve implanted ID's for the military as the forerunner to a nationwide initiative to equip the ID chip for links to other databases. (A front-page news story in August 2006 in the *Washington Post*'s "Examiner" has since confirmed that prediction.)

Finally, there was my international award-winning classic, *Cloning of the American Mind: Eradicating Morality Through Education* (Huntington House 1998)—my response to calls for a more in-depth treatment of the marriage between psychology, education, data transfer, behavior prediction and advertising.

Schools had, by that time, embarked upon a nightmarish partnership with agencies of government and tax-exempt foundations (including some friendly to hostile foreign countries, such as the Aspen Institute for Humanistic Studies). The result discouraged innovative thinkers and encouraged a process mentality. True investigative reporting became the purview of "mavericks" instead of the hallmark of a free press. A kind of political conformity emerged that would have made Adolf Hitler and Vladimir Lenin proud. My 2001 seminar manual, *How To Counter Group Manipulation Tactics* (now in its third update and printing), details how professional provocateurs and agitators have morphed from their Marxist beginnings, manipulating both data and the political process at all levels of government. School curricula and textbooks became symptomatic of this larger effort.

Cloning of the American Mind was a difficult book to write because it meant explaining three facets of a complicated puzzle —computerization, psychological profiling and affective (noncognitive) teaching methodologies—and then showing how these became institutionalized in our nation's schools through the lobbying and legislative processes. It also entailed naming names, nailing down money trails and laying bare the pages of hundreds of old documents and speeches which their originators would just as soon have left buried.

Mandatory drugging of nonconformists, slow learners and naughty kids has since emerged as a fourth component in the massive agenda to engineer uniformity of opinion without appearing blatant about it. While mind-altering drugs are nothing new, they have come a long way since Baby Boomers gave them cultural legitimacy in the late 1960s by assigning recreational value to them. What Boomers didn't realize while they were "giving peace a chance" and "making love not war" was that governments around the world had long had their eye on psychotropic substances for more practical, political reasons. The sticking point, until about 1970, was a lack of general acceptance for mind-altering drugs, much less public enthusiasm, along the lines, for example, that alcoholic beverages have traditionally enjoyed. Even today, the World War II generation, now well on in years, tend to just "suck it up"—or maybe turn to alcohol—before they will accept a drug to ease the pain of their infirmities.

This "stiff upper lip" business seems like nonsense to former beatniks, hippies and their now-grown offspring. On the other hand, once Baby Boomers started reproducing, most were not so keen about "turning on and dropping out." Yet, there was no turning back. Counterculture Boomers had, inadvertently or not, opened a Pandora's Box that would be used against them, their families—and, indeed, the entire free world.

Schools, of course, were perfect incubators for a popular drug culture—and, for that matter, a "popularity" culture. The compulsion to be accepted and admired (based on nothing more than physical appearance or affability) created a time bomb in our post-war, recreation-driven society. Young people were jockeying for popularity points almost from the moment they boarded the school bus. This obsession to be part of the "in" crowd trained them, in effect, to view matters of public policy (as well as candidates for public office) through the lens of trendiness.

Little wonder that adult society soon became consumed with celebrity and the emotional status of its members rather than with larger matters of principle. With the help of the entertainment industry, a Charisma Culture emerged that gradually drifted away from old ideals about individual merit and integrity. Increasingly, people settled for emotionally satisfying, short-term "fixes," both literally and figuratively, leaving life's complex problems to anyone who would take them.

That made it fairly easy to govern by opinion-poll, the stuff from which predictive attitude assessments are made. Soon questionnaires and surveys of every kind were ubiquitous. Twenty- and thirty-somethings could scarcely get enough of them. In an increasingly impersonal society, important people and influential organizations seemed to be soliciting the individual viewpoints of the rank and file. The equivalents of Oprah Winfrey, Jerry Springer, Katie Couric or Barbara Walters were interviewing them *personally*—and Boomers, despite their renowned cynicism, were just naïve enough to believe their opinions would matter. Little did Boomers realize they were non-persons in a gigantic market-research analysis aimed at determining how many people were buying a certain magazine or listening to a particular celebrity.

Their youngsters, meanwhile, were filling out opinion polls and surveys of their own in the classroom—under the umbrella of social studies, health, sex education, and whatnot. Their parents barely gave it a second thought—until the other shoe dropped. Suddenly their kids came home saying that some of the surveys were asking questions about Mom and Dad. About their finances. Their methods of discipline. Their attitudes toward current events. Their medications.

What the heck was going on?

Inquiring parents wanted to know. But once Boomer parents started scrutinizing all this activity, they noticed that computerization was playing a disturbing role in data-gathering, data transfer, data retention, and data analysis. The few mothers and fathers who could afford it decided it was time to do a little data-*laundering* to fight back. They hired programmers to surreptitiously change or expunge embarrassing information. Others challenged schools on the legality and ethics of collecting such information from their children in the first place. What they got for their trouble was the runaround, and even a police escort from the school premises.

When I first brought these matters to the attention of legislators on Capitol Hill, I was told by some that I was being "alarmist." But once the 9/11 attacks on the World Trade Center and the Pentagon catapulted security to the top of the political agenda, citizens suddenly became acquainted with terms like *data-mining*, meaning the collection and (more importantly) the linking of personal information, and *psycho-behavioral profiling*, meaning personality and conduct assessment based on perceptions about connections and relationships, true or not, wrested from computers. Apparently, concerns over computerized data-gathering and cross-matching weren't so "alarmist," after all, and in fact predictive profiling required only a bit of tweaking before going national in a big way.

Capitalizing on the 1995 Texas Medication Algorithm Project (TMAP)—a pilot alliance of individuals from the pharmaceutical industry, the University of Texas, and the mental health and corrections systems of Texas under former governor George W. Bush—a model mental health assessment-and-treatment plan was established with the intent of taking it to the federal level. New and expensive antidepressant and antipsychotic drugs were given a huge public relations boost, with the long-term aim of garnering support for psychological profiling and expanding coercive mental health treatment programs (including the use of mind-altering drugs). The plan was to begin with schoolchildren and teachers, then expand to evaluating parents—through Parts B and C of Individuals With Disabilities Education Act (IDEA). In 2006, the U.S. House Appropriations Committee approved $20 million in new federal monies to revamp TMAP into a nationwide, universal mental health screening program, under the Marxist-like moniker "New Freedom Initiative." For the first time in American history, average citizens worried about being targeted by their own government, not from agents looking down the barrel of a gun, but by behavioral psychologists working the "barrel" of a computer keyboard.

State-level copycat legislation was already in the works—a typical ploy when the federal government badly wants a nationwide initiative. What the feds do is apply pressure and/or offer financial incentives to the state governors, who, in turn, get help crafting the legislative wording through the Commission on Uniform State Laws.

The upshot in this case is that young people are being assessed early on for individualistic tendencies as part of their psycho-behavioral assessments. Controversial opinions, unconventional attitudes or just general quirkiness can exclude pupils from career paths that might lead to positions of influence or leadership.

"Bushwhacking Johnny," featured in this anthology, is an examination of precisely how educators and provocateurs drive a wedge between parents and their children, utilizing a method known to professionals as "scientific coercion" and "cognitive dissonance"—which are key to surreptitiously extracting information and implementing the kinds of values changes that bypass the use of military force.

While this anthology was being compiled and edited, it occurred to me that what I had actually spent 15 years chronicling was something called *psychopolitics*. Once the stuff of science-fiction, *psychopolitics* has assumed a permanent place in daily life—not only in the United States, but throughout the free world. Think of it as Intimidation 101 for the 21st Century. Its purpose: to avoid a military showdown—a civil war—while turning out a population of sitting ducks that thinks with their emotions instead of facts and reason.

The term *psychopolitics* found its way into the American lexicon via Isaac Asimov, still the unsurpassed master of the sci-fi genre, although he may have borrowed it from lesser-known thinkers who alluded to the concept back in the 1930s and 40s. For centuries, various dictators, world leaders, religious extremists and even journalists (such as they were hundreds of years ago) have coveted the capability to somehow coerce a populace into "internalizing" (accepting as though it were one's own idea) whatever attitudes, viewpoints and opinions augmented the ruling elite's vision of how the world ought to be. This typically entailed the use of spies, intimidation, secret police and political (also known as *psychiatric*) prisons.

But now ethically challenged leaders have another option.

Most people have long known, deep down, that computers make it possible to correlate dissimilar and contrasting data points in such a way as to ensure that a person looks bad—by implication, innuendo and insinuation. Key segments of something one said or did can be excised, while non-germane chitchat is woven in amongst a mixture of facts and half-truths, until no one but an expert programmer can prove the difference.

Ratcheting up the pressure a couple of notches, experts began to merge advertising with computer science and psychology, creating a technique known as *psychographics*. This term, well-known in public relations circles, is self-explanatory; it combines psychological, demographic and economic factors to create a sales package that will appeal to a specific group. Once that is accomplished, constructing an advertising campaign targeted to a *single individual* becomes viable.

Suddenly, yesterday's neighborhood junk mail got recast as a pop-up ad on someone's personal computer—a considerable refinement over clumsier attempts to tailor an idea to an audience via old-fashioned whistle-stops and town-hall-style meetings, which are more easily recorded and compared by different demographic blocs. The ultimate advertisement is to target a child through "individualized" school curriculum and entertainment.

Thus did *psychopolitics* "morph" from its incarnation among science-fiction *aficionados* into a tool that allows attitudes to be assessed, predicted, tracked, monitored and possibly modified—from childhood on—all via computer. Because computers can link information and regurgitate it in such a way that any surrounding context is obscured or replaced, the modern educational system serves as a kind of sieve through which a pupil's actions and words are judged. The trend continues into adulthood, owing to an ever-increasing sophistication of computer cross-matching and individual targeting capability.

Twentieth-century programmers were not the first to consider the filtering potential inherent in educational settings. A renowned behavioral eugenicist of the 1920s, Paul Popenoe, foresaw what was at that time just beyond the grasp of his colleagues, the age of the computer being a few short decades away. Prophetically, he insisted that "the education system should be a sieve, through which all the children of [a] country are passed.... It is very desirable that no child escape inspection."

Which brings up the rationale behind the title of my 1998 book, *Cloning of the American Mind* (Popenoe's quote, from the 1926 *Journal of Heredity* appears on the title page). Many people thought the title itself was a play on words mimicking the 1987 best-seller by Allan Bloom—**Closing** *of the American Mind*. Bloom's book was on education, too, and its purpose was to signal the looming intellectual crisis and degenerating moral climate caused by—guess what?—failed schooling. When my publisher suggested the "Cloning" title (I had submitted a different one), I almost rejected it out-of-hand as too gimmicky. But then I happened on an old quote by Gus Hall, USA Communist Party Chief: "The battle [for freedom of speech in America] will be lost, not when freedom of speech is finally taken away, but when Americans become so adjusted or conditioned to 'getting along with the group' that, when they see a threat, they say: 'But I can't afford to be controversial!'"

I concluded that my publisher was right, after all. "Cloning" was precisely the right term because it implies an attempt to homogenize thought, not merely to "sanitize" it through semantic sleights of hand. With the cultural elite firmly entrenched—in this case, wealthy socialists and closet Marxists, including much of government's federal bureaucracy —it is possible to destroy a person's incentive to express a different opinion on "sacred cow" topics that are critical to the larger agenda—because that's what it comes down to once "experts" start deciding which thoughts are acceptable and which ones are not. When it becomes possible, via technology, to track and legislate private opinions—and even to classify those that don't conform as "mental illnesses"—then we have left the realm of politics and are talking about a tool of coercion: psychological coercion. Pragmatism and expediency necessarily become substitutes for independent thought, and presto! Psychopolitics is a *fait accompli*.

In a society that once prided itself on ideals like self-sufficiency, self-determination and independence, it is no small feat to institutionalize political correctness. Yet today, in the United States of America—the "last bastion of hope" and the "beacon of freedom"—livelihoods are made or ruined based upon the equivalent of snippets gathered off editing-room floors. By the time a victim gets around to damage-control, it is too late to salvage one's reputation.

When I wrote my two-part column, "Lost," in January 2006, I realized that the bad guys were winning by a landslide no matter who, technically, was in office. The catastrophic value changes that had assaulted America's unique place in the world since the late 1940s had become virtually unstoppable. The pendulum was not going to swing back, at least nowhere close to my lifetime, and certainly not without help.

Middle America—the folks we once called the "backbone" of society—had waited too long. While a few of the saner heads among the traditionalists and constitutionalists did speak out, they were being overwhelmed by a political correctness and greed factor they seemed powerless to deal with. Inevitably, the "backbone" fractured. Some conservative leaders suddenly developed enormous egos to go along with their trust funds. They were busier defending turf than supporting colleagues.

Limited financial resources played a role—and that should have been a sign right there that we were losing. If patriotic Americans were a majority, why should their resources be "limited"? Clearly the left-wing had no such problem.

Most conservatives never saw what hit them. When I returned to Washington, DC, after a 20-year absence and began applying for entry-level jobs in conservative think-tanks and political action organizations, I was asked to try my hand at answering letters sent in by donors and potential members. An hour or so later I turned in a fist-full of responses and was told that I was "way over-qualified for this job."

Wondering how anyone could be over-qualified for a job like that, I interjected: "But were the letters okay?"

"Way too good for 'okay'," came the response.

Only later did I realize what the game was: The organizations in question had no interest in actually corresponding with the public, or in carrying on a dialogue with the man-in-the-street. It was all about "show me the money." What they wanted was a boilerplate response such as "thank you for taking your time to share your concerns and ideas with us. Do you think you might be able to send an extra donation of $____ this year so that we can get the word out about this?" The blank was to be filled in by checking the computer to see how much the addressee had contributed previously.

Computerized methods that cross-match potential interested parties and create data bases make it easy to send out real and phony survey materials, too. An organization can even go so far as to add a blank marked "Other____" so that an individual might write in a different option or express a concern.

Whether it's the Fraternal Order of Police, Planned Parenthood, or the Republican Party, there is really no interest in what an average donor thinks. Solicitors work from a script, and the person who calls or writes may, in fact, not even be connected with the organization in question.

Like solicitations for high-speed Internet, phone systems and other big-ticket items, mailings are generally composed by a public relations firm. In the case of politics, all returned responses, with or without the coveted donations, are opened at "fulfillment houses." There, envelopes containing polling materials are separated from the checks. Comments in the "Other____" blank usually go into the circular file along with the rest of the survey. Another round of solicitation letters are churned out from the actual donations.

The message seemed clear: If you have at least five figures in spare change lying around, have at it! Be a part of the super-platinum-charter-member-whatever-club. You will be wined and dined. You will be listened to politely, whether or not anyone on the campaign follows up on your suggestion. But, should you have somewhere between $5 and $500 to donate, just fork it over and shut up.

More importantly, predictive behavioral technology (which made "individualized" solicitations possible in the first place) basically cut its teeth in the nation's schools—using nosy questionnaires passed off as being personalized. That, and the fact that one can "test" for things like gullibility, has changed everything from campaign strategy to marketing tactics—which, by the way, are pretty much the same thing. Our technical know-how has outstripped our legal system's ability to deal with it. Only 50 years ago people spoke in terms of laws, constitutional rights and morality; today's courts are enmeshed in the kinds of "technicalities" that depend upon "what the definition of 'is' is."

Initially, the notion of universal screening faced serious privacy concerns, both from the public and state legislators. But with each new violent atrocity, such as the 2007 shootings at Virginia Tech, comes more calls to ferret out "nut cases" before they can inflict serious bodily harm. Unfortunately, mental health screening has a poor track record in uncovering people like Seung-hui Cho at Virginia Tech. One of the reasons can be found in a column by the renowned professor, Walter Williams: "All the things that used to develop character [are] suddenly politically incorrect.... Society's first line of defense—morality—soon bit the dust, and laws, the second line of defense" have mostly been used to target traditionalists. So, if mental health screening is ineffective in identifying the dangerously violent, then it must have an ulterior purpose. That purpose appears to be locating and tracking the politically incorrect as they wend their way from the classroom to the boardroom.

Meanwhile, modifying attitudes is accomplished through media campaigns so subtle that they can spread disinformation, provide "infotainment" instead of news, and "pitch" ideas as either popular or unfashionable. Each new graduating class is increasingly flummoxed by information overload—owing in part to their dumbed-down education. Thus do a majority of Americans wind up "buying" a lot of baloney—from catch-phrases like "global warming" to "sustainable development"—that will cost them dearly down the road, once officials start going through people's trash receptacles for forbidden items, artificially reducing the standard of living, enacting draconian energy and emissions mandates and attempting to reduce the world's population to 300 million people.[a]

Despite the ease of access to research via the Internet—as opposed to trudging to the library and poring over old-fashioned card catalogs to investigate the hard science behind the various claims—most folks have little inclination to sort out the truth from the hype. The crush of spam, computer viruses, worms and "spyware" has further discouraged people from serious inquiry—which could be one motive behind the enormous spike in such assaults to our computers over the past couple of years.

Even though most folks know they aren't getting the whole story, they opt for turning on the television, scanning news magazines, and reading the local newspaper. Parents often go to great lengths to assure that their children get into prestigious universities, imagining their kids will "learn how to think." Instead, they will learn *what* to think—all the while failing to notice a certain pattern when it comes to addressing hot-button topics that *should* be subject to free and open debate, but somehow are not.

Is there truly a field called "political psychology"?

Unbeknownst, apparently, to hundreds of thousands of Americans, there has been a bona fide discipline for at least 22 years (longer if you count government intelligence circles) known as "political psychology." As recently as the November 2007 issue of Washingtonian Magazine, an article by Ken Adelman appeared in which he interviewed Jerrold Post, former CIA analyst, author and founder of the Center for Analysis of

a   "First do no harm," Woody Zimmerman, at-large columnist for the *Atlantic Highlands Herald*, from a letter to the editor piece published in *The Washington Times*, May 27, 2007, p. B-5. Many science writers and best-selling authors like Michael Creighton have pointed to the same agenda items and set out a list of references to check on the subject.

Personality and Political Behavior, who also established a degree program at George Washington University in political psychology. He has testified in his capacity as political psychologist before Congress and the United Nations and written psychological profiles of Osama bin Laden, Saddam Hussein, Hugo Chavez, Mahmoud Ahmadinejad, and Kim Jong Il, among other high-profile, international figures. Mr. Post is taken very seriously, and nobody in his large circle of influence even bats an eye at the term "political psychology." He describes his specialty as the study of "the political personality." The interview in the Washingtonian portrays him as a legitimate observer of what goes into the making of a leader —or, for that matter, a terrorist. It would be hard to argue with some of his observations as described in the article, and there is no hint whatsoever of his ever attempting to use political psychology to either screen youngsters or "dig up dirt," as it were, on average citizens, much less schoolchildren.

Still, his work—and more significantly, his program at George Washington University—points to a disquieting reality: "psychopolitics" is fast becoming a factor that defines a person's legitimacy (or lack thereof)—whether a student, an employee, a journalists or other person of potential influence. So, it should come as no surprise that psychological (or "mental health") profiling is becoming part and parcel of the education experience, or that it has been put to use as a screening mechanism for the future workforce, for candidates running (or being tapped) for public office, or even for parenthood. As long as we have mental "health" profiles—in reality, a combination of psychological, personality and political profiles—we have a troubling potential for dossiers, built on every citizen. The computer's predictive capability—even when it errs—means that nobody any longer has the luxury of changing his or her mind on a topic, because foes can pick and choose from among whatever has been accumulated in past profiles, and throw everything else on the cutting room floor. Furthermore, there is no way one can "prove" that any of the information, correct or not, is purged from all computer systems.

This makes Richard Nixon's so-called "Enemies List" puny by today's standards; it is no stretch to imagine political parties and their heavily funded supporters capitalizing on such information by the time the next election cycle in 2012 comes around.

As mental health profiles are increasingly incorporated into school test and survey instruments, with the goal of molding the opinions of those whose attitudes do not match a pre-ordained "mainstream" of acceptability, the time is fast approaching when individuals who deviate will be "drugged" with psychotropic substances "for the good of society." This, of course, is a recipe for social and political control unlike any the world has previously witnessed. Already, curricula are adjusted, and school counseling programs are transformed, tailored and expanded to accommodate the demand that everyone acquiesce to a psychologically approved version of "conventional wisdom," whether that be global warming, interdependence (as opposed to independence), redistribution-of-wealth schemes or some element of "necessary" historical revisionism.

Moreover, popular wisdom is being engineered, cloned and replicated—even as you read this—especially via the schools and media. That is the essence of psychopolitics.

For example, the very terms *individualist* and *maverick* have become dirty words. Like the word "loner," they imply mental instability. While minor disagreements are permitted, anyone running afoul of so-called "conventional" wisdom is relegated to the fringes of debate, hence the terms *fringe group* and *lunatic fringe*.

Unfortunately, a nation will not find leadership, will not find people "thinking outside the box" or "coming up with innovative ideas" in such an environment, regardless of corporate and government directives to the contrary.

Does this mean that every person, right now, at this moment, is being psychologically tracked and monitored? No. We are not there yet. The resources to do so cannot be expended willy-nilly. Typically what happens is a "red flag" goes up if one irritates somebody important, runs for public office, or promotes an unpopular idea. There is no necessity for some big, humongous central computer when millions of small ones communicate, transfer and share data at the state, local and federal levels.

As the new century comes into its own, it takes a household name like the National Association of Scholars' (NAS) to get the truth to large numbers of people. For example, CASNET, a publication of the California Association of Scholars, keeps track of intimidation tactics against people having traditional views about campus life. On May 7, 2007, CASNET disseminated the press release written by the Foundation for Individual Rights in Education (FIRE): "Professor on Brink of Being Fired for E-Mailing George Washington's Thanksgiving Address."[b] While it's all to the good that our nation still has enough free speech left to accommodate such groups as FIRE and NAS, the need to go to such lengths to give people a "heads-up" on potential threats to their freedom would have been unthinkable just 20 years ago. Readers will find more along these lines in this anthology in a piece entitled "Crimes of Opinion."

Moreover, *Walking Targets* points to an agenda that begins with government-controlled childrearing and force-feeds young people a pseudo-education under the cover of "mental health," "safety," "jobs" and something called "lifelong learning." The "hook" to keep them in school is lax dress codes, sports and entertainment, even as the dropout rate continues to soar. The push to mandate school at ever-younger ages—universal pre-kindergarten—represents a last-ditch effort to lessen the influence of the home and to squelch homeschooling.[c] In the late 1970s and early 80s, career- and recreation-minded Boomers tended to view preschool as "convenient" day care for their runny-nose toddlers. By the 1990s, any employer offering nearby day care was seen as "family-friendly"—a well-sold public relations buzz-term with pleasant connotations. But by 2005, some parents started having doubts. They woke up one morning to see children who were nothing like them—people they didn't know and who didn't share even what few "values" they had left.

To aid the reader, the various articles, columns, lectures and new commentaries in this anthology are assigned to one of five categories: education, family, political correctness and deception, behavioral science and privacy. The glue that holds

---

c See **"Center to help extend school days, calendar: Advocates more time form learning, extracurricular activity,"** by Amy Fagan, *The Washington Times*, Oct. 3, 2007, p. A8. The Boston-based National Center on Time and Learning, "funded with a $1 million grant from the Broad Foundation, and partnering with the Center for American Progress," is using the No Child Left Behind Act as the rationale for further extending the 180-day school year. But the objectives are not necessarily academic; even more time would be spent away from the family to boost already excessive pushes to participate in extracurricular activities. The article cites Center's numerous relationships with members of Congress and influential policy-setting groups within established universities like Harvard.

them all together is *psychopolitics*, which encompasses psycho-behavioral profiling, data collection (attitudinal, job, health, and bank records), trend analysis, electronic transfer systems and attitude manipulation. Any repetition of information you may find in these pages serves to reinforce key concepts that are critical to the reader's understanding, and I opted to retain certain passages for that reason.

Every morning's newspaper, it seems, brings a new discomfort concerning prerogatives we once believed were protected under the Constitution—especially freedom of speech, assembly and conscience. Most readers, I imagine, will likely be individualists seeking answers and a strategy—people already trying to navigate this new world of psychopolitics and process-thinking and finding themselves inexplicably placed "on hold," waiting for their cause to be "processed in the order in which it was received."

To you, I say, please listen (and read) carefully, as all of your options have changed.

B. K. Eakman

PROLOGUE

Data-Mining Begins at School

As many of my readers know, in the 1980s I stumbled on what appeared to be a testing scam in the State of Pennsylvania. I had long since escaped the teaching profession and was working in an unrelated field. But a chance discovery in 1984 led to a 14-year-long investigation of the Mental Health Movement which, I confirmed much later, gave us today's psychologized K-12 education, complete with computer cross-matching capability of personal and family information. This put us firmly on the road to socialism, environmental extremism and, of course, psychopolitics, which, as indicated in the Foreword, includes data-mining. Historically, this comprises the formative stages of a police state—children reporting on their parents to representatives of government.

My curiosity was first piqued by the Educational Quality Assessment, or EQA. The EQA (which later appeared under a different name, pretty much intact) was given every two years. The questions turned out to be fairly representative of assessments given in other states as well, such as:

- I often wish I were someone else. [or] I get upset easily at home. The student checks: [a] Very true of me, [b] Mostly true of me, [c] Mostly untrue of me, [d] Very untrue of me.
- You are asked to dinner at the home of a classmate having a religion much different from yours. In this situation I would feel: [a] Very comfortable, [b] Comfortable, [c] Slightly uncomfortable, [d] Very uncomfortable.
- There is a secret club at school called the Midnight Artists. They go out late at night and paint funny sayings and pictures on buildings. I would JOIN THE CLUB when I knew ... [a] my best friend had asked me to join; [b] Most of the popular students in school were in the club; [c] my parents *would ground me* if they found out I joined.

The Midnight Artist question was clearly a "fishing probe": It assumed that the child <u>would</u> join the club under some circumstance, including the peculiar desire to provoke parents. *What*, I asked myself, were psychologists really asking here? Weren't they asking, in effect: "What do we have to do to get this kid to commit vandalism?"

Looking at the Midnight Artist Question from the vantage point of 2007, one recognizes the seeds of Columbine. Instead of asking what it would take to make a kid commit vandalism, subsequent questionnaires, under the cover of mental health, have been asking pupils what it would take to make them shoot their classmates and teachers.

Test creators have always maintained, of course, that they are not trying to plant suggestions in youngsters' heads. Kevin P. Dwyer, president of the National Association of School Psychologists, who helped develop the mass-screening project in Texas, explains that this is "valuable information, almost impossible to obtain from any other source...."

But triggering conflict and strife is exactly what these hypothetical questions and self-reports wrought. Most adults could see through such a ploy right away—which is why they were never permitted to see these "tests."

But such questionnaires, which today are ubiquitous, do something else, too. They are analyzed by behavioral scientists (educational psychologists), and the conclusions made about children and their families are often wrong—dead wrong. Once a child selects an answer that sends up an alarm bell, anything can happen, from mandatory counseling, to placement in Special Education classes, to drugging and even removal from the home.

The EQA had 375 questions covering attitudes, world views and opinions. There were just enough academic questions to appear credible.

The next shocker was the scoring mechanism. It revealed points given for what was called a "minimum positive attitude." For example, on the "Midnight Artists" question, the preferred response was "**b** — Most of the popular students in school were in the club." Why "**b**"?

The Interpretive Literature, which was, and still is, off limits to laypersons, explained why. The EQA's creators were testing for: the child's "focus of control"; his "willingness to receive stimuli"; his "amenability to change"; and his inclination to "conform to group goals." In plain English this means: Where's the kid coming from? Is he easily influenced? Are his views firm or easy-to-change? Will he "go along to get along"?

Answer "**b**" to the Midnight Artists question was *preferred* because it reflected a "willingness to conform to group goals"— one of the behavioral litmus tests. This is what is meant about triggering an alarm bell. Suddenly, child experts are going to scrutinize a kid with "non-preferred" answers a little more closely, even though his parents might be teaching their child to think for himself instead of necessarily conforming to the fickle demands of the peer group.

In 2005, poor Pennsylvania was again selected as a pilot state for mental health screening—this time of the universal, mandatory variety. But a whistleblower named Allen Jones turned up the heat in Pennsylvania's Office of the Inspector General. He told the *British Medical Journal* and the *New York Times* about the perks enjoyed by some Pennsylvania staffers as well as certain ties to pharmaceutical companies. He was sacked for his trouble.

Just how the onerous piece of federal screening legislation called "New Freedom Initiative" made it through the U.S. House of Representatives despite the questionable goings-on is the subject of the article entitled "What? Are You Crazy?" First published by *Chronicles: A Magazine of the American Culture* in 2005, this article has been disseminated internationally.

My nine years as a classroom teacher, interspersed among other career opportunities, confirmed my initial impression from college: that my role was not to transmit "basics," or literacy, or proficiency at anything, but rather to advance the cause of so-called "mental health." *Accountability* meant satisfying government mandates that never improved education. Nor was my role about answering to parents, or even satisfying local superintendents. No one seemed to care if we knew anything about the subject we were majoring in—the one we were going to teach. Indeed, we were told essentially *not to teach*—**not** to put red marks on pupils' papers, **not** to transmit grammar that might conflict with any substandard usage used at home, because it might somehow hurt a pupil's self-esteem. Instead we were taught to "relate" and be "hip." No one cared about math or the value of "x." In essence, we were called upon to be social workers, the first foot-soldiers in a clandestine movement to transform American values and ideals through a steady series of modifications in the educational structure and in curriculum. The only way, of course, to gauge success was through an ostensible system of testing—primarily of student attitudes, perceptions (including level of gullibility) and opinions.

While I "got" the part about serving as a social worker in the classroom, I didn't really see the whole picture while I was actually teaching. I understood, for example, that fewer and fewer teachers were pursuing an academic major; that most of us were majoring in Education, which meant, quite simply: Psychology—i.e., social work. What I didn't get was the rationale *behind* the Mental Health Movement in the classroom.

"Behavioral science" and "mental health" in the context they are addressed in these pages, has more to do with information-gathering and opinion-molding than with neuropsychology. Neurology, a branch of medicine concerned with the nervous system and its disorders, utilizes psychology in an attempt to assess and repair damage caused by physical diseases, brain trauma or injuries and medically verifiable disorders related to cognitive function (i.e., full utilization of one's perceptual and knowledge-retention faculties).

The concept behind neuropsychology has some admittedly interesting possibilities, especially for victims of strokes, Alzheimer's disease and Down's syndrome. Certainly strides have been made in neurology. But the marriage of that field with psychology has become so hopelessly tangled with little-understood emotional, personality and behavioral factors that it has led to the invention of non-verifiable diseases and even phony disorders, better described as quirks or individual differences.

All people have good days and bad days, and life's experiences inevitably contribute to how a particular individual, child or adult, is going to perceive information or react to events on any given day. For example, many Holocaust survivors who both witnessed and/or underwent torture not only enjoyed professional success once the war ended, but came through their ordeals mentally and spiritually intact. Today's youngsters, on the other hand, are supposedly traumatized by a parent who is "controlling" or a teacher who is harsh. There is no medical explanation for these disparate reactions, but psychology appears determined to find one (Post-Traumatic

Stress Syndrome, various conduct disorders, and other ailments for which no objective test exists).

Why do some people hold onto their "sanity" while others fold? So far, there is no medical answer—and certainly no drug or therapy that has any track record to speak of. Consequently, the best psychiatrists are those who fully recognize (and some do) that objective science dictates first ruling out medical conditions and anomalies that might pertain to a patient's discomfort. In the absence of such, the psychiatrist's ability to help the patient is limited at best. Various drugs, of course, can **blunt** the emotions, which may be helpful in the short term for those who are on emotional overload, so to speak, but in the end, the application of reason and the tenets of faith—summed up in what everyone used to call "character"—is still all that exists.

The term "behavioral science," as I refer to it in these pages is Psychology with a capital P, the one that has been hijacked by a mostly leftist faction and turned into a virtual state religion. This is something based in politics, not in medicine, and it has reared its vicious head down through the years in the form of Hitler's Third Reich and communism's political prisons-cum-psychiatric "hospitals." Unfortunately, the 1940s produced experiments in psychological manipulation—some of which can be classified as torture—that for half a century allowed Psychology to change the political landscape, morphing into a tool of coercion under the deceptive phrase "mental health." This is the Psychology that has infiltrated the schools, the courts, the theological seminaries and to some extent has spread even to medicine itself.

That is why even those few educators who *do* specialize in an academic subject in college often wind up "facilitating" some other subject once they hit the classroom.

Facilitating and *coaching*: That's what teaching is called now. This entails a whole new curricular experience: "survival and coping skills," "anger management," "conflict resolution," "self-esteem," "diversity," and more. Little in the curriculum provides insight into our cultural, constitutional or theological underpinnings. Courses like logic, philosophy, and civics, which once helped kids get a handle on modern issues, are practically gone. Nothing supports ideals like self-reliance, property rights, limited government (especially in the context of regulatory power), or religious morality in society. Physics, chemistry, calculus, and physiology are reserved for the few with very high IQ scores, kids who are then summarily skimmed off the top for what can best be described as ideological studies in political correctness, or else rounded up to "mentor" slower students.

Quite by accident I discovered the specifics of the campaign to re-orient education's purpose. A left-wing cadre of so-called "behaviorist" educators—psychologists like the late Ralph Tyler, Richard Wolf, and Walcott Beatty—began urging their colleagues to abandon traditional concepts about right and wrong. Suddenly something called "high religiosity" was deemed a *risk* factor (a.k.a. *marker*) for mental illness. Religion itself became equated with dogmatism, inflexibility, resistance to change, paranoia, and irrationality—echoing the pronouncements of infamous atheists from the late 1800s to the early 1930s—Erich Fromm, Sigmund Freud, Karl Marx, Franz J. Kallman and John Dewey.

In my 1998 book, *Cloning of the American Mind: Eradicating Morality Through Education*, I spent considerable time discussing the experiments of pioneers in the field of attitude prediction, many of whom also helped establish today's list of "markers" (the *risk factors* or *red flags*) that supposedly signal mental illness—individuals like Wilhelm Reich, Kurt Lewin, Theodor Adorno and Erich Fromm of Germany; A. S. Neill, A. J. Oraje and John Rawlings Rees of Great Britain; Antonio Gramsci of Italy; Anatoly Lunacharsky and Georg Lukacs of Russia, G. Brock Chishom and Ewen Cameron of Canada; and the U.S.'s own Ralph Tyler, Ronald Havelock, Benjamin S. Bloom, and Linda Erlenmeyer-Kimling, the latter being a protégé of Franz J. Kallmann, who once headed Ernst Rüdin's "racial hygiene" program under Adolf Hitler. There followed a slew of others whose work "medicalized" the terminologies of Psychology as a means of establishing a system of numerical codes for computerization. This lent legitimacy to otherwise questionable "illnesses." If insurance companies and government agencies accepted these codes the same as they would for, say, Type II diabetes, then mental illnesses so codified would become credible.

On the computer side, experts like George Hall, Richard M. Jaeger, C. Philip Kearny, David E. Wiley, Willard Wirtz and Archie LaPointe contributed to a system that would eventually ensure political correctness and stigmatize dissenters and resisters as damaged goods. As their methods were refined, behavioral forecasting became a new purpose of testing in the schools—something I didn't recognize while I was teaching.

If most of the names above seem unfamiliar, don't feel badly; for it is not entirely by accident. I discovered that mass-circulation newspapers and newscasts rarely, if ever, reported on advances in fields like behavioral assessment and forecasting or data collection. One can learn all about every bug's and insect's natural habitat, and how man is destroying the planet, but hardly a word appears about the one thing that is vastly changing the nature of our everyday lives—computerized behavioral assessment. Most of what gets published was (and still is) located in hard-to-find professional "working" papers, meaning that they do not reach the larger, glossy publications. A recent exception appeared April 9, 2007, in the *Washington Times*. Reporter Al Webb described how Great Britain has installed some 4.2 million surveillance cameras, many outfitted with loudspeakers in an effort to intimidate and acclimate citizens to having their every movement and activity monitored in real-time. Should a person, say, drop a cigarette or candy wrapper on the sidewalk, the device hollers "pick up that butt" or "put the candy wrapper in the bin," thereby shocking the populace into being lectured for committing what amounts to minor annoyances.[a] It's a short step from this to the establishment of a police state.

Professionals in behavioral forecasting, of course, have always held conferences, given each other awards and otherwise congratulated one another on a regular basis. The tiny few older reports that did actually make the dailies, like A. S. Neill's 50s-era leftist education and childrearing tome, *Summerhill*, occasionally won their authors some face time with the public (Neill was a guest in the 1960s on the old Johnny Carson Show.) But such individuals typically are quickly forgotten and not taken seriously by sleepy viewers. Most sixties-era audiences, for example, never dreamed that somewhere in the lounges of academia, a screwball like Neill, who advocated, among other things, *more* food fights in the school cafeterias, would one day serve as a catalyst for changing the very

---

a   Al Webb, *'Big Brother' scolds scofflaws in Britain, The Washington Times*, April 9, 2007 (www.washtimes.com/world/20070409-122618-3886r.htm).

foundations of schooling—through a combined process of chaos, disobedience and non-assimilation.

In 1981, a "working paper" surfaced from the National Institute of Education. Archie PaPointe and Willard Wirtz's watershed document, "Measuring the Quality of Education," called the goal of excellence "unrealistic" and recommended that it be changed to "functionality." Ideals about excellence soon went the way of "Yes, Ma'am" and "No, Sir" and all the rest of what once was required of children in the way of academic standards and civil behavior. Had people paid attention, it would have come as no surprise to readers of A. S. Neill's *Summerhill* that popularity contests, gangs and peer pressure eventually replaced respect for teachers, parents and other adults, thereby launching what the media dubbed "the Generation Gap."

The various incarnations of the Mental Health Movement during my teaching years — the "humanistic" movement, the self-esteem movement, Schools Without Failure, psycholinguistics, pass-fail grade schemes, the Effective Schools Movement, and finally outcome-based education—all reflected the fads and fancies of child "experts" more than any actual breakthrough in the emotional well-being of children. In the process of "humanizing" education, students were subjected to far worse stress at the hands of their classmates than they had ever experienced under the guidance of caring parents. The new laxness of discipline, eradication of dress codes, disrespect for the flag and the armed services, eradication of prayer in school—all can be traced to the various incarnations of the Mental Health Movement.

Unfortunately, experts have rarely agreed as to the feasibility of their own schemes, so it is no wonder they failed to improve our nation's ranking in basic subjects. In 2007, we remain firmly entrenched at third or fourth place from the bottom of the international heap, depending on which study one is looking at.

By the time I had plowed through some 1,000 pages of the *Behavioral Science Teacher Education Project* (BSTEP), an old education blueprint compiled and published by Michigan State University in 1969, I knew that teachers from that time on had been trained to minister to a mentally "sick" society through the nation's schoolchildren. Even so, I cannot say that the truth had set me entirely free. I did my fair share to promote the buzz-terms "relevant" and "meaningful" in the BSTEP classroom.

For example, during one particular election year, I had my English Literature students reading all kinds of popular claptrap about the political process—mostly to ensure that they *did* read *something*. The students kept asking me whether I was a Democrat or Republican, and I wouldn't tell them. They asked me my religion, and I wouldn't tell them that either, as it was against school policy to proselytize or even appear to do so. At length, I discovered that there was a wager afoot to determine my political and religious affiliations! I thought that was rather funny, and even felt proud of myself for having succeeded in carrying out the school district's directive of neutrality (I was only in my 20s then, so go figure...).

In the teacher's lounge, I recounted my discovery of the wager to my principal and supervisors. They thought it humorous as well—except maybe for the gambling part. So, on the last day I owned up to my students (I was curious, actually, as to how many of my pupils would guess correctly), and sure enough, the majority lost the wager and guessed wrong on both counts, politics and religion.

It was not until some time later that I realized the idiocy of my flirtation with neutrality. I recalled the "I like Ike" campaign buttons of my youth: How my teachers wore them, or the pro-Stevenson counterparts, proudly in the 1950s. How we repeated the Lord's Prayer aloud in three languages every morning—in an international "diplomatic" school that enrolled everyone from Catholics to Hindus to Moslems and Jews. And I wondered: Why did we do this? Why were there no complaints from non-Christians?

The answer was that everyone understood Christianity to be a "given" in the United States of America. While everyone was as free to pursue any of the world's other religions as they were to wear a campaign button, Christianity was nevertheless the basis upon which our Constitution was founded. End of subject.

Today, our religious institutions have been stripped of moral authority and are of little use in the matter. They decided they have bigger fish to fry than reciting the Lord's Prayer, much less deliberate the ethics of phony surveys and questionnaires. Indeed, if our students can be sidetracked from the nation's Judeo-Christian moorings, if the coming generation will accept the "all religions are equally noble" credo (translation: "it's all bunk"), then the ideals that made this nation different—individualism, leadership, morality, self-determination and self-sufficiency—will crumble. Already, traditional churches have lost touch with the everyday concerns of their flock because the left has kept them busy debating patently ridiculous notions like "gay marriage." The truly momentous issues go unaddressed.

Moreover, my experiences in education, combined with copious research for my books and articles—not to mention my various "day" jobs: newspaper writer for NASA; speechwriter for the Voice of America and for a former Chief Justice of the Supreme Court; writer-editor U.S. Department of Justice—all have served in some way as a backdrop for this anthology.

I have reluctantly come to the conclusion that, despite all the warnings of history, our government is poised to make an "enemy combatant" of every politically incorrect parent, child and potential employee via a system of dubious interconnected mental health profiles. We can catch a glimpse of the future through the eyes of human rights activist, Larisa Arap, detained by Russian military police during a routine medical exam on July 5, 2007, after she collaborated on an article describing abuses under the cover of "punitive psychiatry." She was recently released from the Murmansk psychiatric ward, complete with threats to her entire family if she spoke out. Prophetically, she warns: "[E]ven if I kept mum, I would still be a sitting duck. If I don't speak up, the society at large will never learn about the things that are happening...." (See: "Activist tells about torture and captivity," by David R. Sands, the Washington Times, Oct. 16, 2007).

Although readers will find that I submit several alternatives to "fix" what is now clearly broken (especially in our schools), the key question remains: Will the various pieces of legislation that psychologize (and further politicize) our educational institutions prove to be the final nails in the coffin for the "American way of life," turning this nation into a bona fide American gulag?

Education

B. K. Eakman

BLINDSIDED BY EDUCATION'S LEFTISTS:
Republicans Assure Their Own Marginalization

Michael Moore, the leftist originator of "Fahrenheit 9/11," got one thing right when he proclaimed at a June 24 press conference that, despite the Republican control of the White House and Congress, America is liberal. It is a fact. The Republican Party, the only home conservatives have at election time, does not remotely resemble the GOP of Reagan or Goldwater or Nixon or Eisenhower.

Much of the blame can be placed at the feet of conservative "leaders," who continue to shoot themselves in the foot on every issue—environmental extremism, abortion, limited government, crime—because, for 40 years, American public schools have been indoctrinating each class of new high school graduates in leftism.

Many true conservatives were disheartened when Ronald Reagan (and, later, the Newt Gingrich-led "Contract With America") failed to follow through on campaign promises to shut down the U.S. Department of Education — a creation that everyone knew was a sop to the National Education Association (NEA) in 1976 by then-Democratic candidate Jimmy Carter. Today, conservatives continue to be stumped over the continuing reticence of legislators that they elected, in the name of stopping communism and socialism, to take on America's left-leaning education system — not only for the sake of nation, but for the sake of the Republican Party itself. Increasingly, serious conservatives are looking at Third Party options — or just not voting at all.

At least three of Mr. Reagan's senior advisors in the Department of Education warned him about the escalation of left-leaning schools. But neither his appointed education secretary, William Bennett, nor Mr. Bennett's deputies were moved to do anything with the information.

Among the data points these advisors presented was a laundry list of left-leaning foundations, think-tanks, and

31

university researchers to which the Education Department was awarding grants that funded unsound methodologies, controversial programs and counterculture curricula. They uncovered plans written by top officials inside the department's own research arm, the National Institute of Education, to redirect American schools away from excellence toward mere functionality, and they confirmed links between certain federally "validated" curricula and the United Nations Educational, Scientific, and Cultural Organization (UNESCO).

Indeed, two of President Reagan's own children, Patti and Ron, were testaments in the 1980s to the damage inflicted by Marxist educators. The pair noisily rejected both their father and traditional American values — and still do.

I was a young, just-married teacher in Orange County, California, when Ronald Reagan was governor. Having attended a rigorous private academy in Washington, D.C., for most of my life, I was appalled to discover that, in the time it had taken me to complete college, schools were turning out not merely eighth-graders two or three years behind private schools, as before, but youngsters, just ten years my junior, who could not read, spell or do simple arithmetic at all. Nothing in my university teacher-training courses prepared me for the deterioration in learning and conduct I discovered Johnson Intermediate School in Westminister, California — a middle school not much different from others around the nation.

I seemed to be the only one in my district giving essay assignments; most teachers were handing out social adjustment games. There was pressure to hire younger, supposedly "hip" teachers (like me) and to force older, tougher teachers into retirement by saddling them with the worst-behaved classes.

The final two straws came, first, when the dress codes were scrapped and, secondly, when the NEA launched its campaign to hoodwink teachers into joining its soon-to-be consolidated local, state, national unions, which previously had been separate and voluntary. Suddenly, our classrooms were filled with backward baseball caps and gross-out T-shirts that made our jobs even harder. Then, when we got to the teachers' lounge, our mailboxes were stuffed with union leaflets, such as one might find in blue-collar factories, condemning administrators, parents and state policymakers for low salaries and poor benefits.

I was naïve, of course. The money didn't look so bad to me. I would have done worse accepting an entry level position in journalism or technical writing. It bothered me that the NEA was not advocating backup in the office for disciplinary problems or lobbying against relaxed standards of behavior, which by that time included cursing, vandalizing desks, spitting on the floor, and talking back to teachers. The union didn't condemn social promotion, or the excess of drug-and-sex programs, or even the absence of clear-cut benchmarks for each grade level.

If our "professional organization" really had wanted to do something for us, I thought, salaries and benefits were the least of our problems. Union leaders denounced tests of all kinds, calling them "humiliating." They criticized workbooks and drills as "boring" and advocated chaotic "open classrooms." The NEA upheld the doctrine of "moral equivalency" between communist and Christian values, supported the Sandinista government in Nicaragua, and favored socialist economic policies over free-market principles.

In frustration, I wrote a letter to then-Governor Ronald Reagan, explaining the situation as I saw it and describing just how many of the "special activities" and "supplementary curriculums," in particular, were built around anti-American themes. I revealed how some of us who didn't buy in to the union-led rhetoric were seeking out alternate curriculum repositories outside the district just to find suitable materials from which to teach. Often, this meant resurrecting older texts, some of them stamped "obsolete."

My comments to Governor Reagan must have struck a nerve. I received a wonderful, hand-written letter back (which I eventually lost — who knew that he would one day be President, and that the letter would be a collector's item?). He commiserated, theorizing that the Marxist-inspired student demonstrations in the universities were filtering down into elementary and secondary classrooms. He wrote that he was forwarding a copy of my letter to Max Rafferty, then California's superintendent of instruction, with a directive to look into my allegations and get back to him with suggestions.

In due course, I received a personal response from Max Rafferty. It was no form letter. Mr. Rafferty was particularly concerned about forced unionization.

33

Despite the lack of a positive outcome, both Ronald Reagan and Max Rafferty appeared to be sincere. What I do not think they recognized — nor did I, at the time — was that local, state, and federal agencies had already been outmaneuvered. The two teacher unions (the NEA and AFT) had a certain amount of influence with teachers and administrators, of course, but they weren't necessarily calling the shots.

Tax-exempt foundations like the Carnegie Foundation for the Advancement of Teachers (CFAT) were giving the marching orders — and not only to the teachers' unions. It was carefully inserting politically acceptable individuals into the state education agencies and the federal bureaucracy — such entities as the Education Commission of the States and the old Office of Education when it was still under the Department of Health, Education and Welfare.

CFAT also was raking in millions of dollars from its for-profit spin-off, the Educational Testing Service (ETS). ETS was constructing most of the testing instruments in the United States — and beginning to incorporate psychological and opinion-oriented items. Several of ETS's presidents, such as Ralph Tyler, were sitting as Commissioners of the Office of Education, which should have been seen as a conflict of interest. Tyler was also busy creating tests for state after state under separate contracts and helping to formulate what would become the National Assessment of Educational Progress (NAEP).

Since 1947, when UNESCO was launched — with two grants, one each from the NEA and CFAT — the liberal-leftists understood the stakes in institutionalizing a Marxist-based education system. They knew even from the beginning of the European counterculture movement that schools were their ace-in-the-hole, assuring the *overall* success of Marxist socialism, whatever temporary political setbacks might occur from one administration to another in the free world.

Toward that end, UNESCO was able to weave a spider's web across Europe and the United States of highly placed associates to serve as "agents of influence." The term morphed into "agents of change," then "agents of social change," and finally just "change agents."

By contrast, traditionalists, since World War II, were busy playing catch-up. They started about 15 years too late. They failed to anticipate the menace that Marxism posed as far back

34

as the Allies' march to Berlin at the close of World War II, when Gen. George S. Patton was told to wait until the Soviets could meet us and go in together.

Despite attempts by the House Committee on Un-American Activities to turn public opinion against communism, the cult of celebrity greatly influenced the young. The education establishment increasingly called upon left-leaning stars to speak on behalf of various initiatives, such as anti-drug programs. The fact that many, even most, of these celebrities were wolfing down recreational drugs, condemning American policy abroad, and being notoriously promiscuous failed to hurt their credibility because the media had already idolized them.

In 1958, California's Senate Investigating Committee on Education convened hearings on Marxist propagandizing in the schools. The Sixteenth Investigating Committee Report on Education quotes portions of teachers' guides, elementary- and secondary-school curricula, and teacher-training texts, revealing an obvious Marxist slant. Yet, the propagandizing continued.

Erich Fromm, author of *Escape From Freedom*, for example, was lauded in teacher-training classes as an outstanding contributor to modern educational theories — including at the university I attended. It was he who coined the term *authoritarian aggressors* to describe the defenders of traditional norms. His theories form the roots of today's self-esteem movement.

Max Horkheimer echoed Fromm's wisdom in his book *Studies on Authority and the Family*. The family, he wrote, "... produces the attitudes which predispose men for blind submission" — the implication being that families were incubators of Nazism.

This is the kind of pap that still passes for teacher training. Mr. Reagan, his Education Department appointees, and most leaders of conservative think-tanks failed to examine such materials, so they couldn't comprehend the appeal of Marxism to young, college-age students preparing for careers in teaching.

In 1958, Mr. Reagan was just becoming aware of the scope of Marxist influence within his own profession; he had not set his sights on the governor's mansion, much less the White House. There is an even chance he never read the text of California's hearings.

The United States, of course, remained distracted with various crises and issues. Education simply was not a national priority — until the launching of *Sputnik*, when legislators suddenly realized what most parents had already noticed: that the level of hard knowledge was dropping precipitously. Our communist adversaries inflicted damage that went considerably beyond the scrapping of substantive learning, however. Marxist professors and bureaucrats, who began swelling the ranks of the profession, made it their mission to set in place policies that would create a "Lord of the Flies" subculture. By the mid-60's, it would be dubbed a "generation gap." This subculture was endowed with power — and money — and, by 1968, when I started to teach, cultural Marxism was trumping any serious effort to transmit knowledge to America's youth.

Ronald Reagan was blindsided by his fixation on the Soviet Union. Like many of his colleagues, including Max Rafferty, he thought that if the Soviet Union could just be made to break apart, the Marxist underpinnings would fall with it — in the schools, in the media, in the motion picture industry. It would all turn around once everyone could plainly see that Soviet communism had failed.

This proved to be a miscalculation.

Of course, Ronald Reagan had more on his plate than stopping the Soviet arms buildup. He also wanted to curtail "stagflation" and double-digit inflation, inherited from Democrat Jimmy Carter, and rekindle respect for America worldwide. *However, the extent to which cultural Marxist and socialist economic principles had already become institutionalized in the American psyche eluded him.*

Failure to teach and instill free-market concepts has produced a large egalitarian faction that believes the socialist system falls short only when legislation fails to give everyone an equal share of the pie. That someone must first *create* a pie escapes their logic. Economic prosperity requires unleashing the creative energies of enterprising people through the profit motive, but collegiates unschooled in free-market principles viewed pie-making as government's job.

The schools also produced a plethora of amoral elitists who found the strictures of civilized society confining. Even ideals of honor, decency and integrity were rejected in favor of "self-actualization," a me-first mentality.

President Reagan was a rarity in Tinseltown. He never forgot who he was or his humble beginnings. He was, by all reports, a good man. "I believe that man is essentially good," he said, and "that good eventually triumphs over evil." While good may indeed triumph, President Reagan's enthusiasm for such an outcome in the near term may have blinded him to the perverse staying power of cultural Marxism and economic socialism — even with a defunct Soviet Union.

He was not alone. Today, education is the stuff of photo-opportunities — Presidents and their wives sitting among minority children, "making nice." Band-aids like Head Start and testing are hopelessly outweighed by the lack of real teaching skills, leftist propagandizing, and classroom chaos.

By the 1990's, the left went "back to basics." The left realized it had to divert attention from its end-game. It proceeded under the rubric of "mental health." Dr. John Rawlings Rees had pointed the way in a 1940 address to the National Council for Mental Hygiene: "We must aim to make [psychology] permeate every educational activity in our national life.... [W]e have [already] made a useful attack on a number of professions. The two easiest of them naturally are the teaching profession and the Church .... I think we must imitate the Totalitarians and organize some kind of fifth column activity."

An early guru of the Mental Health Movement, Dr. Paul Popenoe, put it another way: "The school should be a sieve through which all the children of the country are passed.... It is very desirable that no child escape inspection."

Having set in motion the contempt for authority that eventually gave us Columbine, the left started launching programs ostensibly aimed at "prevention" — i.e., screening for troubled youth — masking its agenda of inspecting for political correctness. The strategy combined the burgeoning new field of computerized cross-matching with psychological profiling. The inauguration of Dr. Rees's proposal could not have been timed better. Conservatives, at this point largely marginalized by the media, were completely blindsided.

George W. Bush, like his father, knew America's education system was in trouble. He thought that, if only he could mandate testing in reading and math, he would force the hand of "progressive" educators. They would have no choice but to re-establish standards — especially in reading and math. In that rationale, he made three errors. First, he was convinced by his neoconservative allies that tests were, well, actually tests. The term *assessment* was lost on both Bush presidencies, in particular the fact that assessments measured opinions more than academics. Secondly, even the few standards that emerged (such as the Standards of Learning in Virginia and the Profiles of Learning in Minnesota) were initiated more as a way to force teachers to bring minority children from lower income families up to the mediocre level of their middle-class peers. Of course, no such thing occurred. Standards soon had to be lowered across the board to avoid a political backlash.

George W. Bush also inherited his father's bias toward the United Nations, which had helped establish the elder Mr. Bush's credibility on the world stage. Even though the United Nations thumbed its nose at the President's War on Terror, the President re-endorsed UNESCO, undermining any chance he might have had to improve America's schools.

Even the most prestigious conservative think tanks and advisory organizations do not seem to understand that the interests of the Republican Party are not being served when schools are turning out little socialists year after year. They somehow expect that curricula which denigrate self-reliance and individualism, play down national sovereignty, scoff at the existence of a Creator, and advocate socialistic solutions to problems like health care and unemployment are going to produce conservative Republicans.

Exactly how is teacher preparation that is geared to promote Marxist-socialist ideals supposed to energize the electorate to vote Republican? Or advance traditional values? The questions conservative organizations and think-tanks should be asking are: How can we remove the red tape so that private-school startup costs are lessened, thereby providing more supply to meet the demand? What are the "breakthrough" methodologies that would revolutionize, without stigma, the teaching of basic subjects? Can we support these techniques through the universities — instead of writing each state a blank check? How can we penalize the teachers' unions so that they cannot masquerade as "professional associations"?

In the end, axing the U.S. Department of Education became a no-go, while dozens of vested interests helped sustain a *quid pro quo* between the Department and agencies of the left — all committed to Marxist socialism.

Conservatives will continue to redouble their efforts while missing their aim as long as they refuse to take on the education behemoth. How long before young graduates are no longer schooled well enough in the principles of liberty to bother *defending* them?

B. K. Eakman

IT'S ABOUT MENTAL HEALTH, STUPID!

Oh, great! Another school year; America's still near the bottom of the global heap, according to the Educational Testing Service, in math, science, and reading comprehension; but The Washington Post runs an article glamorizing the fact that academics are out, and more touchy-feely, privacy-invading mush is in ["Phonics Is Out, Fairy Tales Are In," *The Washington Post*, Sept. 8, 1993]. Just what we need!

According to the article, first-graders in a Washington suburb will learn to spell by looking at familiar shopping labels – Nordstrom's, Cheerios, etc. They will learn to read, Lord knows how, since teachers will "eschew most phonics ... and plunge into the world of 'children's literature' – fairy tales, fables, and classic stories ... [and] read stories such as The Little Red Hen to one another." The youngsters will "keep a written journal ... and be 'assessed,' not graded, on the basis of portfolios of their writing."

"Children [beginning at first grade] have to be given autonomy; they have to be given ownership of their learning," chirped the Dranesville, Md., teacher quoted.

As a former teacher, let me tell you exactly what the kids are going to get out of this:

The children will learn to spell "gleam" g-l-e-e-m, just like the toothpaste – if they have a good visual memory. If they don't, they'll migrate to the back of the room and decline to participate. By failing to learn phonics – which most teachers today have no idea how to teach – these students will be denied the tools for deciphering the "code," the rules of English spelling, which covers more than 85 percent of the words in our language.

The child may be able to make out the traffic signs as he whizzes along the freeway (and possibly pass a driving test), but he will not be able to do anything more advanced than follow a dumbed-down set of directions or write an incoherent paragraph about the importance of safe driving. If he's bright

40

enough, this look-say, or "whole language," approach to reading may make him literate, in that he will recognize enough words to get by, but reading, per se, will be of little practical use to him, and all his school subjects eventually will be affected. Unless the pupil has excellent visual memory, he will never read effortlessly and fluently, which is a prerequisite for lifelong learning, reading for pleasure, and decision making in a democratic republic.

The child won't know he lives in a democratic republic, but that's another issue.

His journal and diary writing will be examined not so much for academic knowledge, but for psychological "defects" and home-family problems. His teachers will be asked to look for signs of emotional disturbance, and the school psychologist and/or counselor will take it from there.

The term "assessed," as opposed to graded, is the only thing the article in the Post got right. It's part and parcel of the "whole child" theory of education. What a youngster believes and feels and thinks is assessed for "appropriateness"; what he knows will become increasingly insignificant.

So when the Educational Testing Service says test scores are going up, down, or sideways, you had better ask what kinds of questions they're talking about. If they specify math and science, so be it. But assessment questions are not the same as academic questions. Here's a sample from Pennsylvania's Educational Quality Assessment, put out by the E.T.S. in 1984:

- "I feel I don't have much chance to control things that happen to me." Check: [a] Very true of me, [b] Mostly true of me, [c] Mostly untrue of me, [d] Very untrue of me.
- You are asked to sit at a table with retarded students. In this situation, I would feel: [a] Very comfortable, [b] Comfortable, [c] Slightly uncomfortable, [d] Very uncomfortable.
- A person in a crowd is standing on a street corner. They are protesting about something. Some people pick up rocks and start throwing them at windows. I would also throw rocks when I knew: [a] There was no chance of getting caught, [b] I agreed with what they were protesting about, or [c] My closest friend decided to throw rocks.
- There is a secret club at school called the Midnight Artists. They go out late at night and paint funny sayings and pictures on buildings. A student is asked to join the club. In this situation, I would join the club when I knew: [a] My best

friend asked me to join, [b] The most popular students were in the club, [c] My parents would ground me if they found out I joined.

The only "appropriate" answers for these types of questions on the E.Q.A. test appear to be those indicative of a conformist mentality, either to please the group or to avoid punishment. Most states use similar tests, put out by E.T.S. and other testing contractors, such as Psychological Corporation. Most tests are "slugged," so as to be identifiable down to the individual child and classroom. The results (even the responses themselves) are entered into cross-referenceable databanks at first the state, then federal, levels. The "portfolios" the Post article mentions are more than likely electronic portfolios, not the old manila folders.

If a majority of students in a school district give "inappropriate" responses to the same questions, "remedial" mini-courses, called "strands," are brought into the various hard-subject areas to improve scores. In other words, personal opinions are being assessed for "correct" responses in a pluralistic society that supposedly treasures the concept of individual differences.

What happens to a youngster's self-esteem as a result of all this foolishness? Look at two random sentences taken from typical academic textbooks:

1. Thomas Jefferson was the first President to be inaugurated in Washington.

2. As the Spirit of St. Louis touched down on the turf, the crowds surged toward it.

Using the currently voguish "whole language" (the old "look-say") approach, based on sight memory and context clues, the minimally competent students turned out in these classes will, by 7th grade, read the lines above as follows:

1. Thomas Jefferson was the first President to be assassinated in Washington.

2. As the Spirit of St. Louis rolled along the surf, the cowards surged toward it.

Naturally, the student will do poorly on academic tests. Because of the nature of his errors, the rest of the selections will make no sense to him. Why was Thomas Jefferson assassinated? the student will wonder. The rest of the paragraph seems to indicate the man lived on a good while! And did the Spirit of St. Louis have water-landing gear? Why did cowards go up to it instead of away from it? And so on.

Passed on from grade to grade, this student eventually will throw up his hands in exasperation because nothing in any of his classes makes sense.

What kind of self-esteem do you think he will have?

How long are parents going to put up with this nonsense? American taxpayers – not to mention schoolchildren – have endured one fiasco after another for 30 years in the name of psycho-behavioral calisthenics passed off as "education reform."

The American public has been amazingly patient through all this. It gave up a method of reading instruction that had 70 years of experimental research behind it and which was successful in producing a literate population (remember those soldiers' letters in Ken Burns's award-winning Civil War documentary?). We exchanged that method for one having only a smattering of subjective, anecdotal research.

We relinquished proven techniques for teaching mathematics, nearly all instruction in geography, penmanship, essay writing, English grammar, and chronological history. Parents acquiesced on the issues of school dances for preteens, lax dress codes, graphic sex education as a separate course (that is, separate from biology and physiology), and cheerfully exchanged civics for insipid pap called "social studies."

Moreover, America gave up the three R's and got back the three I's: ignorance, illiteracy, and illegitimacy.

Parents of the postwar years wanted a "kinder and gentler nation," just like former President Bush. They had just been through the horrors of World War II, and they were in no mood for a repeat performance. Americans were vulnerable, therefore, to the arguments of behavioral psychologists, which came at them, first through articles and books touting appealing but unworkable philosophies of child management that eschewed adult guidance and leadership. These messages were later repeated through colleges of education in the form of courses in "educational psychology."

Suddenly grades were "dehumanizing." Lecturing was passé. Tests were traumatizing. Drills, practice, and rote learning were judged "dull." Homework undermined family life. (That's a howl, now, isn't it?) Workbooks were "too expensive" and "impersonal." Criticism "frustrated pupils," and red markings

B. K. Eakman

on students' papers were "insulting." Geography, penmanship, study hall, and physiology were out; plush sports facilities, educational games, and sex clinics were in.

Establishment educators in expensive think tanks questioned whether the ability to spell correctly was worth the price of a traumatized adult. Learning was always supposed to be easy and fun. It occurred through some mystical process of intellectual osmosis; if you were in the same room together it somehow seeped in through your brain cells.

The rationale, of course, was that nobody should have his personality "warped" by failure. Do you want your child to be a Hitler or a Mussolini? psychologists challenged. Nobody did.

Graduate and in-service education classes I took in the 1970's admonished us teachers to forgo standards of excellence in favor of "giving everybody a taste of success." But the upshot was that public schools and even some private ones coasted downhill on the sled of mediocrity, sapping the incentive of students and teachers as they went. Instead of encouraging pupils to try harder so they could keep getting this wonderful "positive feedback," the instant-success syndrome had a demoralizing effect and led to apathy. Many students began choosing as much idleness as possible as a way of life. We teachers, frustrated and emotionally drained from spending our days as babysitters and entertainers, reacted predictably. Some, like me, changed professions; others lashed out at parents and administrators. This spurred union membership. From teachers' unions like the National Education Association emanated a never-ending stream of rabble-rousing leaflets in teachers' mailboxes (I remember them well), which in the end further alienated parents from their schools.

The rest, as the saying goes, is history. Gradually, social adjustment and behavioral goals took the place of academics.

The bottom line is that today, education is not about literacy. It is not about proficiency at anything. It is not about basics, or core curriculum, or skills, or jobs.

It's about mental health, stupid!

Copyright © 1993, Education Week, Reprinted with permission

UNCLE SAM'S CLASSROOM

Yolanda and Raul Salazar of Miami, Florida, naturalized citizens who escaped Castro's Cuba, found out the hard way that Uncle Sam's classrooms are not about proficiency at anything, or literacy, or basics. America's schools aren't extensions of the home, where families are held sacred and parents are valued. Instead, American education is about "mental hygiene," defined by psychologists as "preventive psychotherapy."

Case in point: Daniel Salazar, age ten, who had been, as of the year 2000, in the Dade County School system for eight years.

The multitude of psychosocial, behavioral, intelligence, and personality tests that make up a typical child's school record today reveal that Daniel was once an "active, sociable, happy, alert, affectionate, and playful" little boy. Between the ages of two and five, Daniel's motor development and language skills were advanced compared to those of other children his age. His kindergarten and first grade records describe Daniel as enjoying school, having no peer, absence, or disciplinary problems, and maintaining a positive relationship with his parents. He had bridged the gap smoothly from Spanish to English. He wasn't even a finicky eater or afraid of the dark.

By the time the school got through with him three years later, the picture had changed. Daniel had turned into a hostile and unhappy child whom teachers pitted against the people who loved him most: his mother and father.

Daniel's sins? Well, it seems that Daniel suddenly had trouble reading in the third grade. He occasionally skipped letters in words. When his voice became hoarse, the school sent the boy for psychometric testing. Bewildered, Daniel was subjected to a battery of vision tests, hearing tests, behavior-rating scales, and strange assessments such as the Kinetic Family Drawing.

Art not being his forte, Daniel drew a picture of a man, presumably his father, watching television. This was

45

interpreted by the school psychologist as indicating a lack of attention at home. When Daniel said he couldn't draw his mother, this was taken as "possible feelings of ambivalence toward her," not as an honest statement that he was no good at drawing people. Questioned ad nauseam about his relationships, he commented that he liked the food his father often brought home after work – thus, the "expert" judgment that food was the only positive thing he associated with his parents.

Meanwhile, the classroom teacher singled out Daniel for preferential seating, assigned him a "buddy," and bribed him with computer time. The combination of interrogation, testing, and special treatment sent an unmistakable message: Something was wrong with him. As Daniel became increasingly apprehensive about the scrutiny (who wouldn't?) he found himself distracted, edgy, and negative concerning his studies. His classmates started teasing him, which made him defensive. Daniel longed to escape his stressful environment, where his every move and gesture were taken out of context. He started complaining that he felt sick, a typical reaction to daily unpleasantness.

The school tagged Daniel with the usual panoply of fashionable (if contradictory) psychiatric labels – Attention Deficit Disorder, dyslexia, hyperactivity, anxiety, emotionally handicapped, learning disabled, low self-concept, depression. Advised that a smaller class would allow Daniel to get the individualized attention he needed to improve his reading, Mrs. Salazar agreed to it. She was presented with an Individualized Education Plan (IEP), which seemed to mean the school would tailor a program to her son's needs until Daniel was confident enough to return to a regular class.

Little did the Salazars suspect that, once in the "special class," there was virtually no possibility that Daniel would ever get out. Moreover, he would be saddled with psychiatric labels that didn't apply to him for the remainder of his school career, and possibly for life. Nor did they understand that, in signing the IEP, they had essentially given up the right to make any further educational decisions concerning their son. They had given the school carte blanche to do what it pleased – *in loco parentis*.

Daniel's teachers noticed him rocking back and forth in his seat. This resulted in further psychiatric screening and "counseling." Eventually, Daniel stopped cooperating and became argumentative. He didn't tell the counselor when his beloved grandfather died or when his best friend was badly injured in an accident – it was none of the counselor's business, after all.

Daniel was placed in a class for the "severely emotionally disturbed" (SED), a warehouse environment where little of an academic nature occurred. A pressure-cooker was the last thing Daniel needed. The only way to survive was to adopt an aura of aloofness (in the vernacular of psychologists, "to act out").

Not surprisingly, Daniel's reading and other academic skills declined further, and he became too upset to focus on studying. His parents were angry; his teachers were disinterested; the kids bullied him; and the counselors intimidated him.

By the time the Salazars saw through the scam and balked, the school had attained the upper hand. The final straw came when Mrs. Salazar was threatened under the Baker Act (removal of a child from his home) unless she agreed to put Daniel on psychiatric drugs. She retaliated by taking the school district to court and her story to the press.

"Is this America or not?" she asked television reporters outside a Miami courthouse on February 8. "We left Cuba to get away from a totalitarian state. But now we see the same thing right here. The school staff lied to me about the nature of the class. They invaded my privacy. They took advantage of my child's innocence. They lied again in the courtroom. The more they lie, the more money they get. What's going on here?"

What was going on is politely called "covering your behind." Caught in their own web of deceit, the school district brought in every one but the janitor to testify on its behalf, including teachers who had never taught Daniel. The district wasted so much of the court's time that expert witnesses for the Salazars, brought in to testify on a variety of relevant legal and professional issues, finally had to return home. What should have been a clear-cut case of parental rights became a circus orchestrated by educrats who arguably had a greater stake in the outcome than either Daniel or his parents. If the Salazars managed to overturn the "emotionally handicapped" determination and remove their child from the SED class, other parents would be emboldened. Such a precedent could not be tolerated.

The school district, of course, had an entire arsenal at its disposal – the teachers' union and a cottage industry of mental-health specialists consisting of social workers, special-education resource agencies, behavioral-research institutes, and the American Psychological Association, all of which stand to benefit financially and politically from a burgeoning "at-risk" population. Teams of legal advisors for the school district worked to disallow testimony from any expert witness for the Salazars who might threaten their case (for example, pediatric neurologist Dr. Fred Baughman, on the grounds that he wasn't an expert in learning disabilities).

Like most people, the judge was not expected to know much about the behavioral "sciences." A pediatric neurologist should have been a shoo-in as an expert witness since the school's own "psycho-educational evaluation" had justified massive intrusions into Daniel's family on the grounds that neurological factors might be contributing to the boy's problem. But Dr. Baughman's testimony was disallowed just as he was about to take the witness stand.

The Salazars' ace-in-the-hole was a professional tutor, Barbara Rivera, a petite, blonde dynamo who has never met an "uneducable" child. Having successfully homeschooled her own children, she discovered that they enjoyed seeking out the least fortunate and bringing them hope and concrete educational, financial, and social opportunities. Dozens of big stores contributed surplus items to the Riveras' literacy project. Within five years, the Riveras were taking in the homeless, stocking the bare kitchens of people they hardly knew, nursing other people's sick children back to health, and enlisting the enthusiastic aid of dozens of "uneducable" kids to do likewise.

A down-home woman with a sense of humor, Mrs. Rivera explained to the court that Daniel Salazar didn't have a learning problem. He was simply overwhelmed by a large campus; a seemingly unpredictable environment; and hundreds of little bodies running all over the place. For a child who is already a bit flustered, she explained, the first task he has trouble mastering can sometimes shake his confidence and compromise further learning. Rivera's successes center on recapturing that first botched assignment, then moving on in a small, nurturing environment.

If the school had paid attention to its own case-study evaluation, Mrs. Rivera pointed out, someone would have capitalized on Daniel's strengths, such as higher-than-normal computation skills, an aptitude for music, above-average rote memory, successes with drill and repetition, and increased comprehension when concrete examples are used to explain something. Daniel also had good spatial orientation and above-average auditory memory. The problem was visual perception. But because the old skill drills of previous eras have been discredited by the education establishment (workbooks, for example, are no longer used), teachers have forgotten how to build the self-confidence of kids like Daniel – specifically, by having him repeat tasks he did well in a variety of formats. Punctuation and grammar, for example, improve markedly when children with good sight memories rewrite sentences so that just the nouns or verbs change each time, rather like practicing a favorite football play using different scenarios.

But prospective teachers don't learn these techniques in their university classes now. Proficiency and excellence are not priorities. Indeed, teaching children how to learn isn't a priority. Instead, the primary focus in education is psychology and its close relative, social work. "Ed psych," as education majors call it, indoctrinates naive college students into the cult of group-think, a scheme that plays out in the classroom as "cooperative learning," "social promotion," "gradeflation," "process orientation," and "interdependence."

The Salazar case underscores the way in which education policymakers perceive students – "labor force management," "human capital," and "human resources." These labels, like the ones applied to Daniel Salazar, equate human beings with inanimate objects which occasionally "malfunction." Conversely, the ubiquitous surveys, questionnaires, and opinion polls are so personal in nature that children and parents believe that someone important cares what ordinary people think. But the surveys are only marketing tools, implying an autonomy nobody possesses any longer.

A whole range of characteristics never before viewed as destructive, such as strong religious conviction, today are regarded as markers (risk factors) for mental illness. Every raised eyebrow and grimace is scrutinized for some sinister meaning by battalions of professional paranoids who call themselves "scientists." Red-flag behaviors, such as rocking in a chair or swinging one's foot, are matched against arbitrary designations on a checklist drawn up by behavioral-research institutes. These psychological screening instruments are sold to school districts, government agencies, and corporations to help them "assess" their "human resources."

Beginning at increasingly younger ages, those with unfashionable beliefs and unique character traits are treated as "defectives" – rigid, uncooperative, or unstable blobs who either must be rehabilitated or weeded out of the job pool. Elementary and secondary schoolteachers play into the hands of bloated bureaucracies vying for government tax breaks, contracts, grants, or partnerships to help carry the unfunded mandate of political correctness.

Thus, schools today promote success without achievement, ethics without religion, and character without morals. Educators proclaim the message of self-esteem, but any attempt to pull ahead of the crowd is discouraged (except in sports and entertainment) because it might make everyone else feel deficient. Amid all the noisy chatter about "relevancy" and "real-world" experiences, our schools have obliterated the concept of failure.

Clinical-sounding labels such as "emotionally handicapped" may make failure more palatable. They certainly make it more permanent.

Meanwhile, the common pantheon of heroes and villains, poems and stories, paintings and documents that gave a diverse people unity and a common voice and heritage are disappearing. Even basic reading and computation have been made so convoluted and controversial that average parents can no longer follow their children's lessons.

On June 2, 2000, the judge handed down a precedent-setting decision in the Salazar Case. She determined that the psychiatric examination of Daniel was invalid since it was not conducted by a medical doctor, which is illegal under state law. She agreed that the parents had been misled as to the nature of the "special class" in which the youngster had been placed and ordered that he be returned to a normal educational setting. Apparently, the judge saw through the thinly veiled attempts to intimidate the Salazars into drugging Daniel, as well as the efforts to keep expert witnesses for the parents from testifying in court. Since May, when the judge ordered Daniel placed in regular classes on an ad hoc basis before the final decision, his behavior has completely turned around.

Daniel will understand eventually, if he doesn't already, that he was a pawn; another victim of an educational system that calls itself "child-centered" but is actually centered on money and politics. In the 1930's, behavioral eugenist Paul Popenoe of the American Eugenics Society (later renamed "the Society for the Study of Social Biology") declared that "the educational system should be a sieve, through which all the children of a country are passed. It is highly desirable that no child escape inspection."

The landmark, federally subsidized Behavioral Science Teacher Education Project (BSTEP), launched in 1969 at Michigan State University, set this nation on the course described by Popenoe. BSTEP changed education from a ticket to self-determination to a management tool of the state.

Today's "humanized" educational environment is short on transmission of knowledge and long on market research, human experimentation, and psychobabble. Experts with behavioral-science degrees, not education credentials, are merging psychology with computer technology – and in so doing, they are delivering the Holy Grail of social engineering.

No child today dare march to the beat of a different drummer. The sexpots and studs of the 1960's who thumbed their noses at the rules, called police "pigs," and mocked traditional standards of morality are now hell-bent on micromanaging every facet of people's lives. They dot every "i" and cross every "t," but they never rethink their ultimate objective. They know that the perfect crime is not getting away with something even after one is caught red-handed; the perfect crime is the one that nobody knows has been committed. In education, this has meant launching an army of misguided educators-cum-social workers to examine everything from our opinions to our medical records and bank accounts. All the Einsteins who ever flunked algebra, all the Beethovens who ever composed without hearing, all the mavericks who somehow catapulted civilization thousands of years beyond where it would have been – to the asylum with them. Gently, if possible. Kicking and screaming, if necessary. Resistance is futile.

Or is it? The Salazars' case might teach us a thing or two about the virtues of resistance.

TERMS OF EMPOWERMENT

Imagine, if you can, thousands of parents last January insisting that the Fairfax County, Virginia school board distribute a 169-question sex survey to their 13-, 15-, and 17-year-olds. Envision legions of taxpayers falling all over themselves to divert $60,000 earmarked for educational purposes to ask students about oral sex, number of sexual partners, depression, and suicide.

Children behaving badly isn't news, of course. The question here is, Who – and, more importantly, how many – are those promoting tell-all polls in the classroom?

A close examination of news accounts reveals the answer: special interests, especially social "service" agencies and other organized causes feasting on greenbacks from federal, state, and local governments. Every foundation, association, and Center-for-Whatever – from the Sex Information and Education Council of the United States (SIECUS) to Planned Parenthood – is hot to get its pet nonacademic program into the schools, particularly if it focuses on sex, race, the failures of parents, or mental illness.

Powerful incentives exist to goad as many children as possible into "confessing" antisocial and unhealthy attitudes. Kevin P. Dwyer, president of the National Association of School Psychologists, defends psychological pop quizzes, explaining that this "valuable information [is] almost impossible to obtain from any other source ... " He worries that a negative court ruling might prompt legislators to nix all questionnaires.

Fairfax's survey is only the latest flap. The furor of 2002, for example, was over Ridgewood (New Jersey) High School's 156-question survey: "Profiles of Student Life: Attitudes and Behaviors." This brainchild of the Minneapolis-based Search Institute received, not coincidentally, major funding for "prevention" projects from several government agencies.

A Fairfax County Board of Supervisors' task force, the Youth Survey Working Group, launched the Virginia survey. Committee members knew perfectly well that asking minors to divulge information of an intimate, political, or unlawful nature without parental knowledge or consent is unethical and usually illegal and that repeating questions in various formats to ensure that the information compromises the respondents is tantamount to entrapment. In any case, most school officials are aware that students' responses are not really anonymous but "confidential" – i.e., that responses are typically "slugged" (preidentified) and disclosed on a need-to-know basis.

Parents are deemed nuisances to be circumvented, not cooperating partners. Dr. Karen Effrem, parent and pediatrician with the Maple River Education Coalition in St. Paul, Minnesota, testified at a recent hearing before her state legislature that the No Child Left Behind Act threatens parental authority.

"If parents are really cooperative," stated Dr. Effrem, "federal and state government will allow them to participate in the educational decisions regarding their own children." This is the key issue: The state and the education establishment, in collusion with the hydra-headed mental-health industry, have decided that most parents are unwilling or unable to provide meaningful guidance to their children.

No sooner had Dr. Effrem presented her testimony than officials in Lebanon, Pennsylvania, announced they would become a pilot district for a new initiative – to disseminate parent report cards. Parents in the 4,200-student district would earn grades based on attendance at parent-teacher conferences, returning papers with the required signatures, and seeing that their youngsters come to school healthy – all admirable goals, no doubt, but insulting to parents who routinely fulfill their responsibilities. Might a parent receive a low mark for, say, objecting to the sex questionnaire in Virginia or for promoting "intolerant" attitudes about single parenthood and "alternative lifestyles"?

Coercive personal surveys permeate today's classrooms, from health to history classes. Nearly all carry political overtones and affect curricula. Some questionnaires include items asking what newspapers and magazines are found in students' homes and solicit information on parents' health or finances. The formats typically are a mixture of true/false, "what would-you-do-if," and "how-do-you-feel-when" queries. That is why newspapers are able to report that "16 percent of 12-year-olds say they have" done this or that in the past month.

Not only is such information frequently individually identifiable, but much of it is cross-referenceable with other computerized data. With the increasing interoperability of local, state, and federal computer systems – under the mandate of information-sharing – comes the specter of citizen dossiers.

Is such extensive record-keeping already underway?

That depends on who needs it. Electronic cross-matching (a.k.a. "data-trafficking" and "data-mining") is expensive and time-consuming. Should an individual sufficiently irritate someone important, aspire to public office, or become a whistle-blower, however, all kinds of data, including political and social views, are trotted out. As info-matching services become more lucrative and national-ID proposals take on new urgency in the name of security, the sheer frequency and volume of data collection is potentially evolving into a political litmus test.

Today's questionnaires and screening instruments amount to psychological profiling. The presumption is that if people have nothing to hide, they will comply. The term voluntary suggests the freedom to opt out. In practice, there are implied repercussions for refusing. Thus, most school surveys do not make the headlines. Consent forms, if any exist, usually find their way home after the fact. Invasive questionnaires may even be incorporated in an academic test or appear as part of a curriculum or school activity.

In one Philadelphia-area Christian school, pupils were asked questions similar to those on the Fairfax survey. The school, while private, received some tax support, which was all it took to launch the survey – to compile government-mandated health statistics. Many times, questions are formulated by contractors with ties to such organizations as SIECUS and Planned Parenthood, which favor graphic sex curricula, aggressive mental-health interventions, and extremist political causes.

Pennsylvania has been awash in phony testing and survey scandals since 1973, when the American Civil Liberties Union first took the state education agency's Division of Testing to task for asking personal questions on standardized tests without parental knowledge or consent. The suit was dropped when the state agreed to provide written notice. By 1984, however, unauthorized fishing expeditions into students' private lives were again a source of controversy. The state was caught red-handed tying curriculum and federal dollars to the "test" questions. Today the practice is ubiquitous, and another survey is headed for Pennsylvania's public schools (see "Survey Will Ask Students about Private Family Matters," www.pennlive.corn/news/patriotnews).

Alison Delsite, spokeswoman for the Pennsylvania Crime and Delinquency Commission, told the Patriot News that "[t]he questionnaire is designed to find out how many young people are at risk for drug abuse, violence and other problems. The information is used to target state and local money and prevention efforts."

Why is state and local money being funneled into prevention efforts in schools? Because the federal dollars received by each state's Department of Education are tied to "violence prevention." These monies are passed on to local school districts through such entities as Pennsylvania's Crime and Delinquency Commission.

Who is behind the Pennsylvania survey? The "Channing Bete Company, a Massachusetts firm that markets Communities That Care, a youth violence prevention effort." The organization was paid by the federal government to develop a survey and receive even more money for administering it. (A version of the survey can be viewed at: www.pccd.state.pa.us/Stats/does/PAYS2001.)

In response to a legal challenge by parents, Fairfax County Attorney David Bobzien determined in February that the survey asking high school students about their sex experiences *is* legal, that it does not violate Chapter 31, Title 20, Section 1232h of the U.S. Code, which states that "no student shall be required, as part of any applicable program, to submit to a survey, analysis, or evaluation that reveals information concerning ... sex behavior and attitudes ... without the prior consent of the parent."

Huh? The rationale for this determination was that the survey was a *local* initiative and did not involve *federal funds*. "U.S. Code" means federal law.

This is a typical response to lawsuits from parent groups. The burden – financial and otherwise – falls to parents to uncover the federal funding behind such surveys, resulting in huge legal fees for discovery. Attorneys usually can pursue the money trail far enough to locate the "incentives" and "technical assistance" that federal agencies and their subgrantees provide. It can be a long, daunting process, however.

There is an even more subtle disincentive to take on the system. Beginning in their youngsters' elementary-school years, parents are urged to "get involved" – serve on curriculum committees, task forces, in the PTA. The illusion is that their views really matter. Parents soon discover, however, that, unless their values conform to the predetermined "consensus," they are ostracized. The "approved opinions" always seem to emanate from well-heeled special interests – like SIECUS.

So just how did those nasty little questionnaires get into the Fairfax and Ridgewood schools? The answer is consensus-building.

Such methods as the Delphi Technique, among others, originated years ago as a means of moving contentious business meetings along. Gradually, these strategies evolved into something more manipulative.

Special interests know that only those controversial initiatives judged to be "in the interest of the state" and to have community support will survive. For example, the federal government is prohibited by law from becoming involved in determining curricula – unless some subject is deemed "in the interest of the state." Teen pregnancy, school violence, sexually transmitted diseases, and a whole range of social objectives fall into that category – but not such basic subjects as spelling, math, or geography. Initiatives likely to be rejected by the public require careful nurturing. But by creating an impression of voter support, legislators and school officials can be convinced to implement projects that most parents dislike, even abhor.

Parents who balk are "Delphied" out. Posing as unbiased moderators of a discussion, trained "facilitators" representing the special interest are sent to communities to engineer a phony consensus. After ascertaining the various factions within the target group, the facilitator deftly pits one against the other until only the pre-approved view is left standing. Alternative opinions are rejected as backward, extreme, or reactionary – by "consensus." Principle is dumped in favor of group-think, which is the adult form of peer pressure.

Consider what are characterized today as majority views on sex and cohabitation. The special-interest groups would have us believe that most people accept illegitimacy and sex outside of marriage and that modern birth-control methods have made abstinence and monogamy obsolete. According to Zogby International, however, by a 2.4 to 1 margin, parents disapprove of comprehensive sex education. Even more condemn the "safe-sex" curricula promoted by the Centers for Disease Control and Prevention. Two thirds of parents disapprove of telling children aged five to eight details of sexual intercourse or self-arousal, of telling youngsters between the ages of nine and 12 that homosexual relationships are satisfying, and of teaching 12- to 15-year-olds that cohabitation is as good as marriage. Parents feel strongly that "sexual or physical intimacy should occur between two people involved in a lifelong, mutually faithful marriage commitment." They approve teaching abstinence as a primary response to epidemic STD's, out-of-wedlock pregnancies, and abortions.

For years, groups such as SIECUS, Planned Parenthood, the Alan Guttmancher Institute, the National Education Association, the CDC, and Advocates for Youth, among others, have claimed that between 80 and 90 percent of parents support "comprehensive" sex-education programs for young children. How did these groups achieve such a misrepresentation of public opinion? By conducting manipulative focus groups and disseminating surveys that describe explicit sex education in vague, even compassionate, language.

Most people do not realize that self-determination is removed in the process of consensus-building. Those who oppose coercive surveys could shut down the process, take back the discussion, and reframe the debate – if they knew how. The less time our schools actually spend teaching, however, the less graduates can hold on to, or argue for, their personal, beliefs – a self-perpetuating problem that becomes deadly for representative democracy.

This is the real tragedy of our declining schools – where "consensus" is sold as "empowerment."

FIXING OUR SCHOOLS:
A REAL "NO-BRAINER"

How many education majors are specializing in any of the following: visual and auditory memory, visual identification, spatial and abstract reasoning, mental stamina (i.e., concentration), perceptual speed, hand-eye coordination, and thought-expression synchronization?

Don't bother looking. You probably won't find any. High-priced learning centers, on the other hand, make increasing use of cutting-edge scientific research to train their staffs in establishing a substructure of learning skills *first*, before trying to remediate anything. That's how these places stay in business — for parents who can afford them when their offspring start foundering.

Suppose, for example, a child thinks ¼ is bigger than ½ based on the logic that 4 is bigger than 2. This is a fairly sure-fire indication that the student has an abstract or spatial reasoning problem. He'll try to memorize his way through math. By fifth grade, he'll crash. He'll struggle with tax and budget issues. He will find that his memory, no matter how spectacular, will take him only so far in mathematics.

Or, consider reading. By the third grade, every child should be able to do it fluently and nearly effortlessly. But if the child has difficulty recalling sounds, he will need intensive and systematic phonics to enhance his auditory memory. Suppose his eye movement pattern, left to right, is laborious and jerky. If so, his visual speed is impaired and a machine that literally trains the eyes to move increasingly faster, left-to-right, in tiny increments, can remedy the youngster's problem until he or she is proficient at doing what most children are naturally adept at.

So, which of these nine areas above are the most important? Perceptual speed? Spatial reasoning?

If you answered "none," move to the head of the class.

Nearly all of us are weak in *at least* one of these areas. The good news is that every single deficiency is remediable, *without drugs*, especially if caught early.

Now, suppose every child took a *real* diagnostic test to find his or her weakest learning element. Suppose, on day one of first grade or kindergarten every child was matched with a teacher whose lesson plans revolved around one of those elements on the list.

Well, after a year or so, the child who is weak in, say, spatial reasoning wouldn't have that problem anymore. And what's even better, there would be no stigma whatsoever. Neither the student nor his classmates would know why he spent a year with teacher Smith instead of instructor Jones.

Instead of doing what *real* educational experts have spent years perfecting based on the latest research and technologies, we (and, alas, other nations as well) have bought into the failed "mental illness" paradigm, which says, essentially, that academic success or failure is traceable to personality, upbringing and social factors. Accordingly, we slap stigmatizing labels on a seven-year-old because he can't draw a stick figure of his mother (or something equally ridiculous), the implication being that the pupil has "issues" involving Mom that somehow affect the ability to add or spell. Then we throw the poor kid into an environment geared to *behavior* problems, **not** learning problems, and call it "Special Education." There, he gets zero remedial help for the three R's (teachers aren't schooled in the basic learning elements, remember?), but he spends a whole lot of time engaged in the three F's — frustration, fightin' and fidgetin'.

To survive in the Special Education environment, the child adapts — either by becoming apathetic (i.e., "thick skinned" enough to tolerate any sort of abuse) or super-aggressive (so as to win never-ending turf battles with out-of-control peers). The losers emerge from this toxic environment either drugged with psychotropic cocktails or hating school or both.

If a child is drugged, the brain chemistry will change over time in ways not fully understood. Some become mentally challenged in earnest, another responds with anger to the point of violence, and still more children suffer bizarre, life-altering side-effects, such as an absent sex drive, frequently associated with antidepressants. By the teenage years, a drugged child may well be "unreachable."

If you wonder why teens and young adults are committing crimes unheard of 50 years ago — microwaving their babies, bombing their schools, shooting coworkers — you might want to consider the academic climate they are being exposed to in school. Even some of the "model" curriculums are virtual sales pitches for bad behavior.

Bullying per se isn't new; it has *always* existed in one form or another. But psychotropic drugs and Special Ed *are* relatively new phenomena. How much good has either of these approaches accomplished?

Over the years, the primary so-called professional association for educators, the National Education Association (NEA), has amassed some 300 policy positions, itemized as annual resolutions and set out in a published Legislative Agenda. The publication purportedly reflects *all* educators' beliefs on assorted issues, from homosexual advocacy to abortion "rights" to condemning capital punishment. Parents, religious leaders, and even many teachers themselves have winced at the increasingly bellicose demands of NEA leaders, who, since 1948, have consistently taken the most extreme positions on domestic and international issues and spent their members' dues on political advocacy.

The one thing the NEA *hasn't* done is to make the job of teaching easier for teachers — or, in fact, even to take the job of instruction seriously.

From college onward, prospective and practicing teachers are told that they need to be part of their "professional association" (e.g., either the NEA or its lone competitor, the American Federation of Teachers (AFT), which is almost as bad) to be considered true professionals. The unions, for their part, rarely take on a teacher's case unless it involves either a salary dispute or promotes one of the union's pet political causes.

Despite sporadic dissent, the NEA managed to consolidate its hold through a rigid, three-tiered membership scheme in the early 1970s, trammeling the rights of any heretic within the profession who dared express a viewpoint contrary to the union's "approved" stance, and pitting teachers against their administrations in an ongoing battle for supremacy. They forced every school district to choose between the NEA and the AFT as their collective bargaining agent, and woe be unto anyone trying to become a "free agent."

Consequently, the NEA has been able to run its state and local affiliates like little fiefdoms using Stasi-style efficiency through such adjunct organizations as "Uniserve" — spying on teachers and thwarting the careers of any educator reputed to be on the wrong side of NEA politics.

Each new crop of teachers, ever less educated than the ones before them, believes the NEA and the AFT are standing up for them when they call for things like increased funding of Special Education and "universal mental health screening." What these educators fail to see is that this sort of activity adds to their workload and makes schools even more chaotic and violent.

For example, most teachers have been talked into the idea that mental health screening will help isolate potentially violent children (ignore for a moment that segregation, in *any* context, is unlawful). What they don't see is that it's not only school psychologists who will be doing the screening, but teachers, too. They now have a whole other job to add to their workday.

The NEA also doesn't point out the long-term repercussions of screening, or that embedded in the mandate is a plan to examine teachers, too.

Psychological screening is a profiling mechanism. It's sure to turn political (and ugly) once the entire initiative is in place, stigmatizing the politically incorrect (whatever that is in 20 years) along with the "loner" and the "genius." Every person, in essence, will be punished for daring to think for himself.

Meanwhile, taxes increase to provide extracurricular goodies that educrats hope will "keep kids in school" — instead of with their families, whose childrearing once centered on Judeo-Christian standards that countered humanity's baser instincts. With the parenting function all but transferred to the therapist via the state, using the school to "professionalize" parenting, mothers and fathers are relegated to breeding and feeding and providing financial support, but little else. Already, parents are deemed "amateurs," while schoolteachers and psychologists are sold as "unbiased" and "professional."

With four high-profile scandals involving the NEA and its gofers in 2003 alone, one would have thought there was a window of opportunity to de-fang a major leftist headache that has been helping to churn out good little socialists for decades. Stealing money outright from members, credit-card scandals at the highest levels, inciting students to march for abortion and protest the "War on Terrorism" in the aftermath of Sept. 11.

These did not make good press. Yet, even teachers themselves, to say nothing of congressional oversight committees, were afraid to pull the plug on the union's tax-exempt status.

Which brings us back to those nine, make-or-break elements of learning.

The NEA and the AFT could have had at their disposal insights from thousands of teachers and educational experts (the ones with actual track records). These might have translated into better teacher-education courses, productive education research, and effective policymaking at the state and local levels.

Instead, the two unions chose the lower route of yellow journalism, pitting teachers against management, teachers against parents, and finally teachers against students. Now the educator stands alone, amid an onslaught of rotten apples from all directions.

Principals and superintendents no longer go to bat for classroom teachers, parents neither respect nor trust them, and pupils view their instructors as babysitters.

Why is this enormously large behemoth that ridiculously calls itself a "professional organization" being allowed to continue letting kids and teachers down? Why are politicians so afraid of an organization with such a horrendous record of scandal? Why are teacher-delegates to the NEA's own annual convention still balking at some of the leadership's various *diktats*, even when they get rudely sidelined? What do Americans have to show for the kinds of institutional settings both unions have advocated and lobbied for — the dropped dress codes, the lax discipline, the biased curriculums, the graphic sex questionnaires? Why do we continue to throw tax dollars at failure-ridden social programs?

More to the point, why do we continue to label social programs "education" and psychological profiling "tests"?

The two teachers' unions have played the American public for suckers. They frittered away their chance to "make a difference" — first out of financial greed; then, for raw political power. They have turned two generations of educators into social workers, and now our nation's leaders have the audacity to wonder "what went wrong".

Yikes! Talk about a no-brainer!

Building character and demonstrating knowledge-based proficiency are the only two endeavors that matter in childhood.

Maybe it's time government re-thought its strategy ... ya think?

ALTER EGO

Since 1970 'ed psych' has taken over education. Baby Boomers, meet John Dewey.

It was the year of the nation's Bicentennial, 1976, when education's high priests finally succeeded in their struggle (which had been going on since the heyday of John Dewey's "progressive education" in the 1920s) to shift schools away from academics and toward socialization and guardianship. Teachers threw out stuffy old books, tests and curricula were dumbed down, and once-neat rows of desks were replaced by "open classrooms."

The increasingly powerful teachers' unions solidified their gains by insisting that teachers be treated as "experts" and "professionals." The tactic swelled union membership rolls as classrooms dissolved into chaos. But the upshot of unionization was that it launched an us-against-them mentality. Frustrated teachers lashed out at their superiors and at the mothers and fathers who expected so much from them. Meanwhile, the new variety of school principal pushed teachers to pass failing students and "relate to youngsters on their own terms." Grade inflation became rampant.

So along came "accountability" legislation. Accountability meant developing a process by which we teachers would prove statistically each term that so much learning had transpired in our classrooms. This sounded professional and hard-nosed. But since there was no longer any hint as to what a child ought to know by such-and-such a grade, department heads told us to write our objectives accordingly. If we set our goals too high, they said, we were the ones who would look bad.

Besides concern for promotions and funding, the schools' rationale was that nobody should have his personality "warped" by failure. Education psychologists in expensive think tanks questioned whether the ability to spell correctly was worth the price of a traumatized student. (They didn't ask if the license to spell incorrectly was worth the price of a traumatized adult.) Psychologists challenged: Do you want your child to be a Hitler?

A Mussolini? This struck a chord with the World War II generation.

By 1978, day care was a booming business, and educators had become "agents of social change" and "facilitators of learning." Psychiatrists touted the day-care concept as being not only beneficial to parents, but a boon to a child's socialization and school readiness. The reality, of course, was less positive. Day-care centers overstimulated toddlers and made them nervous; they transmitted diseases like hepatitis; and they weakened the bond between parent and child. But the groundwork had been laid. Institutions of "learning" had now taken on a new function: that of substitute parent.

Unsurprisingly, by the 1980s American teachers were no longer able to take pleasure or pride in their work – and the quality of new teachers suffered accordingly. Many couldn't do simple math; some didn't know their history or geography; others couldn't punctuate or spell correctly. Of course, by that time many of the experienced instructors of yesteryear had been weeded out, leaving young people who knew more about "ed psych" than their subject area. Child psychology, adolescent psychology, educational psychology, behavioral psychology – when I left graduate school in 1972, psychology courses already had superseded scholarly pursuits for America's prospective educators.

By 1990, the teacher had become almost indistinguishable from the National Education Association's far-Left political agenda to the majority of taxpayers. That agenda was dominated by the Human Potential Movement, which, in turn, was directed by many of the same behavioral psychologists who had orchestrated the shift of education's focus in the first place – people such as Ralph Tyler (1903-1994), former U.S. Commissioner of Education. His forte was educational testing, which was typically long on attitudes and opinions and short on substance. For example, in Pennsylvania's Education Quality Assessment, 61 per cent of the questions were in the following vein:

"I feel I don't have much chance to control things that happen to me." Check: (a) Very true of me. (b) Mostly true of me. (c) Mostly untrue of me. (d) Very untrue of me.

You are asked to sit at a table with retarded students. In this situation you would feel: (a) Very comfortable. (b) Comfortable. (c) Slightly uncomfortable. (d) Very uncomfortable.

If a majority of students in a school district gave "inappropriate" responses to the same questions, then "remedial" minicourses were brought in to improve scores. In other words, personal opinions were being assessed for "correctness," then "remediated" if they didn't pass muster. Furthermore, most tests are "slugged" so as to be identifiable down to the individual child – so much for anonymity.

Despite periodic protests by parents' groups, the practice has been largely ignored by legislators – until February 9, 1996, when the Pittsburgh Tribune-Review's Dennis Barbagello scooped the rest of the media with a story concerning three Pennsylvania school districts targeted to be part of a psychological experiment. He revealed that the National Institutes of Mental Health had made a grant to Western Psychiatric Institute for a study of pharmaceutical and psychosocial treatments of Attention Deficit Disorder.

Neither parents nor school boards had been fully apprised of the effort; they had to find out for themselves. As a result, one district (Shaaler) refused to participate, another (Gateway) quit after six weeks. Only low-income Duquesne fully participated.

Although Western Psychiatric vehemently denies administering any experimental drugs — that part of the charge is still being investigated — the psychological questionnaires are in hand. Records exist of particular children having been seen and perhaps treated by a psychiatrist. Insurance companies, potential employers, or political opponents would find such information useful. State Rep. Sam Rohrer spearheaded an investigation, then penned a potentially precedent-setting "opt-out" bill for parents.

It was Ralph Tyler's "whole-child" approach to education that brought us to this point. In theory "whole-child" education meant targeting the child's emotions, feelings, and beliefs as well as his intellect. In practice, what the child believed and felt became more important than what he knew, and schooling became a process of "changing students' fixed beliefs" (to use the phrase coined by Tyler's colleague Benjamin Bloom) instead of imparting substantive knowledge.

As Tyler's theme was picked up and promulgated, the primary thrust was to develop strategies for inculcating "appropriate responses" to life's challenges. The primary method was "behavioral conditioning" — a technique advanced by B. F. Skinner (and pioneered by Pavlov and his famous dog).

Various labels have been applied to behavioral conditioning — from "effective schools movement" and "humanizing education" in the 1970s to "mastery learning" in the 1980s and "outcome-based education" (OBE) in the 1990s. But all reflect a socialization agenda John Dewey would have approved.

Banking on the fact that most people (including teachers) will never investigate the semantics, education heavyweights at the NEA and the Department of Education continue to call what they are doing "cognitive learning" and insist that the goals and outcomes of OBE are going to usher in a new era of tough "standards."

The words "cognitive" and "standards" sound like English, and the average person translates this as "academics" — i.e., the sort of facts transmitted through a traditional curriculum: Where is the equator? If a 60 days note of $950 is discounted at a bank at 5½ per cent, what are the proceeds? But in the technical terminology used by behavioral psychologists, "cognitive" means that curricula dealing primarily with attitudes, opinions, viewpoints, and beliefs constitute "basic" subject matter.

The public also misinterprets terms like modifying behavior, targeting attitudes, and outcomes. Because of the massive problem of disruptive students, the public assumes that behavior means "conduct," that attitude means "temperament," and that outcomes mean "standards." Not so. In the jargon of psychology, modifying behavior means "altering beliefs," attitude is synonymous with "viewpoint," and outcomes are the automatic, subconscious responses a child is supposed to have when he leaves school.

Because we have allowed psychology to become education's alter ego, the entire school-age population is deemed "at risk" for one reason or another — while good, caring parents abandon the system in droves. Miscreants are provided with all manner of special programs and enticements, while disciplined and motivated children are forced to tutor the pupils who won't buckle down.

The overriding concern of school authorities is to keep disruptive students from dropping out, not to produce leaders for tomorrow.

FINAL SOLUTION:
The Hostile Takeover of America's Schools

The Alliance for the Separation of School and State ("SepCon") is just one of several organizations nationwide to recognize that a government powerful enough to feed, burp and entertain the nation's children all day is also potent enough to hold their futures hostage to whatever may be politically correct. The Alliance, in conjunction with the Frontline Ministry's Exodus Mandate Project (motto: "get the kids out"), seeks to devise a mass exit strategy from so-called public schools. "So-called" because the "public" has long since been removed from any decision-making prerogatives.

Parents at SepCon's November 2004 conference explored a variety of alternatives to vouchers, charter, and magnet facilities, which were viewed as overly attached to government funding sources and, thus, beholden to the same special interests and directives as tax-supported institutions. Younger parents had learned from their older counterparts: They could "pay now or pay later." Once a child comes home traumatized, bored or just plain hating school, the chances of turning it all around is just about nil.

Public education exacerbates today's toxic youth subculture. The combined forces of advertisers, television, teen magazines, and Internet spammers already have lured our nation's youth into lives of promiscuity. Government schools add incompetence and dependency to the mix—all wrapped in a façade of "learning" and "testing" packages.

Government education, unfortunately, never quite met the promised ideal. One reason is that the "free" schooling, as everyone's birthright (*ergo*, entitlement), runs counter to it being a privilege.

Even so, as lately as 1950, public schools were mostly "creating unity out of diversity and nationalism out of particularism." Historian Henry Steele Commager noted that year in a piece for Time, Inc., that the goal of American schooling was still centered on passing along a "common body of knowledge," which children could then take into whatever profession or avocation they fancied. "Poets like Bryant, Longfellow and Whittier; painters like Trumball, Stuart and Peale; historians like Jared Sparks and George Bancroft; schoolmen like Noah Webster with his Spellers, William H. McGuffey with his Readers—these and scores of others popularized that common group of heroes and villains, ... images and values, of which national spirit is born," he wrote.

How many graduates recognize even half of these famous Americans today? And why do government educrats not view it as necessary that they should?

Many youngsters no longer know enough about America's past to value ideals like "national spirit." Worse, vast numbers of immigrant children are not mainstreaming as they once did. And they have no desire to do so.

Recent attempts to scrap teaching of the Declaration of Independence underscore how leftist organizers are ratcheting up their intimidation of federal and state education bureaucracies in an attempt to redirect the allegiances of the next generation. Diaries and correspondences of George Washington, John Adams, Thomas Jefferson and William Penn are presently deemed inappropriate requirements, because they contain references to a Creator. Ditto the Pledge of Allegiance.

The Internet news service, WorldNetDaily, was first to report on November 23, 2004, that Patricia Vidmar, principal of Stevens Creek School in the Cupertino Union School District of greater Oakland, California, ordered a Christian teacher, Stephen Williams, to henceforth submit his lesson plans and supplemental handouts for advance approval *because he gave copies of the Declaration and other writings by the Founding Fathers to his American history students*. Attorneys for the Alliance Defense Fund filed suit on Mr. Williams's behalf. Federal law and California's Education Code *do* allow "references to religion or references to or the use of religious literature," said ADF Senior Counsel Gary McCaleb, "... when such references or uses are incidental to, or illustrative of, matters properly included in the course of study."

The massive effort to expunge all references to Christianity in particular, and to theistic religion in general, has been underway for years. One cause is the entanglement of tax-exempt advocacy groups with state and federal governments.

Take, for example, the Fordham Foundation and Achieve, Inc., both frequent federal grant recipients. Erich Martel, a Washington D.C.-based social studies teacher who writes for both entities, called it an "historical error" to include the Declaration among America's founding documents. Steve Kelley, Minnesota's State Senator and Chairman of its Education Committee, abruptly concurred, stating: "The Declaration of Independence has no legal status in defining people's rights and privileges." This is tantamount to censoring the document.

November's SepCon conference revealed a widening contingent of parents that is fed up with government schools. Many attendees were politically liberal and non-Christian, with advanced degrees in physics, medicine, engineering, law, and history. They resented wacky courses like:

- "constructivist math" (also called "guess-and-check");
- "whole language" (reading);
- "inventive spelling";
- "Ebonics" (street grammar);
- "multicultural history" at the expense of Western civilization;
- "junk science" (hypotheses taught as facts, such as global warming/cooling;) and
- "situational ethics," an updated version of the old "values clarification" without reference to philosophy or religion.

Apologists for today's government schools justify the de-emphasis on Western culture and English grammar by complaining that names from, say, Third World countries could have been added to Commager's list of influential people.

But did that make it necessary to denigrate the rest of them?

Through similar experiences and curricula, the young people of yesteryear came to see themselves as part of one nation. Immigrants, no matter how they got here, were "Americanized"; the United States absorbed an unprecedented number of racial and ethnic stocks, not to mention religious faiths, each decade from 1840-1950. Commager writes how youngsters took home with them the speech, standards of fair play and free-market values they picked up at school.

Beginning about 1965, the goals of public education made a U-turn. Counterculture Marxists exploited their carefully planted Fifth Column forces to radicalize America's government schools, couching their mission in terms of "social conscience" and "mental health."

All at once, out of nationalism we got particularism. Nonstandard and substandard speech were held up as a models to be emulated, instead of being respected for what they were: vanishing dialects that once were part of our culture, and possibly worthy of study on their own merits, much as Latin used to be, but not intended as exemplars of social or professional communication today.

Concepts about merit dissolved, save in sports; ostensibly to "level the playing field." This objective was articulated at the highest levels of government. *The* definitive paper, "Measuring the Quality of Education," penned by National Institute of Education's Archie LaPointe and Willard Wirtz, maintained that "[a] different kind of assessment would help correct the tilt in ... educational standards ... toward functional literacy and away from excellence"—i.e., *functional literacy* was deemed more realistic than the former ideal of a well-rounded, educated person.

Meanwhile, tasks once the domain of the home and church were usurped by the school. Parents were encouraged to abdicate their childrearing responsibilities—first, via day care centers (which didn't exist, as such, until about 1977); then extended kindergarten programs, pushed by "early-childhood-education" advocates; and finally nonstop after-school activities that ran parents ragged. Family meals became impossible, as parents chauffeured their offspring from one event to another, blindly accepting the experts' view that socialization was key to college acceptance—and to life itself.

By the time parents started trying to reclaim their authority, in the 1990's, they found themselves shut out.

Child advocacy agencies started running amok under the cover of "protecting kids." Today, parents live in fear that even the most ordinary occurrence—such as in Michigan, when a youngster remarked to his teacher that "mommy dropped a thermometer last night in the bathroom"—may result in school staff alerting Child Protective Service agents to check out their homes and demand all kinds of expensive, excessive and unnecessary "precautions" (in this case, replacing every single tile in the bathroom, even though it had been thoroughly cleaned). The implicit threat is that the child can be forcefully removed unless a parent fully *and cheerfully* complies.

Such intimidation sends a sobering message to youngsters—that parents are incompetent, and their counsel need not be heeded.

Commager observed in 1950 that "[s]chools reflect the society they serve." "A society ... indifferent to its own heritage cannot expect schools to make good the indifference. A society that slurs over fundamental principles cannot demand that its schools instruct in abiding moral values."

But if the school can be transformed into a mini-society that substitutes the authority of peers and teacher/caretakers for actual parents, then the family will *not be able* to pass along its heritage or principles. This, coupled to unsound teaching, is how the left facilitated inculcation of new, "preferred" values.

Today, when parents admonish their children to think for themselves, the school undercuts them by reminding youngsters that consensus is more important than whatever principle might be at stake. When mothers and fathers tell their kids to be "true to themselves," the school tells pupils to be flexible instead. When clergymen explain about timeless truths, educators say that change is the *only* absolute.

Moreover, students learn all about life's "gray" areas before they understand the "black and white" ones. So, what can parents expect later, when educators broach tougher topics like euthanasia, end-of-life pain alleviation, abortion, stem-cell research, reproductive fertility methods, DNA monitoring, and microchip tracking? Free and thoughtful deliberation?

In November 2004, *Time Magazine*'s Michelle Cottle wrote that "[w]hile the Bush White House may be on the side of social conservatives, time is not.... Day to day, liberals have the luxury of ignoring conservative America.... Social conservatives, by contrast, cannot escape the world view of blue staters. Every time they go to the movies or turn on the television or open their child's schoolbooks they're reminded that traditional values ain't what they used to be."

(See also the Washington Times, Nov. 30, report at www.washtimes.com/national/inpolitics.htm.)

Cottle's remarks echo leftist film-maker Michael Moore's June 2004 comment, insisting, in effect, that the Marxist world view is now thoroughly entrenched ("despite Republican control of the White House and Congress, America is liberal").

Meanwhile, the left is working overtime to avoid a Reaganesque backslide into traditionalism. It is pulling out all the stops—frivolous lawsuits, appalling textbooks, and mandatory mental "health" screening—in an effort to assure an emerging generation of easy targets for demagoguery. Even the new college entrance exams (SATs and ACTs) require essay questions that probe student worldviews (see *New York Times* article "Federal Plan to Keep Data on Students Worries Some," Nov. 29, 2004). Responses will become part of a pupil's permanent record.

The left is doing what totalitarian elites always do: cutting off the escape routes. The road to college and jobs is littered with obstacles, from deceptive "exams" to scavenging for parents' viewpoints. Home schools are scrutinized for "child abuse."

However, the sudden shrillness of the homosexual movement, together with increasingly lascivious sex education, has shocked even the most "progressive" parents to their senses. Gay/lesbian incursions into government schools, in an era where AIDS and other sexually transmitted diseases are rampant, signal a full-scale assault.

Paul Simao (Reuters News Service) cited a federal study on December 1, 2004, showing a precipitous rise in new cases of AIDS and HIV infection among gay and bisexual men ("HIV, AIDS Cases Rise Among U.S. Gay, Bisexual Men"). The report by the Centers for Disease Control, released in connection with World AIDS Day, said new HIV and AIDS diagnoses in 32 U.S. states rose 11 percent among gay and bisexual men between 2000 and 2003. "Men who have sex with men continue to constitute a substantial proportion of HIV/AIDS cases," admitted the CDC.

The news has not been lost on parents.

Additionally, health departments nationwide report an upsurge in other sexually transmitted diseases. This makes agitation for graphic sex talk and homosexual "tolerance" even more contentious. The implicit message seems clear: Since the public continues to defeat counterculture causes at the polls, leftists are stepping up their campaign of bullying the nation's schoolchildren into accepting sex as a purely recreational sport.

In the four weeks following Election 2004, parents saw four hostile offensives by old-guard Communist front organizations like the American Civil Liberties Union:

- a lawsuit against Kentucky's Boyd County School District over its failure to force students into attending gender-identity "tolerance training" classes;

73

B. K. Eakman

- intimidation of the Defense Department into ending sponsorship of the Boy Scouts;
- a threatened lawsuit against an abstinence-education website; and
- support for a Missouri high-schooler wearing a "gay pride" T-shirt to class.

Sex "education," of course, is the most notorious example of dishonest intellectualism in government schools. Typically, it is folded into a course called "Health." Parents know that little about actual health is disseminated, even during those few weeks when sex and drugs are not the main topics of discussion.

Barely a word is uttered, for example, about the link between gingivitis and periodontal disease—a serious malady that results in the early loss of gums, underlying bone, and teeth. It is largely preventable with today's oral hygiene procedures, but youngsters remain ignorant about infection signals or their remedies. General physiology, once a mainstay of middle- and high-school academia, is essentially reduced to a year-long focus on genitalia.

Today's sex education is grossly biased toward indiscriminate behavior with multiple partners. "Mainstream" folks like Montgomery County, Maryland's school board president, Sharon W. Cox, says that exposing eighth-graders to topics like flavored condoms and sexual orientation are necessary because these represent "reality." The "reality" is that sex educators are contributing to the delinquency of minors and child sex-abuse. Dr. Judith Reisman, president of the Institute for Media Education and author of Kinsey, Crimes & Consequences, writes that some 58,200 children under age 18 were kidnapped in 1999, *not by family members*, but from the streets. Those that returned home were usually sexually abused. Add to that a 418 percent increase in forcible rape, and 523 percent increase in unmarried births from 1960 to 1999.

Educator Donna Garner of Texas says that even "many of the multicultural novels, which have become a regular diet for today's public school students, contain [vulgarity], graphic sex, and violence."

Here is just one sample (for more, go to www.pabbis.com) from a 2003 book entitled *33 Snowfish*, now in Fairfax, Virginia schools:

"On top of everything else, Boobie's got the clap," begins [this] dark tale about three runaways who understand hatred and violence better than love. Custis, an orphan, is fleeing from his "owner," a producer of pornography and snuff films. Custis is accompanied by Curl, a child prostitute, and her boyfriend, Boobie, who has just murdered his parents and kidnapped his baby brother to sell on the streets."

And that's just the review in the Fairfax (Virginia) County Public Schools library catalog)! An excerpt from actual the book goes:

"...made like four films together. The best one was called Girl Eats Boy, *where Bob Motley puts this black pillow case over his head and pretends like he's cutting me with the electric saw. Then he grinds up my legs in a hamburger maker and feeds me to this little girl who lives under the kitchen sink. The little girl's name was Wendy Sue. She was like seven or some sh_t. I think she belonged to one of Bob Motley's boys, but I ain't sure."*

By the end of the book two runaways are dead. The word "sh_t" is used over 163 times; the racial slur, "n_gger," 55 times.

Yet, *33 Snowfish* won an American Library Association (ALA) award for "Top 10 Best Young Adult Book" of the year, a category that extends to 12-year-olds.

Another sample (also copyrighted in 2003), *Boy Meets Boy*, is in eleven Fairfax, Virginia, high schools. The FCPS library catalog summarizes it as a romantic comedy, a "gay love story," revolving around two high school characters. "A drag queen named Infinite Darlene" reigns as "both star quarterback and homecoming queen." The Boy Scouts are renamed the "Joy Scouts."

Parents usually find out about such materials (required and supplemental) midway into the school year. Of course, counterculture advocates know full well that once children have seen something inappropriate, they can't simply "un-see" it. Youngsters may even be cautioned *against* discussing the content of a curriculum with parents, using the sex-abuse excuse.

Schools justify these offerings by pointing out that sex-soaked fare is ubiquitous, and therefore it is in the interest of students for schools to provide "accurate" information.

But government schools do not present accurate information. If educators actually disclosed the particulars of homosexual activity and its consequences, for example—internal bleeding, permanent incontinence, chronic diarrhea, and incurable mouth diseases—most youngsters, no doubt, would be "turned off." So, schools gloss over the gross parts and incite youngsters to experiment.

Just how government schools can "worry" about child sexual abuse, while instructing adolescents in the techniques of perversion and instituting "gay clubs" (there are now some 3,000), is a mystery.

Well, not quite. It doesn't take a rocket scientist to figure out that an increased demand can be created for pornography, sex-"enhancing" products, psychological screening instruments and even psychotherapy given an aggressive enough campaign of legitimized sodomy and promiscuity cloaked in appealing packages like health, tolerance and diversity.

Moreover, under the cover of nonjudgmentalism, diversity, and the Establishment Clause, a hostile takeover of our country is underway—a kind of "final solution" by the forces of the left. If our nation's leaders are too blind or corrupt to acknowledge the fact, then government education has surely outlived its usefulness.

AIN'T EDUCATIN'

On February 7th I got a surprising e-mail from a public high school student. She must have obtained my name on the Internet. This 11th-grade girl asked me to help her with a class project. The young lady sounded like a dutiful pupil, in that she was attempting to fulfill her responsibility to complete an assignment, such as it was. But I was so taken aback by her query I really did not know how to respond, or even if I should. With only the girl's name and school changed (to protect her privacy), I present here, for the reader's enlightenment, the youngster's e-mail verbatim, complete with misspellings and convoluted verbiage:

My name is Mary Jenkins. I am from Banning High School and We are doing a trial on Lord of the Flies. I was wondering if you could help me with some questions? One is "What is the needs of children?" "To what extreme would dominance reach?" "Can any action a child my take be a result in being in these situations and aren't of the child's personal will?" "Could a child control these actions?" "What happens to children mentally without adult supervision?" Please E-mail me back if you can be of any help. Than You, Mary Jenkins

The letter from this student speaks volumes about what is wrong with today's public education system (and a few private ones, too). The errors in capitalization, punctuation, grammar and spelling speak for themselves, of course, and the girl may even be considered "computer literate" on some level.

But was she incapable of utilizing the "spellchecker" and grammar-correction functions, which are provided automatically by most computer programs using red or green underlined prompts?

Obviously, this child had been taught to "just get the thoughts out there" without bothering about tedious spelling and grammatical concerns. This is the way students have been encouraged to write for the past two decades. I ought to know; I was once a classroom teacher. The rationale is that youngsters will not write at all if they are constantly pestered about particulars, so teachers wait – endlessly, it would seem – until such time as their young charges appear "ready" to pursue a more polished piece of work.

To hear schools of teacher preparation tell it, educators are supposed to focus on "critical thinking skills" rather than on boring, repetitive exercises in grammar, spelling and punctuation (not to mention addition, subtraction, multiplication and division). Thus, no doubt, the teacher's assignment: a "trial on *Lord of the Flies*," as opposed, say, to an essay, or maybe a book report.

A trial? To borrow a quip from Jay Leno: "What's that all about?" This doesn't sound like a written assignment at all, but another of those infamous "class activities" – glorified jam sessions during which kids flap their jaws without having to sit down and organize a logical sequence of thoughts.

Speaking of logic: Look again at this 11th-grade student's second question:

"To what extreme would dominance reach?"

Huh?

"Can any action a child my take be a result in being in these situations and aren't of the child's personal will?"

Does she mean to ask whether a child in this circumstance is responsible for his/her actions?

The only question that really makes sense is the last one: "What happens to children mentally without adult supervision?"

Now, that's one I can answer! Obviously, the student's teacher has provided little, if any, "adult" supervision in the conduct of this assignment. What has happened to this pupil, mentally, is that she has been rendered incapable of producing a single coherent thought, thanks to years of gross educational malpractice, yet the teacher is prodding these youngsters to conduct a "trial," the defendants being, presumably, the cast of culprits in the *Lord of the Flies*.

Most of today's 11th-graders, whose grammar- and junior-high-school years have consisted mainly of encounter sessions, condom demonstrations, and Britney Spears/Eminem-style primping, are incapable of debating or analyzing anything on the level of *Lord of the Flies*. In fact, I doubt, from the student's e-mail, that the pupils in her class ever read the book; they probably viewed the film version, brought into the school as a "supplementary exercise."

If the administration—any administration: present or future—should get to the point where it is legitimately interested in improving basic skill levels (beginning, by definition, with reading) and in slashing educational spending for programs that aren't showing a significant bang for the buck (some $4 billion dollars' worth at this writing), then we have *real* experts who already know how to do that. For example, we know how to teach basic reading successfully—via a combination of intensive, systematic phonics and updated technologies, which include incrementally adjustable fast-forward screens that train the eye (and brain) to read faster and more accurately (reminiscent of the difficulty-level settings on today's video games). Increasingly, parents realize that their children are way below 1950s-era grade-level equivalents in reading and math and are investing thousands of dollars in remediation at learning centers that employ these time-tested methodologies. The incremental fast-forward technology, for example, has been around since the 1950s, when the military used them as simulators and for reflex training. These were later modified for entertainment, which generated a predictable down-side with violent video games. But there has been a positive aspect to the technology as well, and the "reading trainer" is one of them.

As for scrapping expensive, but essentially worthless, programs, that's a no-brainer, too:

- Get rid of the phony-baloney, politically correct junk science and stick to the basics.
- Trash all the sex education programs and replace them with a single unit (that's o-n-e) on the reproductive system, which in turn is incorporated into a three-month course in what used to be called "physiology" – a subdivision of "science." That's all children require to become informed about what will likely happen to individuals who engage in any sort of promiscuous sex. If students "do it anyway," as the left assures us they will, that is not the fault of the schools. (Yes, there are good sex education programs out there that send an abstinence/monogamy message. But because they are necessarily in continuous conflict with programs offered by their liberal adversaries, the school environment is further polarized in a way that spends far too much time discussing sex.)
- Get rid of drug "education" programs and fold these, too, into a unit on physiology and anatomy. The time and expense

expended on what has become a counterproductive battle against drugs is ill-spent. Kids know very well what drug-abuse is. There is no need to belabor the issue so that youngsters are literally fixated on the subject.

- Critically examine all those "supplementary activities" (curricula) that come to schools via the National Diffusion Network database from special interest groups. They are time-wasters that consume billions of taxpayer dollars in the form of grant solicitations that go to special interests to devise curricula and other school activities. Many of these activities come under the heading of "socialization" and even "character education." But the kind of "ethics" espoused by such paragons of vice as Advocates for Youth, the Alan Guttmacher Instititute, the Education Commission of the States, the Carnegie Foundation, the Kettering Foundation, the Rockefeller Foundation, the Sex Information and Education Council of the United States, and dozens of other politically motivated institutes with fine-sounding names are not the kinds of entities that intend to help children become responsible citizens.

- Re-instate workbooks, drills, and repetitive exercises at the elementary levels because (surprise, surprise...) younger children actually like these activities. Have you ever seen little kids singing the same verses or repeating the same phrases over and over until they drive their parents nuts? Well, you see, preschoolers and grade-school children like to do that. Successful repetition results in (surprise again!) self-confidence. If schools miss this window of opportunity, they cannot get it back in high school.

- Cut back on sports programs, which have become grossly over-emphasized to the detriment of real education. Sports are nice and do teach sportsmanship, but they are primarily recreational, not educational. Parents who want more sports for their children can do what parents are doing now when they want more music, dance, or art: Enroll their kids in specialized recreational programs outside of school. The fact is, schools actually could do with more emphasis on music, dance and art and less on sports. Sports do not teach kids about their heritage, or to appreciate refined cultural pursuits. No wonder they listen to trash like rap "music." Most youngsters wouldn't know a complex harmony or an impressionist art work if it hit them in the face. (Nor would they recognize a noun or a verb, for that matter.)

The President apparently is completely enamored of his No Child Left Behind initiative, which purports to produce "clear results" by testing youngsters periodically in reading and mathematics. He either will not, or cannot (for political reasons), acknowledge that without totally revamping teacher training. Regardless, no testing program – even if it really does measure academics, as claimed – will boost the base of common knowledge among our youth without wholesale, systemic change.

Today's youngsters already are inundated with surveys: "health" (sex) questionnaires, mental health screenings, behavioral screenings, and personality profiles – most of which pose as legitimate academic instruments, to a greater or lesser extent. What, exactly, have any of these accomplished? Here are some recent samples, compliments of Andrea Peyser in a February 8, 2005, front-page New York Post article titled "Guinea Pig Kids: Paid $25 to rat on parents" (online version Feb. 6: SHOCK QUIZ PAYS GUINEA-PIG KIDS.) According to the article, "[h]undreds of Manhattan sixth-graders are being recruited – in their classrooms – with $25 cash payments to serve as guinea pigs in a psychological study that some parents are calling blatantly racist," wrote Peyser:

- "How much does your father or mother like or love you?" [multiple choice]
- "How often do you feel that adults treat you like you're NOT smart because of your race or ethnicity?" [list of possibilities follows]
- "We have given you a list of the names of all the kids in your grade. Who gets picked on a lot? Who is not liked by teachers?"

Parents and teachers also get a turn. Mothers evidently get paid up to $180 to unload about their children. "And teachers rake in $3 a head for writing student behavioral evaluations – illegal if done during school hours, an education official warned."

This is the very type of activity I first exposed in my 1991 book, *Educating for the New World Order*, warning that such illicit activities would only escalate, which they did. In my 1998 book, *Cloning of the American Mind*, I included even more examples. About once every three months I receive explicit survey questions from parents, teachers and dissenting experts.

State and federal governments are investing a bundle in this nonsense that has yet to prove effective and violates both freedom of conscience and family privacy.

President George W. Bush is not the first to surround himself with the same "experts" who gave us education's current state. Nor is he the first President, Republican or Democrat, to cave in to leftists in Congress, such as Senator Ted Kennedy (the real architect of NCLB), presumably to score points toward other issues the administration wants even more (but rarely gets, in the long run). Moreover, education has become a political football in which the students are viewed as "disposable."

But the ideals articulated in the Constitution are not disposable. If we expect to extend freedom around the world into the next century, as per George W. Bush's 2005 State of the Union speech, we had better get serious about getting our education house in order instead of throwing money at it.

The National Assessment of Educational Progress (NAEP), originally called the Nation's Report Card, used to be voluntary for each state. In 2003, it became mandatory, as every educational researcher worth his or her salt knew it would.

The definitions of "proficiency" are tortured, to say the least, and they vary from state to state, as each pretends to be administering its own exams and setting its own performance standards when in reality they are slightly reworded clones reflecting a nationwide, counterculture agenda.

The fact is that tax-supported schools are not about proficiency at all. At best, "educational" facilities are warehouses to keep kids off the streets, entertained, and out of their parents' hair. At worst, they are politically correct centers of indoctrination under a banner of "mental health."

Until and unless this administration chucks the psychobabble and the fluff, forcefully rejects politicization of the educating process, and gets real experts (including, despite all odds, a few remarkably good teachers, with excellent track records) to lay out a strategy for overhauling schools from top to bottom, we can bring in new Secretaries of Education till the cows come home and still have an institutional behemoth that runs on "empty."

The bottom line: American schools still "ain't educatin'!"

Copyright © 2005, NewsWithViews.com, Reprinted with permission

SO YOU WANT TO BE
AN "EDUCATION" CANDIDATE

Former presidential-challenger Al Gore once challenged his presidential rival by announcing that "[t]he time for generalities without specifics is just about over." It's "time to put up or shut up," he said.

So let's fling down the gauntlet in education, still a campaign issue, by all accounts. Dispense with the sound bites about "school choice," "national standards," "safe schools," and "investing in the future." Here's an opportunity for our education candidates to test their knowledge on the top 20 education issues that real people are talking about, posed here as Q and A's (grading scale follows).

1. Why are school tests (including those from previous years) held tighter than the Pentagon Papers (i.e., exempted from the Freedom of Information Act) so that parents are refused access even after-the-fact?

2. What is it called when school tests and surveys ask children what magazines are in their homes, whether parents have a dishwasher, and the family's favorite vacation spots?

3. What is "predictive computer technology," and how is it useful to experts in determining a student's future employability under School-to-Work legislation?

4. What is the primary focus of college course work for prospective educators, including curriculum and testing specialists?

5. Describe a process called "thought disruption" and explain how it affects learning.

6. What is "cognitive dissonance," and how does it compromise parent-school cooperation?

7. How have terms like "remedial" and "handicap" been redefined so that parents erroneously believe their child will get special help?

8. How "individualized" is an IEP (Individual Education Plan), and what rights do parents have once they sign it?

9. What legal loophole permits the federal government to become involved in state and local curriculum?

10. What is a psychological "marker" (used in behavioral screening devices), and why is "strong religious belief" considered a marker for mental illness?

11. What level of privacy does the term "confidential" confer?

12. What federal law prevents Information Brokers from combing secure databases for "value and lifestyle" information and cross-matching it with political criteria or other public and private records?

13. What is "data-laundering"?

14. Describe the scope of school-related computer cross-matching.

15. How are the principles of advertising harnessed by educators, and what are the two primary advertising axioms?

16. How could schools assure nondiscriminatory testing and placement?

17. Explain the most important ethic that today's teachers are expected to transmit.

18. What links Goals 2000, Outcome-Based Education, School-to-Work and Workforce 2000?

19. What are the long-term effects of psychiatric drugs on growing bodies?

20. What do education experts consider the primary purpose of education?

ANSWERS:

1. The rationale is that the validity of all tests and surveys will be compromised if a layperson sees any of them.

2. *Psychographics*: "the study of social class based on the demographics of income, race, religion and personality traits."

3. By combining responses pupils provide via self-reports and situation-based questionnaires with psychographic data, statisticians can predict how a child will likely react to events in future years. This capability can be turned into a political litmus test by college and job recruiters.

4. Behavioral psychology.

5. "Thought disruption," a technique launched in 1940s Germany, means interrupting the train of thought so that logic cannot proceed. The continual interruptions built into the school day impede a child's ability to concentrate.

6. "Cognitive dissonance" means an unresolvable conflict resulting from attempts to reconcile two opposing "truths" simultaneously. When educators discredit parental teachings, youngsters cannot choose between two opposing "authorities."

7. These are buzz-terms for warehousing kids deemed "uneducable" by the system. Teacher training deals with emotions, not learning methodology.

8. Signing an IEP gives the school control over future education-related decisions and provides virtually no individualized help.

9. "Compelling state interest."

10. *Markers* are "risk factors." Firm religious belief has been linked to the dogmatic, authoritarian, and delusional personality.

11. *Confidential* means "need to know," not "anonymous." Data, including a person's identity, are shared with "approved" entities.

12. No federal law currently prevents database searches and cross-matches. Legal experts are having trouble writing a law that differentiates between legitimate and illegitimate cross-matching.

13. "Data-laundering" means deleting or changing existing data surreptitiously to circumvent #12, above.

14. The SPEEDE/ExPRESS is the largest school collection-and-transfer "engine." WORKLINK, developed by the Educational Testing Service, provides a link to employers.

15. Advertisers were the first to employ psychographics as a means of targeting a market. The primary axioms are: (1) "All consumer behavior is predictable," and (2) "Consumer behavior can be changed." The key is finding what makes the target population tick. School "tests" and surveys, rife with opinion-oriented questions, provide this key. Curriculum becomes the advertising package for social change.

16. Class placement, curriculum, and teacher training built around learning processes (spatial reasoning, perceptual speed, auditory memory, etc.) is nondiscriminatory.

17. "Interdependence": The group is more important than the individual and consensus more important than principle.

18. Funding: Legislators who vote for one, vote for all four.

19. Psychiatric drugs haven't been around long enough to know.

20. "To change the students' fixed beliefs." – Dr. Benjamin Bloom

GRADING SCALE:

19-20 correct = Fit for public office

17-18 correct = Study up for debates

14-16 correct = Easily manipulated by special interests

12-13 correct = Frankly, my dear, you don't know diddly about schools.

SENDING WASHINGTON
AN "EDUCATIONAL" MESSAGE

In case someone out there still can't see the urgency of yanking the kiddies out of public schools—either home-schooling them or placing them in a good private school—you might just want to take a look at last week's newspapers.

Let's see: In Virginia, we have sex felon Edward Lee Hopkins, 18, convicted of sodomizing a 12-year-old boy last February. Hopkins somehow had his 21-year prison sentence completely suspended so that he might undergo psychiatric "treatment" instead. Meanwhile, he's back at George Wythe High School, caught Wednesday, June 2nd, engaging in "consensual" sodomy with another 16-year-old Special Education student right in the classroom!

Where was the teacher? Who knows?

Then we have two teenagers from Oxen Hill High School in Suitland, Maryland, arrested for the murder of senior student, Michael Bassett, over a girl he was innocently offering to buy a Slurpee for at a local 7-Eleven store.

Two middle school 14-year-olds in Winder, Georgia, have just been found guilty of a May 14 conspiracy to pull off a Columbine-inspired mass murder. Two girls testified they saw a gun in one of the boys' lockers. These fine young gentlemen reportedly planned to kill as many people as possible. Their punishment—pending a "social history" on them by psychiatrists: At-home confinement and ankle monitoring bracelets! Doesn't that make you feel warm and fuzzy?

Count on these fellows being back in class next year.

Over the past four weeks, there have been three incidents in the District of Columbia involving warring gang-members, most of whom share classrooms (whenever it suits them) with children just like yours. Remember, the Individuals With Disabilities Education Act precludes expelling delinquents—on the grounds that they may be suffering from mental illness. The stray bullets from these "troubled" students' guns have shattered neighborhood windows, killing innocent children as they watch television and adults going about their daily chores.

I've lost count of the reports involving teachers raping students; pupils assaulting teachers; administrators and teachers dealing in child pornography; kids downloading porn into their classroom computers; and curricular activities built around topics like homophobia, condoms, racial tension, suicide, depression and, well, just about everything except solid academics.

And we won't even talk about dress codes out of Lower Slobovia. One 11-year-old, Ella Gunderson, of Redmond, Washington, was so fed up with hooker-chic that she wrote a letter to the head of Nordstrom's Department Store complaining that the only things she could find to wear in her size and department were low-riding jeans and skin-tight tops. She said the implication was that there is "only one look"—that girls "are supposed to walk around half naked."

Well, of course. That's what public schools have been, in effect, subsidizing for years.

The bottom line is that the government schools are completely out of control in most localities—and even where they aren't, there's a pervasive, anti-intellectualism and spiteful kiddy subculture that are part and parcel of the school environment. All public school students have to contend with this toxic culture.

The Southern Baptists, whose Project Rescue 2010 is encouraging parents not to send their kids back to the public schools next fall (www.GetTheKidsOut.org), are not the only ones who have "had it" with government-subsidized education. Even liberal parents and agnostics increasingly are recognizing that public schools are dangerous places, physically and emotionally, and that their youngsters don't know nearly as much as their parents did at the same grade levels.

Here in the Washington, DC, metropolitan area—among the most politically liberal localities in the nation—there are, ironically, hundreds of private schools from which to choose, and the competition to get a child accepted is fierce. In fact, that is pretty much the case in major metropolitan areas up and down the East Coast. Parents soon learn that they need to start applying and interviewing while their children are still toddlers if they expect to place them in a non-public-school environment.

Even that may not suffice. The process is grueling, with dozens of visitations, forms, references and parent-written essays for each school on a father's or mother's "wish list." No longer is entrance a simple matter of obtaining literature and selecting from the various promotional materials.

Why would liberal parents, especially those in Congress who pretend to be such strong supporters of public education, go to all this trouble? Simple. They don't want their own children saddled with that mess! Yet, they loudly condemn school choice schemes like vouchers and tuition tax credits.

Of course, vouchers, like charter and magnet schools, introduce tax money into schools. This eventually turns the schools that choose to accept pupils from such programs into carbon copies of the public schools—i.e., entities without autonomy. But that is not the reason liberals don't support vouchers and other schemes that would allow less well-endowed parents to choose better options. Liberal politics is all about perception, and liberal legislators think if they pretend to support public education, they will get the support of teacher unions. They gamble that most voters won't ask where legislators send their own kids.

The best approach, of course, would be for Congress and the state legislatures to remove the red tape from launching private schools and to stop interfering in home schools. That way, the supply of alternatives would multiply and eventually bring down costs. But liberals don't like free-market concepts such as supply-and-demand; they prefer elitism—with themselves at the top.

Unfortunately, the long-term solution of non-interference doesn't help the majority of parents right now, regardless of where they happen to be on the political, religious or socio-economic spectrum. American taxpayers have put up with one fiasco after another in the name of improving education for 40 years. Yet, it has not improved. Not the curriculum. Not the tests. Not the learning environment. Not the quality of teachers. (Indeed, who, in their right mind, would even want to teach in a public school these days?)

Meanwhile, Liberty Legal Institute's chief counsel, Kelly Shackelford, has been reciting to a U.S. Senate panel a virtual laundry list of previously unheard-of anti-religion abuses, a war waged under the umbrella of "state-sponsored religion": schoolchildren prohibited from handing out candy or cards bearing religious messages (or anything that might be interpreted as a religious message), public school districts that bar administrators from sending their own children to Christian schools, and religious seminaries punished for failing to get state approval of their boards and curricula.

The message in this plethora of anti-religion legislation is clear: Religious tenets carry no authority and, therefore, even the appearance of legitimacy must be scuttled. What does government have to offer as substitutes? Ankle bracelets. Metal detectors. Suspended sentences. Jailhouse-chic dress codes.

No wonder the recent news items from Virginia, Maryland, Georgia and the District of Columbia are becoming par for the course nationwide.

It's time for responsible adults to draw a line in the sand. Parents must start saying "no," and do it right now. It's summertime; you have time to plan for this. The only way Washington and the state legislatures are going to get the message that America's backbone, its real tax base, isn't putting up with bad schools any more is to take the kids out en masse.

Even if you have to send your children to a private boarding school, or get a group together and home school them, your children—and you—will be better off in the long run.

Look at it this way: You can pay now, or you can pay later—when your kids are traumatized, in trouble, can't get into college, can't get a job ... or are dead. That's what it has come down to.

IF YOU STILL NEED A REASON
TO REJECT GOVERNMENT SCHOOLS

It didn't surprise me when an Associated Press story appeared August 25th announcing that the expulsion of 14-year-old Anthony Latour from a Pennsylvania school for writing vulgar and violent rap lyrics last March had just been overturned by a U.S. District Judge on First Amendment grounds, and that the lad was ordered readmitted at the start of classes the following week. No doubt the youngster's classmates will benefit greatly from his presence in their classroom.

While allusions to Christianity — spoken, written or visual — are forcefully and noisily removed from government-school premises, the malicious and disdainful lyrics of rap "artists" and their disciples are enshrined in constitutional holiness.

Of course, the omnipresent leftist organization, the American Civil Liberties Union (ACLU), was on-hand in a heartbeat to represent the reprehensible young devotee of so-called "battle-rap," a term used to dignify this ridiculous "music genre," in which wannabe rock stars compete for their admirers' attention using violent and lurid insults.

Given that this particular ditty included verbiage about shooting up classrooms and other students, even the usually tolerant education administrators were put off and cited "terrorist threats" to get rid of Anthony. Had they been in London, England, this August instead of in Riverside Beaver County, USA, last March, such a charge might have flown, inasmuch as incitement to terror in England, after the subway bombing scare, is presently deemed a criminal act. But, alas, the "caring professions," which have invaded our nation's judicial system along with the schools, have determined that while concepts about sin and guilt necessarily lead to neurosis, agitation to violence and delivery of non-stop put-downs are somehow healthy expressions of merriment. And so, the school was instructed — not asked — to stop taking the language of thugs so seriously and readmit the miscreant.

On the same day, joyful news on the education front emerged from Illinois. Now understand, first of all, that schools need to raise state and property taxes nearly every year to ensure that "learning" facilities are both attractive and learning-friendly. Well, last February, an 18-year-old Chicago boy (legal adult?) emptied the contents of a can of gasoline on papers in his locker and set them on fire — with the stated objective of being expelled! The school was evacuated and classes were canceled for the day. Facing felony charges for carrying (and detonating) explosives, Gianluca DeMarco cut a deal to plead guilty, which resulted in parole and his being allowed to continue his "education" in college, where no doubt the predominantly left-leaning professors will ply him with additional incentives to mayhem.

Almost daily — and not just in inner-city neighborhoods — we read about, or watch newscasts, concerning ongoing horror stories involving our public schools. This, of course, doesn't mean that nothing bad ever happens at private and parochial schools, but with one overriding difference: the real threat of expulsion and punishment. The Individuals With Disabilities Education Act (IDEA), in particular, has morphed into a revolving door for young criminals and scoundrels who have no interest in learning. IDEA has vastly expanded the concept of "disability" in tax-supported settings.

This means that no matter how responsible you are in disciplining and monitoring your own child, you have no control whatsoever over the behavior of the pupil sitting next to him, much less over the hypocritical and counterproductive policies promulgated by the school district and its cohorts in the state and federal bureaucracies. Government educators and bureaucrats really don't care what you think. At school's opening, they may pretend to care, but even the pretense typically is dropped by Christmastime — excuse me, "Winter Vacation."

In the 1960s, parents were irate over the increasing laxity of discipline and the disappearance of substantive learning. Even 20 years ago, one could get several hundred or even a thousand Baby-Boomer parents to a district-wide meeting over trendy notions like outcome-based education; global studies; graphic sex education; pass-fail grading schemes; abolished dress codes; "transformational grammar"; the dissolution of proven teaching techniques (like phonics, memorization, drills, and workbooks); the marginalization of geography and penmanship; excessive emphasis on sports; and immoral or delinquent acts by students or teachers. Today, the buzz-terms have changed, and Boomers are the grandparents, not the parents. One can barely get a handful of citizens to turn out, even for gross offenses (most of them predictable by-products of one or more of the aforementioned fads). Nowadays, parents don't bother themselves unless something really grabs their attention — i.e., a massacre on the order of Littleton, Colorado.

In the years between 1965 and 1988, scholars foresaw that outcome-based education, for example, would end "academics" as we knew it and bring in the kind of touchy-feely fare that currently passes for learning — mainly psychological calisthenics in the form of tell-all surveys, junk science, revised history, social adjustment activities, and exercises in self-esteem. Scores of experts warned that graphic sex education for high-school students would inevitably filter down to the kindergarten level, with rape and sexually provocative conduct played out daily in elementary school classrooms; that sexual activity would no longer be merely an option for children, but a right.

Parents who once rolled their eyes at curricular atrocities like "new math" and "look-say" reading programs have, of course, been vindicated. And dissenting administrators who, in the 1970s, questioned the wisdom of allowing kids who cheated on their exams to remain in school, much less remain at the helm of coveted school committees and events, have long since been replaced by more "open-minded" officials.

Today, neither teachers nor their administrators need any longer experience nightmares over the prospect of merit incentives. They are more concerned with getting hazard-duty compensation than merit pay. They worry about being kicked or even killed by their students; they obsess over parents converging on their classrooms and demanding that little Suzy's grade be raised. They agonize over the ability to keep some semblance of order among their students – completely oblivious to the reasons why their forebears didn't seem to have such troubles.

And then, of course, there are those teachers who have to contend with the likes of parents John and Denise Latour, who, by their very lawsuit at the behest of the ACLU against Riverside Beaver School District, effectively condone vile and

93

repugnant behavior, further stifling the educational process and compromising the school environment (such as it is).

It is a sad commentary on our society that the majority of mothers and fathers have grown so accustomed to their prerogatives being usurped and the education of their children being forfeited that they don't even trouble themselves to fight anymore.

Perhaps some watched their own parents' hard-fought battles in the 1970s and 80s, and noticed just how little their efforts succeeded in the end. Those are the parents, I suspect, who escape — if they can — to private schools, parochial schools, home schools. But more and more, it appears that modern parents simply no longer recognize the values their parents and grandparents fought for as being the "big deals" they once were. The so-called conservative movement, meaning the ideals with which that term is today associated — honor, propriety, merit, tact, principle, integrity, modesty, graciousness, sincerity, individualism, resiliency, sacrifice, humility, virtue, morality, justice, decency — all of those things, at least for the time being, are dead or marginalized, no matter who or what political party is holding the reins of power.

As the new school year looms, if you still are wrestling with the question of whether to take advantage of "free" government-supported schooling, you might want to consider just which delinquents the courts may have recycled back into your child's class.

WALL STREET BLUES:
CONTRACEPTIVES, DRUGS...

A news flash from Wall Street: Retail outlets for all things typically associated with the school year and the K-12 youth market are still reporting disappointing sales at Christmas. Even school clothing—such as it is—has experienced a downturn.

Stephanie Woods of PBS' highly rated Nightly Business Report first alerted investors to expect bad news in a back-to-school segment in August of 2003: "For the true back-to-school basics: pens, paper and notebooks ... the average family spends about $75. [A]dd in electronics, clothes, and all those other extras and the National Retail Federation expects the average family to spend ... only $10 more than families spent last year. Analysts say it's not just a slow economy that's keeping shoppers cautious, retailers say there are no really trendy items this year."

No trendy items?

As soon as I heard this news, I did some checking on the Web (am I ever going to pay for this in spam!). My findings surely will hearten "family life" educators, school counselors, and maybe even a few teachers worried about out-of-control kids and pupils with learning problems. But parents, administration officials and taxpayers already fretting over the last round of test scores, global competitiveness and the dwindling base of common knowledge among America's youth will find little to cheer about in the 2004 school spending department.

Here's what's trendy: Cell phone accessories (especially videophones); condoms (flavored and unflavored); the new generation of MP3s (advertisement: "rockin' to class" for $139-$299); Ortho Evra's "the Patch" (a long-lasting alternative to the once-daily pill); and a new generation of psychiatric drugs to cover everything from hyperactivity and attention "deficits" to impulsiveness and bullying.

NASDAQ and the Dow, still stuck in the values (if not the ethics) of the 1950's, may not have thought to categorize items on the above list as back-to-school, um, staples. But marketing moguls, being less backward, spent the whole summer hyping these wares in teen magazines, teen movie ads, over the Internet, and in other venues frequented by the typical unsupervised youngster.

Where are their parents? At work, of course, struggling to pay for these gadgets, both gross and frivolous, that will enable their little Jordan (daughter) or Jordan (son)—gender-specific names are out—to fit in, get by, and keep quiet.

Parents figure it's a lose-lose situation. They can pay now (i.e., purchase whatever their little darlings and/or teachers want) or pay later (i.e., to the psychiatrist once their offspring are sufficiently "stressed"). Rarely does it occur to these people that what's stressing children is not the demands of educators and parents, but the cruel expectations of other youngsters.

What do we make of the kiddie trends today? A few observations:

One hears that kids are maturing earlier. As a former teacher, I can assure you that yes, youngsters can draw more spectacular pornographic pictures on their desks. And no doubt children are exposed to more violence and debauchery than their Baby Boomer parents. And with increased immigration and mixed marriages, many American girls, statistically speaking, menstruate somewhat earlier and exhibit secondary sex characteristics a year or so sooner. But parents of Hispanic, Middle Eastern and Asian descent, for example, are quite accustomed to 10-year-olds wearing bras and having periods. For that reason, as late as the 1970's most of these parents were still making sure their daughters were chaperoned in their native countries whenever they ventured into activities where both sexes would be in attendance. Unlike the so-called enlightened parents of American extraction, these folks knew—not to put too fine a point on it—that an elevated bra size does not necessarily translate to "maturity" in higher parts of the anatomy. Twelve and 14-year-olds are still children in the head.

Scientists recently announced they have found the brain chemical responsible for the high-risk, daredevil behaviors so characteristic of youth. But didn't we already have thousands of years of experience admonishing us to expect excesses from youth's recklessness, hotheadedness and indiscretion?

Today, parenting strategies like chaperones are laughed at and condemned as "overprotective." School counselors are often the first to inform parents that "children must be allowed to make their own mistakes." Much better, I suppose, to go to court and take out a restraining order on a daughter's manipulative boyfriend or to play grandmother to a 13-year-old's illegitimate baby. That's right. Several such incidences were described in a July 30, 2003 segment on 60 Minutes II.

Instead of going to bed ready for a good night's sleep, today's kids are "revved up," as Jenny Crompton's murderous boyfriend, Mark Smith, now describes his actions of 17 years ago on the 60 Minutes II segment—from a jail cell, where he will spend the rest of his life. To hear him talk, he's had a change of heart—a.k.a. "maturity"—but that doesn't bring back 15-year-old Jenny, whom Smith stabbed to death right before homecoming in retaliation for her ending their year-long relationship, begun when she was only 14 and he, 17.

I walk away from "infotainment" like 60 Minutes with less outrage toward the miscreants than at a society that deliberately puts vulnerable children in harm's way. What is a 14-year-old girl doing dating a 17-year-old boy? Thanks to the plethora of child experts that have been spouting nonsense since the mid-1950's, parents and other authority figures continue to let their young charges down, promoting activities that encourage early dating and age-inappropriate intimacies. In effect, they have spent 40 years subsidizing the Lord-of-the-Flies subculture we have today. Our best response to this mess is, like Jenny Crompton's mother, to go around "raising awareness" about teen violence—i.e., substituting useless social programs for genuine instruction, and endless talk for serious limit-setting.

Meanwhile, today's truly responsible parents try, as best they can, to "get involved." They attend meetings and volunteer till they're blue in the face, but there doesn't seem to be a thing they can do to change the school's—or society's—sorry approach to child guidance.

Of course, schools have long undercut parents' better judgment about such things starting in the 1950s, when they promoted dances for pre-teens. Never mind the thousands of "late bloomers" who really weren't interested in "hooking up." Today, the outrages have come full circle. Health and physical education teachers, under the auspices of "sex education," shower elementary students with a panoply of sex toys and surveys, birth control devices, HIV campaigns, even bringing in "reformed" prostitutes and drug addicts to "raise the awareness" of children who, in their innocence, still equate sex with love. School policymakers legitimize grade-school-age girls coming to school dressed like streetwalkers. They let boys roam the hallways looking like something out of "Nightmare on Elm Street." Even government-sponsored anti-drug ads depict ghoulish, body-pierced teens as merely demonstrating their identity.

Television programs were into selling false realities long before "Survivor," with young people repeatedly thrust into adult-like situations—always pressured to do things that, in real life, carry long-term dangers.

Pity the poor parent who tries to shield a youngster from the combined effects of media excess, violent games and toys, and schools that put sex above grammar, and race-and-gender issues over substantive learning. Parents will circumvent these offensives only by dedicating roughly 100 percent of the time to childrearing. Never has there been a worse time for Mom and Dad to consume themselves with career advancement, "self-actualizing," and upward mobility. Yet, paradoxically, never has there been a time when parents required such elevated incomes —to shield their youngsters from the ravages of a public school system and media industry that stand determined to undermine decency, propriety and virtue.

Today, unsupervised children are assumed to be lazing around, getting into trouble. We call them "latchkey kids." But most home-alone kids, circa pre-1960s, had something to do called "chores." They fixed meals, did laundry, cleaned house, set the table. To earn extra money, they mowed lawns, babysat, raked leaves and shoveled sidewalks—and then did hours of homework.

Nowadays, we call that "exploitation."

In pre-sixties America there were no medications for "learning disabilities," either. Youngsters were expected to pay attention, concentrate and control themselves. Ditto for colds, headaches, menstrual cramps and all the rest of life's transient physical discomforts.

How could such things be "better"? some may ask.

Well, there was an irritating little expression back then called "building character," which none of us Boomers appreciated at the time. But those of our elders who took their adult roles seriously used it with maddening frequency. Today, every little ache and pain is treated as a cataclysmic event. Children grow up with the expectation that adulthood is cushy. They resent suggestions about applying self-discipline or tempering wants. Of course, when grown-up children wind up jobless, divorced and depressed, they move back in with their parents.

There's a term for these overgrown adolescents, too —"boomerang kids." And they're making their parents' golden years miserable.

So, just what are financial planners making of the Christmas season's "gloomy" back-to-school economy? Apparently, economists are taking it in the same spirit that retailers themselves have reserved for Christmas, Easter and other solemn traditions. They simply reduce all to the ultimate *reductio ad absurdum*: "Show me the money."

B. K. Eakman

MARXIST EDUCATION
AND THE WAR ON TERROR

I don't often get into foreign policy issues, but today is an exception. As most people know by now, Spain's conservative Prime Minister, José Maria Aznar, was defeated in a surprise upset immediately following the terrorist attacks on Madrid's subway trains. The winner instead was socialist José Luis Rodriguez Zapatero, who probably rightly accused Mr. Aznar of deliberately deflecting suspicion from al-Qaeda as the mastermind behind the attacks. The conservative party no doubt feared that its support of the United States in the Iraq War would turn voters against Mr. Aznar in the wake of such a devastating attack.

The leaders of al-Qaeda knew the psychology of their targets well. And now that they have succeeded in changing one country's leadership by initiating terrorist attacks, they will surely try it again.

There is a lesson here for the entire free world, but especially for the United States, which has stubbornly refused, in the face of irrefutable evidence, to concede the deleterious effect of UNESCO's, and other, Marxist-based incursions into not only our own education system, but into school curriculums worldwide.

What does education—Marxist or not—have to do with the Spanish vote and/or the war in Iraq?

Quite a bit, actually. Education in the Marxist-socialist vein has always been more about attitudes, values and feelings (technically called "affective" education) than about substance, proficiency or academics. Through UNESCO, which has influenced schools globally since 1947, educators have been delivering the appeasement-"peacenik" mantra to two generations of young people, many of whom of course are now voters. Courses in logic, rhetoric, debate, philosophy and other courses that focus on mental discipline and reason have been stripped away. "Fluff" classes, such as those in women's studies, sexology, and scientifically questionable environmental studies, have taken their places, injecting large doses of radicalism and propaganda along with their psychological thrust. Testing has increasingly included a plethora of psychological, personality and political questions, while those of a scholarly and intellectual nature have diminished or been "dumbed down."

So, while al-Qaeda leaders may be described more as religious zealots and anarchists than Marxists, men like Osama bin Laden, himself the product of a wealthy family and a good education, are not so dumb as to overlook the fact that today's voters in the "Westernized" target countries think with their emotions instead of their rational minds—or that the populations of free-world nations are essentially soft and unaccustomed to displays of backbone. Vomiting teddy bears and flowers at the site of the latest atrocity, while heart-warming, is not the same as standing on principle for something important.

If Spanish voters had been thinking rationally, they might have wondered, upon hearing about a tape in which al-Qaeda called the attacks retribution for Spain's support of the U.S.-led war in Iraq, just why Iraq was of so much interest to al-Qaeda. If the tape had said the attack was al-Qaeda's answer for Afghanistan, the connection would have been obvious. If they had cited "a war against Islam"—even though that is not technically correct—one might concede the point from their perspective, given al-Queda's radical brand of Islam. If they had used the term "war on terror," even that would have been generic enough to circumvent the question. But they said Iraq. So, a logical person has to ask: "Exactly how much contact and what kind of collusion has there been between al-Qaeda and the former government of Iraq?" Maybe, just maybe, we are in the right place, after all.

There are other questions that should occur irrespective of one's views on the Iraq War: What kind of message does the successful ouster of a regime in Spain send to terrorists elsewhere? Not just from al-Qaeda terrorists, but any kind of terrorists, or even "wannabe" terrorists? How successful has the strategy of appeasement been at any time, anywhere in history? And, of course, what kind of track record has the United Nations had in peacemaking anywhere in the world?

Voters in Spain, like most voters in the United States, were raised on a diet of "conflict resolution," in which all the players are moral equivalents who bring to the table only their differing perspectives. In the wake of Columbine and copycat atrocities, of course, Americans have rediscovered the fact that bullies exist, and that they don't care about bringing anything to the table. Undeterred, educators expect psychological counseling to do the trick.

They, and the entire mental health industry, are oblivious to the fact that individuals like Dr. Ayman al Zawahiri, bin Laden's right-hand man and personal doctor, is a psychiatrist, not a mere surgeon, and that he therefore has all the psychiatric training he needs—including a working knowledge of conditioning and drugging techniques, to alter the personality and sanity of his followers and supporters. Likewise, Ali A. Mohamed, the Egyptian psychologist and army officer who pleaded guilty to his role in the American embassy bombings in Kenya and Tanzania, was a top al-Qaeda motivational leader and trainer. In addition to his bomb-making expertise, Mohamed taught his charges to masquerade as "average" Americans and (in his own words) "create cell structures that could be used for operations." He was a master double-agent (he graduated from the elite U.S. Army Special Forces school for foreign officers in Fort Bragg, North Carolina) who penned dozens of training manuals on terror for al-Qaeda.

The trouble with school courses like "conflict resolution" is that young students fail to learn that some people don't want to bring their grievances to a peace table. Such people are not "mentally ill." Their "sickness" is one of spirit. They have not lost their mind, they have lost their conscience. And for that reason, such individuals and groups must be stopped—by force, if necessary. There is no choice. It's a matter of self-defense.

As Baby Boomers worldwide approach their senior years, they have passed along—inadvertently, in some cases—an irresponsible and even deadly legacy of non-reason. They have internalized the psycho-political message of appeasement passed along to them by UNESCO and its Marxist cohorts.

This mind-set carries long-term ramifications, not only for the War on Terror, vis-à-vis the Western nations and al-Qaeda, Hezbollah, and so on, but in policies and initiatives much closer to home. Gay "marriage," removal of religion under the banner of the Establishment clause, school voucher programs, illegal alien amnesty and dozens of other issues wedded to the security of our society and the longevity of our Constitution are being debated in a logical framework that looks like Swiss cheese. The arguments are full of holes; the reasoning seemingly devoid of any perception of cause-and-effect. The masses read or listen to one paragraph concerning the issues of the day and imagine themselves "informed." There is little or no attempt to find out what the other side, especially the conservative side, actually says—because it tends to be too difficult, screened out or censored as it is by the "mainstream" media. So, the public settles for what they believe the other side says, as gleaned through the filter of the liberal-leftist press.

Unfortunately, this is not a phenomenon peculiar to the United States. It is a global phenomenon, bequeathed to Westernized nations largely through UNESCO. UNESCO was established with a joint grant in 1947 from the Carnegie Foundation and ultra-left National Education Association. Remember them? The folks who ruined our schools, promoted anarchy, gave us social engineering, dubbed homeschoolers "child-abusers," and condemned serious learning? Well, now we have something else to thank them for—the success of terrorism.

What goes around, comes around.

B. K. Eakman

EMBEDDED WITH THE PROTESTERS

With a well-synchronized pro-"choice" rally in full throttle last month in Washington, D.C.—co-sponsored by America's largest teacher union, National Education Association (NEA)—it occurred to me that a former teacher-turned-writer, and a native Washingtonian at that, might make the perfect "embedded" journalist right here in the Nation's Capitol.

Expecting to hear at least a few well-thought-out arguments, on April 18 I passed myself off as just another 60's-era radical, darting among the noisy sea of aging hippies, student zealots, anarchists, and even a gay rights activist here and there, asking questions. Behold the composite results, verbatim:

Me: How'd you hear about this rally?

Protester #1: School bulletin board.

Protester #2 (high school student): My teacher.

Protester #3: An NEA flyer.

Protester #4 (another student): Planned Parenthood.

Protestor #5: NOW [National Organization for Women] leaflet.

Protestor #6: ACLU [American Civil Liberties Union].

Me: Did you come with a group or by yourself?

Responses: A group—via vans, minibuses, and Metrorail [subway].

Me: Who put the announcements on school bulletin boards to get the students involved? I thought just teachers were demonstrating.

#2: I dunno.

Me: Who funds Planned Parenthood?

#4: Uh, parents?

Me: And the ACLU?

#2: Environmentalists, I guess....

Me: Just how strongly do you feel about the freedom to choose abortion?

#4: Oh, I hate Bush. He didn't really win the election, you know.

Me: Really? I wasn't aware of that. Wasn't there an investigation?

#4: Oh, that was trumped up. Gore won.

Me: I see. How'd you find out?

#4: Everyone knows. Even our teachers talk about it.

Me: Speaking of teachers, I used to be a teacher.

#2: No kidding.... What'd you teach?

Me: Among other things, debate team and rhetoric.

#2: What?

Me: Debate team and rhetoric.

#2: What's that?

Me: What's what?

#2: What you just said.

Me: Well, both debate team and rhetoric involve speaking skills.

#4: Oh, like drama.

Me: Um, no. Rhetoric's a cross between philosophy and speech. Debate hones your knowledge of history in the context of current events.

#4: Debate does what to knowledge?

Me: Hones it.

#2: What's "hone"? Where'd you say you taught?

Me: Southern California—Los Angeles area. I also taught in a suburb of Houston, where NASA's Johnson Space Center is.

#4: Houston's in Texas, right?

Me: Last I checked. But back to this march. Aside from who won the election, why is abortion rights an issue?

#4: Because Bush is going to get a lot of women killed who don't want to have babies.

Me: He is? What about birth control, or just not being sexually active?

#3: Oh, come on ....

Me: Well? How is the President interfering with birth control and abstaining from sex?

#3: Those are not feasible options. Really ....

Me: Humor me. Why aren't they feasible?

#2: (giggling) Because, you know, stuff breaks and sometimes doesn't work, and you forget .... You know. (turning around) Hey, Mrs. H___, we are getting community service credit for this, aren't we? Response muffled.

#5: Besides, the UN is supposed to deal with that, not Bush.

Me: How's the UN supposed to deal with it?

#5: Hey, you're the teacher. They have whole teams to provide free birth control to undeveloped countries.

Me: What does that have to do with abortion in the USA?

#5: Well, yeah, but Bush wants to force people to get married, and he's trying to pass a law against gay marriage, and -.

Me: Huh? I'm sorry. I'm a little confused here. I just want to know why you support abortion.

#6: You're not for Bush, are you?

Me: I thought the rally was about "choice," not Bush.

#4 (squealing): Omigosh! She is for Bush. I bet she's a Bushie!!!

Me: I'm just an embedded journalist here.

#4 (still squealing): You mean you were inside Iraq?!

Me: Um, no. Inside Washington. I was being facetious.

#4: Being what?

Me: Facetious. Kidding. Joking....

#4: Oh.... You talk funny, you know that?

Me (walking away): Well, enjoy the constitutional right to vent your spleen.

#4: To what? Bent what?

Me (shouting to be heard): Vent. Vent your spleen—uh, air your grievances ... sort of.

#4: Uh, yeah. Well, you too.

Me: Oh, any of you heard of someone named Vladimir Lenin?

#2: Sounds familiar, but sorry, I don't know 'im.

Me: Well, if you run into him, say that Education Secretary Rod Paige sends his congratulations on a first-rate job.

#2: Wanda Page. Sends congratulations to um, John Lennon?

Me: No, no. Vladimir L-e-n-i-n. Gotta go; get some more interviews.

#2: (writing) Okay, Wanda. Bye.

Amusing? Perhaps. But this little exchange carries strategic lessons for conservatives in the upcoming election.

With assorted leftist political intervention groups (PIGs)—the ethically challenged teachers unions, assorted feminist organizations, and the ACLU—lobbying on behalf of education policy, plus a predominantly left-leaning bureaucracy still firmly ensconced within the education establishment, the "defunct" Marxists of Soviet-era notoriety continue to mold successive generations of Americans into the useful idiots of Lenin's dreams, continually aiding and abetting the enemies of freedom.

These large, well-funded entities are undermining every conservative Republican candidate, by helping to ensure that educators and their students toe the liberal line. Until the leftist hammerlock is broken and dismantled, we will not have schools that reflect our founding, constitutional values; we will not promote academic excellence; and teachers who would take our side on the issues won't be given the opportunity to do so.

When everything from teacher training, to textbooks to standardized test questions systematically twists what our nation stands for, it's America itself that gets left behind.

B. K. Eakman

FAMILY

(CHILDREARING, DISCIPLINE, ETHICS & MORALITY)

B. K. Eakman

STOP LEGITIMIZING DISORDERS

Trusted publications like *Scientific American,* reputable columnists like Mona Charen, and even level-headed clinicians — like the American Enterprise Institute's Dr. Sally Satel — all seem to agree: An accelerating epidemic is striking young children — attention-deficit/hyperactivity disorder (ADD-ADHD). Symptoms include inability to concentrate and lack of focus. "Hyperactivity" adds a deleterious mix of social ineptness, impatience, absent-mindedness, disruptiveness and nonstop energy, supposedly rendering sufferers nearly dysfunctional without medication.

First popularized in the early 1950s as a bona fide disorder, tolerance of the phenomenon's more irritating manifestations waned as schools consolidated and class sizes swelled, as parents became dual wage-earners and as day care became ubiquitous. Left with disinterested caretakers from near-infancy, kids returned to their homes nervous, excitable, and clamoring for attention.

Few questioned whether the new holding-tank environments might be over-stimulating youngsters, whether kids were becoming overly dependent on "pre-fab" games, or if staff were requiring youngsters to complete anything or put toys away.

Dissenting medical doctors — among them, pediatric neurologist Dr. Fred Baughman, pediatrician Dr. Karen Effrem, and nutritionist Dr. Mary Ann Block — point out that not a single organic anomaly marks ADD-ADHD — until a psychotropic drug is introduced. In particular, long-term use of Ritalin shows X-ray evidence of atrophying brain tissue. A groundswell of mad-as-hell parents is embarking on legal action.

Children diagnosed with ADD-ADHD frequently are prescribed a panoply of mind-altering drugs, many countering the effects of the other. It's not uncommon to see youngsters taking anti-depressants like Prozac, stimulants like Ritalin, tranquilizers like Valium and anti-anxiety drugs like Xanax at different hours of the day. Schools literally disseminate substance-abuse surveys with one hand and dangerous drugs with the other.

As a youngster in 1950s Washington, I was one of those precocious kids on perpetual overdrive. If there was trouble afoot, I was the first (and most likely) suspect. Impressed with some TV doctor show, I tried to "inoculate" the whole third grade with the "syringe" from my Playskool doctor's kit — except that I replaced the plastic "needle" with a hat pin and carried it around in a jar of goo.

Was I out of my mind? Not really. In my child's view, the hatpin looked more realistic than its "dumb" Playskool counterpart.

When our fourth-grade class broached the topic of World War II cryptography, I concocted a "code" that had my classmates twitching in their seats, making wild gesticulations and weird faces for two weeks — until teachers nabbed my code book.

How disruptive! Did I have ADHD? No, just an active imagination.

Then there was my first piece of "real" jewelry. Captivated by what I perceived to be its intricacy, I brought boxes full of straight pins, gimp and beads to school and spent every spare moment crafting — and selling — well, lots of sparkly junk. Inevitably, pins landed on the floor and the play yard.

Yes, I was a real pain in the . . . well, you get the point. But, alas, I got no excuses for my trouble. My elders only called me "naughty."

If the term "hyperactive" had been in vogue, I would no doubt have found my niche. But thanks to no-nonsense parents, and educators who reinforced their efforts, I learned to channel my energy and put business first. First off, they insisted that I finish one project before starting another. There were consequences when I failed to finish chores; no arguments about TV on school nights (my parents unplugged the set and kept the cord).

Today, I laugh when people say how "organized" I am. Because I still have to remind myself: "Finish the dishes; then you can write your article." My "problem," quite simply, boiled down to bad habits, not "disorders."

Within a mere 30 years, however, the concept of self-discipline has been abandoned, and schools are subject to horrors never previously experienced. It was only after psychologists started launching counterproductive philosophies of child-management that bizarre behaviors spun out of control.

The mix of bad advice, irresponsible entertainment, and psychiatric drugs exacerbate these incidents. But once there's a shooting, suddenly parents are blamed for failing to do all those things experts admonished them against.

Our legislators need to ask some tough questions before they allow schools to intimidate any more parents into drugging their kids into submission. Questions like: What kinds of kickbacks are pharmaceutical companies making off of these "disorders"? Are school psychologists and counselors helping to create killer kids?

Looking at my own childhood in the rearview mirror, I'd say it's time to stop legitimizing so many "disorders" and give the mental health industry a leave of absence from our nation's homes and schools.

OUTSOURCING PARENTHOOD
Thou Hast Conquered, O Boomer

Two categories of parents emerged in the 1970's: those who wanted to rear children and those who merely wanted to have them. I first became aware of the distinction in 1972, about the time the feminist revolution was beginning its blitzkrieg through university campuses. I had been married about four years, and the stark differences in outlook between the two factions had a profound effect not only on the way I viewed starting a family but on my approach to teaching—my chosen career before escaping the profession for more satisfying pursuits.

My husband and I were among the first wave of baby boomers, born in 1946, at the end of World War II. Thus, we wound up oscillating, intellectually and emotionally, between the pre-war belief system and the advancing era of antiauthoritarianism. For me, the former attitude was summed up in the popular lyrics to the theme song of a 1963 film, Wives and Lovers:

Hey, little girl, comb your hair, fix your makeup;
Soon he will open the door.
Don't think because there's a ring on your finger,
You needn't try anymore.
For wives should always be lovers, too.
Run to his arms the moment he comes home to you
I'm warning you.

Day after day, there are girls at the office
And men will always be men
Don't send him off with your hair still in curlers;
You may not see him again.

Translation: Real women don't wear jeans—blue, stonewashed, or otherwise!

I can still remember the words to every verse, though I never saw the actual movie. At 16, the lyrics alone made a huge impression on me. So, unsurprisingly, as a young wife, I sequestered myself in another room if I was going to do my hair; never left anything as crass as a razor on the ledge of the bathtub; and tried, even when I was working, to have dinner fixed, the table set with candles, and to look presentable, no matter how tired I might have been. Some 60's-era wives were literally terrified of "losing their looks" to pregnancy.

But a different view was emerging. I was aware that, at other colleges, girls were throwing away their curlers along with their brassieres, wearing torn blue jeans, and eschewing makeup. A few even called guys for dates. Most had not quite reached the stage where they did not welcome flowers and an opened door.

Nevertheless, there were powerful pressures to buck convention. A youth-obsessed media was catering to, and actively spurring, rebellion against parents and societal norms. Whereas, in the 1950's, teen magazines and children's literature fed a young girl's desire to be "grown up" like Mommy —to wear high heels, maybe sneak a cigarette, dress up for dinner-dances, receive corsages, become proficient at something, marry, and rear children—by the 1970's, these notions had been stood on their head. The goals had changed for both sexes—to dressing like a bum; resisting formal attire for every occasion; drinking until one threw up; sleeping around; and indulging in as much idleness as possible while still living off the largess of one's parents.

That lasted until boomers became parents themselves, at which point their own elders smiled and said, "Sayonara." What nobody counted on (except Pope Paul VI, who has more than been vindicated) was that the new attitude, combined with practicable contraception, would change the face of parenthood and family, and not for the better.

About the time my husband and I had been treated to the umpteenth display of childbirth films and breast-feeding from now-grown school chums and coworkers' wives—all of whom, it seemed, wound up divorced within five years—we realized a trend was afoot that would challenge our lifestyle and threaten our privacy. It may have been the Age of Aquarius, but the philosophical divide that resulted was neither free nor victimless. Sex came to be viewed as a recreational sport, and any babies became virtual trophies announcing an active sex life.

Exactly when we traditionalists, at first dubbed naive and impractical by cynical professors and the media, morphed into "repressive, paternalistic reactionaries" is unclear, but these pejoratives seemed to peak with the Vietnam War.

Couples who wanted to rear children were (and still are) interested in watching their offspring discover an exciting and bountiful world; seeing them take their first tentative steps, and not only in a physical sense; and passing on the values, culture, customs, and traditions that compose what is often referred to as the "extended family" experience.

Couples who sought merely to have children were (and still are) interested in proving their sexual attractiveness. No matter what celebrities of this faction said to the contrary, they were, in reality, advocating outsourced parenthood. Such couples either gave no thought to childrearing, or they adopted the socialist belief that "parenting" (as it came to be called) is best left to professionals. After the initial hullabaloo of giving birth wore off, they inevitably carried on with endeavors more appealing than changing diapers and wiping runny noses. The "extended family" was just one more thing to get away from—unless, of course, one wound up down-and-out with no better alternatives.

In the late 1970's, the more well-to-do went further in their justification, explaining that youngsters were inevitably having more fun with their peers than with adults, thereby institutionalizing what the media had already manufactured as the "generation gap." These "free-thinking" mothers felt they had done their job; they had "proved" their sexuality by enduring pregnancy and childbirth (and had carefully recorded these private moments on film for public display).

By 1978, daycare was big business, and, by the mid-1980's, child experts were aggressively encouraging parents to enroll their children in "early childhood" programs so that the youngsters would be "socialized" and "ready to learn."

But a strange thing happened. Not only were the offspring of the boomers not "socialized"—in the sense of becoming gregarious, well mannered, tactful, polite, fun, or even able to carry on a conversation—they were nervous, uptight, anxious, and torn by the mixed messages emanating from their various preoccupied guardians. They cried more, threw more temper-tantrums, fell ill when separated from their parents or peers, and were plagued with learning "disabilities." The more obnoxious they were, the less their parents wanted them.

I remember a particularly enlightening experience when we invited a couple from my husband's office to a barbecue at our home in 1978. As was customary (we thought), we invited the whole family. The wife asked, very tentatively: "Are you sure you want us to bring the children?" There were three of them, aged five to nine. I did not see a problem. "Well," the wife demurred, "they can be a little rowdy and inconsiderate."

Oh, c'mon, I thought. I teach ninth-graders. How bad can it be?

After they arrived, one child immediately set about opening all the cola bottles he found stored in our closet. The other young man kicked the coffee table repeatedly, right in front of his parents. The four-year-old girl interrupted and carried on continually; she finally settled for the company of our two dogs and, captivated, did not give us, or the dogs, any trouble. The couple spent the entire afternoon disciplining, or attempting to. We adults could barely communicate, much less channel the children into various activities.

"Good Lord," we said almost simultaneously after our guests had left. Is this what we have to look forward to as parents?

As a teacher, I was already beginning to have misgivings, but I chalked them up to having been an only child myself. When I was little, if a child merely cried in a restaurant, parents automatically took the youngster elsewhere so as not to disturb other customers. I could remember being four, trying to get my mother's attention on a bus while she was in conversation with another rider. Frustrated, I finally yelled at the top of my voice. I was summarily yanked off the bus and spanked right there on the sidewalk. Embarrassed and chastened, I decided such behavior was not a winner. Today, my mother would be arrested for child abuse, and my behavior undoubtedly would have escalated to more audacious acts of defiance.

By the mid-1990's, long after I had left teaching, the other shoe dropped. Teachers and care givers could not stand these kids, either. Adults were being kicked, bitten, and spat upon by children as young as three. Teachers complained that six-year-olds came to first grade unable to count to ten, name the colors, or recite the alphabet, much less use scissors or sit still for ten minutes—yet most had been "socialized" in nursery programs aimed at making sure youngsters were "ready to learn."

At that point, the couples who had, all these years, actually coveted the company of their children were suddenly looked upon with suspicion. "Doing something for children" was supposed to mean donating money or volunteering. In an era when most parents stopped attending even the open-house rituals promoted by schools, the notion of actually teaching one's children at home was, well, just weird.

Traditionalist women were particularly weird. Homemakers (much less homeschoolers) "didn't have a life." Increasingly, such mothers were viewed as living through their children, not rearing them. Virtually no one, not even traditionalists themselves, foresaw the ramifications of this worldview. Then there was the "sexy" issue. Traditional women (even those who did not "pump gas") were not sexy. They were "desperate housewives," without the money.

By 2000, the established view was that parenthood was too much for a mere parent, married or otherwise—unless he had advanced degrees in behavioral psychology.

Few parents were aware of a thousand-plus-page landmark treatise in 1969 entitled the Behavioral Science Teacher Education Project (BSTEP), compiled by Michigan State University, one of the government's official research centers for teacher training. BSTEP's purpose was to determine what kind of future world teachers should be preparing. The document predicted that, by the 21st century, drugs would be available to control behavior, alter mood, and even raise intelligence. It forecast that teachers would be "clinicians" and that education would be "based in the behavioral sciences."

Government quietly began taking steps to ensure this outcome—from its treatment of parents in the courts, to the content of tests and surveys in the classroom, to the placement of psychologists in every public school (via the Elementary and Secondary Education Act of 1965). Within 30 years of BSTEP, every quirky conduct, and a few that could not even qualify as idiosyncratic, was remediable with "professional counseling" and a psychotropic drug. All a behavior needed to be was inconvenient or bothersome.

However, there was a catch. The parent who refused such treatments could be cited for "medical neglect." To child "protection" agencies and the family courts, this was no different from denying insulin to a diabetic on religious grounds. In effect, parents no longer had legal standing.

Montgomery County gained distinction earlier this year for revisions to its eighth-through-tenth-grade sex-education curriculum, which included a video of a young female demonstrating how to fit a condom onto a cucumber and warned of the dangers of unprotected sex and cheap condoms that break. It also taught that "sex play with friends of the same gender is not uncommon during early adolescence" and, of course, that homosexuality is not a chosen lifestyle but a "given." Through the ensuing protests, the Montgomery County School Board insisted that parents still had plenty of time to provide input, yet no opinion contrary to the board's was considered. Although established policy actually encouraged parents to visit classrooms, it was trumped by newer state and federal codes that view parents essentially as breeders and feeders. As of this writing, public outrage has resulted in the curriculum being shelved for one year—after which the usual suspects will no doubt try another tactic to exhaust opponents, emotionally and financially.

Clueless boomer parents made their bed; today, all parents must lie in it. Boomers wanted to prove themselves as sexy breeders; 30 years later, these goods are being delivered. Once the boomers started outsourcing parenthood, government did what government does best: It took the whole nine yards.

HAS AMERICA LOST HER MORAL GAG REFLEX?

Since 1935, a branch of psychiatry specializing in hereditary illnesses and abnormalities known as "behavioral eugenics" has been warning of rampant mental illness. Dr. Franz J. Kallmann, who came to America in the mid-1930's, after having served under Ernst Rüdin, head of Hitler's "racial hygiene" program, argued in favor of "psychiatric genetics" even after he arrived on American shores to escape the Third Reich's henchmen. He claimed that, if something were not done soon, schizophrenics would outnumber normal individuals. He and several likeminded colleagues advised initiating a screening program to "counsel against" reproductive rights for those showing evidence of, or suspected of being at future risk of, *any form* of mental illness.

What is and is not symptomatic of "mental illness" is open to interpretation. According to Dr. Kallmann, for example, schizophrenia included "daydreamers, cranks, being cold-hearted or unsociable, persons showing sudden urges in temperament, emotional inadequacy, obstinacy, or superstition." In just the past couple of years, however, television has been awash in advertisements for drugs like Paxil and Zoloft, marketed for "social inadequacy," a term eerily reminiscent of Kallmann's terminology. Like most categories of mental afflictions listed in the *Diagnostic and Statistical Manual of Mental Disorders* (DSM), the ever-expanding bible of the psychiatric profession, such symptoms are highly subjective.

Despite his outlandish pronouncements, accolades surrounded Kallmann in this country, even in such prestigious publications as the *New York Times*. As Nazi atrocities increasingly came to light after the war, however, wiser heads prevailed. Both "psychiatric genetics" and mass screening were quietly shelved until the 1960's and early 70's, when Kenneth Boulding, Carl Bajema and Linda Erlenmeyer-Kimling

(Kallmann's protégé and former president of the American Eugenics Society), among others, brought it up again.

By 1971, the American Eugenics Society (AES) had exchanged its name for the less-intimidating Society for the Study of Social Biology, and its flagship publication, *Eugenics Quarterly*, had adopted a new title, *Social Biology*. Erlenmeyer-Kimling secured large grants, mainly from the National Institute for Mental Health, to pursue her contention that certain "bio-behavioral markers" in "psychiatrically normal children" could be used to predict mental illness. She devised tests that could be used to identify youngsters supposedly predisposed to passing on aberrant traits, with a view to intervention and "counseling." She secured some ten million dollars over the years to continue what was essentially the mission of the old AES: to launch "a program of negative genetics" by controlling who "should and should not have children."

The same year, Carl Bajema, secretary of the old AES, proposed that couples be given a preliminary license to have exactly two children. He assumed that not everyone would want that many children anyway, and those who did could apply for a waiver based on "proof of genetic superiority" in the arts, mental ability, personality, athletics, or business. (How one might "prove" superiority in personality remains a mystery.) Referring to Bajema's waiver concept, Kenneth Boulding lauded *Roe v. Wade*, writing in the Spring 1975 issue of *Social Biology* that it "makes the problem of enforcement much easier...since abortion provides a mechanism for prior elimination of many potential unlicensed babies." However, he cautioned that, while Bajema's waiver might make for "a marketable licensing system," "the political acceptability of this compromise proposal is more questionable than that of a ... system that does not attempt *explicit* eugenic control" (emphasis mine). He went on to propose the development of a mandatory, long-standing contraceptive implant that all females must accept at puberty. "[T]he reversal of the implant's sterilizing effect would be obtainable upon surrendering of a childbearing license," Boulding wrote.

Remember this is coming from specialists in the United States for use on her own citizens, not from the Soviet Union, Germany, or China. Coincidentally, the first serious mood-enhancing drugs were in the pipeline. They happened to have a potent side-effect – lowering of the sex drive.

In 1972, Erlenmeyer-Kimling stated that "attending to the long-term quality of the gene pool was a long-term necessity," and she decided that "society is more likely to tolerate an emphasis on a eugenic attitude that preserves the status quo of the gene pool or prevents it from deteriorating." In other words, she thought that the American public was more apt to buy into eugenics if it didn't have to actually kill anybody but, rather, merely keep the nonconformists and oddballs from having children.

"Who's minding the quality of the gene pool?" Erlenmeyer-Kimling asked.

The essence of evolution is natural selection; the essence of eugenics is the replacement of "natural" selection by conscious, premeditated, or artificial selection in the hope of speeding up the evolution of "desirable" characteristics and the elimination of "undesirable" ones.

To that end, she urged abandoning the "fixation on IQ as the trait to be maximized in our species in favor of an Index of Social Value (or ISV)," never stopping to consider, apparently, the short leap from "desirable characteristics" to "desirable opinions." Given the hasty escape of her mentor, Franz Kallmann, from Nazi clutches, she should have known better.

In any case, Erlenmeyer-Kimling concentrated on attention-deficit disorder as the primary predictor of mental illness. Clarke J. Kestenbaum, describing Erlenmeyer-Kimling's work in the *American Handbook of Psychiatry*, wrote in 1981 that "the children with early [attention-related] deficits...become increasingly deviant behaviorally as they get older [which] supports the hypothesis that attentional dysfunctions serve as early predictors of later pathology." He concurred that "early intervention should include genetic counseling."

Moreover, "negative eugenics" efforts continued under the umbrellas of population control, child care, and mental health.

But the timing of public statements to that effect still was not right in the 1970's and 80's. The emergence of the civil-rights movement meant that the notion of government controlling who should and should not have children on such bases as "social handicap" or "deviance in thought" smacked too much of racial prejudice. Indeed, at the heart of the eugenics movement is the notion of black inferiority and criminality (i.e., "race-specific lifetime...rates of delinquency [and] unwed motherhood"), which in turn is based on something called "bad gene" theory. Sheldon

Segal, former director both of the Population Council and the old AES, and Erlenmeyer-Kimling were among those calling loudest for "control" of "black fertility."

The idea was deferred again.

The prominence during the 1990's of such so-called mental health issues as depression, road rage, school violence, high illegitimacy rates, child sex abuse, and post-partum suicides/murders had, by the year 2000, resulted in aggressive scrutiny of parents, not only by child protective service agencies, but by university mental health researchers marketing new psychiatric-screening instruments to school districts. These instruments increasingly found their way into the classroom, sometimes in conjunction with standardized academic tests, other times as stand-alone questionnaires disguised as health surveys and opinion polls. While some parents balked, most caved in, finding little or no support for their grievances either in their school districts or from the education establishment and fearing, correctly, that failure to acquiesce would blight their children's records. Today, the controversial parent component of the New Freedom Initiative on Mental Health – a nationwide project to screen the entire U.S. population for mental illness and provide a cradle-to-grave continuum of quasi-mandatory therapeutic "services" for those identified as mentally ill *or even at risk of becoming so* – has added to these fears.

The latter legislative atrocity, which I reported on at length in *Chronicles* ("What? Are You Crazy?" October 2004), makes the school the hub of a mass-screening process. (Other authors, such as Dr. Dennis L. Cuddy and Paul Walter on *NewsWithViews.com* and Dr. Karen Effrem of Minnesota's ED-WATCH, have discussed this legislation as well.) Assessment of parents and pregnant women is integral to the plan. Similar pieces of legislation, such as Illinois' "Children's Mental Health Plan/Partnership" and Pennsylvania's "Ounce of Prevention," have passed in various states, so that, when it comes time to fully implement the nationwide directive, most of the country will already be on board.

Now two frightening documents have surfaced. The first articulates a convincing rationale by established psychologists and psychiatrists for resurrecting the concept of parent licensing. A November/December 1996 issue of the social science journal *Society* is suddenly making the rounds—not only among professionals but in Congress. The issue covers a symposium on parent licensing that took place earlier that year. The gist of the proceedings was that increased psychopathy and sociopathy, along with accompanying crime waves, could be vastly reduced if parents were screened for markers of mental illness and counseled against, *even prevented from,* having children. Licensure would carry with it "sanctions," according to several contributors, such as Robert A. Gordon, sociology professor at Johns Hopkins University and a fellow of the American Psychological Association.

Sanctions, of course, inevitably entail the force of law.

Another notable contributor, child psychiatrist Jack C. Westman, M.D. (author of *Licensing Parents: Can We Prevent Child Abuse and Neglect?*), estimated that each sociopath costs society about three million dollars over the course of his lifetime. He called for a long-term solution to require would-be parents to "meet the kind of requirements that one expects of prospective adoptive parents." He suggested that parent-licensing "be handled through the channels of marriage licensing, prenatal care, and birth registration since it essentially would be a question of credentialing." He further endorsed "parent competency testing," describing it as "large-scale testing for signs of parental incompetence...to predict the parenting potential of pregnant women."

A distinction should be made between people who are brain-injured, severely retarded, or otherwise unmistakably brain-damaged, and those who are "mentally ill." In the latter category, there exists no blood test, X-ray, or other examination that can prove a person is of unsound mind. That has left the field wide open to charlatans with ulterior motives for categorizing individuals as "crazy." Indeed, the entire insanity defense has been criticized for years on the grounds that it is subjective and predisposed to deliberate misinterpretation.

Although Westman admitted that large-scale screening was not feasible in 1996, he defended the principle: "A parent license," he wrote, "would validate parental rights and focus public policies on supporting competent parenting and on remedying or replacing incompetent parenting." Westman, however, does not appear to place much stock in "remedying."

"We cannot rely upon every irresponsible person becoming responsible through persuasion, education, or treatment," Westman writes. He cites "the case with habitual criminals,

[who] do not respond to education or persuasion." Yet, it has been an article of liberal faith since the 1960's that education, not punishment, is the answer to criminality. So, is this liberal ideology, mere hypocrisy, or something more frightening?

On October 4, 2004, another staggering pronouncement from the mental health community was made at a Texas Committee hearing on Psychotropic Drugs and Foster Care Children. Even some politically liberal human-rights advocates were stunned when psychiatrist Joe Burkett informed the committee, which was investigating allegations of mass-drugging of children in foster care, that one of the main reasons so many foster kids need to be on psychotropic drugs is that they are from a bad gene pool. Another psychiatrist, Dr. John Sargent, professor of psychiatry and pediatrics at the Baylor College of Medicine and former dean of the Karl Menninger School of Psychiatry and Mental Health Sciences, reiterated the "bad gene" claim, insisting that aggressive psychiatric care is imperative.

At about the same time, (October 9-13, 2004), the 12th World Congress on Psychiatric Genetics was held in Dublin, Ireland. It featured world-renowned speakers and educational workshops, sponsored in large part by drug manufacturing companies with a major interest in psychiatric pharmaceuticals. But there was a surprise from the Institute of German Genetics of Bonn, Germany. In its paper, the Institute backed away from conventional wisdom by stating:

"Whereas complex traits in other fields of medicine are being successfully pinned down to the molecular level, psychiatric genetics still awaits a major breakthrough. It has to be analyzed why mental disorders are obviously harder to tackle."

So, while neurobiological and neuropsychiatric research, including drug treatment, continues unabated, often using normal children under less-than-upfront circumstances, it appears that the field of predictive psychiatry has a long way to go.

Which leaves us exactly where? Back in the 1930's, with politicized psychiatry.

Author Tom Clancy brought the debate into focus in his 2003 work, *Sea of Fire,* by having his protagonist wonder aloud how a government can possibly stop somebody from, say, contaminating the money supply with botulism *via* an ATM machine, or bringing water laced with acid onto a jetliner; he wonders whether such acts can be prevented by screening for

potential psychopaths and sociopaths before they can act –
indeed before they are even born. The character's counterpart
in the story speculates that such an effort on a massive scale
might trigger a "moral gag reflex" in the public at large.

The goal of parent licensing, Westman insists, is noble: It
would acknowledge – by government fiat, if necessary – the
United Nations tenet that "all persons, including children,
should be free from abuse, oppression, and rejection." Westman
assures us that only "a small percentage of parents would not
qualify."

Many of his colleagues go further, however, arguing that
"society must move beyond the notion that children are the
property of their biological parents."

Eugenics has come full circle: from elimination of the feeble-
minded, the criminally inclined, alcoholics and schizophrenics,
to the purging of more modern rejects (the hyperactive, the
attention-challenged, the substance abuser, and a variety of so-
called learning disabled) through "pro-active, reproductive
counseling" in birth control, abortion, and sterilization.

Proponents of parent licensing like David Lykken (whose 1995
book, *The Antisocial Personalities*, focuses on the biological
susceptibility of sociopathy) admit a racial bias in the scheme to
license parents in the 21st century. This, according to both
Lykken and Gordon, is largely because of the high incidence of
single parenthood (illegitimacy) among the black population.
Lykken views single mothering as *the* primary exacerbating
circumstance leading to full-blown sociopathy which, he says,
accounts for much of the difference in crime rate between
blacks and whites.

Most traditionalists would agree that illegitimacy has negative
consequences for children. But Lykken's analysis is misleading.
The increase of single parenthood over the past 30 years has
indeed made parent licensing an easier sell, but it is not an
entirely natural development: society has positively condoned
illegitimacy by removing the social stigma. Single blacks are a
particularly easy target because their lower socio-economic
status makes them less able to fight parent licensing. But once
the effort to target blacks for "parent malpractice" becomes
pervasive, a backlash will occur among African-Americans who
have made their way into the professional ranks and joined the
upper middle-class. Once this outcry begins, the entire
population will be caught up in the licensing web to avoid the

taint of race. "Risk factors" will inevitably take on a political dimension, threatening freedom on every level.

Professor Gordon demonstrates experts' awareness of this eventuality when he cautions his colleagues against overzealousness, correctly citing examples such as the Wenatchee (Washington State) and other harebrained prosecutions of parents or childcare workers for concocted allegations of child abuse, in which supposed experts and other professionals have brought the very concept of expertise into disrepute.

"One must," he writes, "approach child protection as the goal of intervention with extreme caution, lest it come under fire for being politically motivated. Conservatives, recall, are already up in arms over sex education in schools, school questionnaires about home activities that ask about the contents of medicine cabinets, and other intrusions into family privacy that they have come to recognize, not without ample justification, as expanding beyond their original supposed intent."

With that statement, Gordon unwittingly nails the argument against parent licensing, whether he agrees with the conservative position or not. His observations above tell us, first, that: school testing firms (staffed by behavioral psychologists) have always known full well that "test" questions and follow-up curricula significantly intrude into students' beliefs, contrary to their public statements otherwise, and, second, that these "educators" always knew they were on thin legal ice.

Like Drs. Kallmann, Erlenmeyer-Kimling, Boulding, Lykken, Allen, Wender, and Westman, dozens of eugenicists still hold on, expressly or not, to the bold notion first iterated in Genesis, "Ye shall be as gods." According to Catholic University Law School's G. P. Smith (from "Genetic enhancement technologies and the new society," Catholic University Law School, Med Law Int. 2000;4(2):85-95):

> "Genetic planning and eugenic programming are more rational and humane alternatives to population regulation than death by famine and war. Genetic enhancement technologies and the scientific research undertaken to advance them should be viewed as...a tool for enhancing the

B. K. Eakman

health of a Nation's citizens by engineering man's
genetic weaknesses out of the line of inheritance."

Such arrogance, coming down simultaneously with the new
mass-mental-health screening legislation, euphemistically
called the New Freedom Initiative, should activate Americans'
"moral gag reflex" if, indeed, anything, at this point, can do so.

*NOTE TO READERS: On November 9, 2007, PBS' Nightly
Business Report again ran a segment in some localities on
"America's Changing Demographics," raising the specter of
parent licensing within approximately 30 years. The segment
cited out-of-control behavior problems exhibited among modern
children as one reason. This follows a March 1997 program on
"Frontline," which ran a segment entitled "Little Criminals: The
Rationale and Feasibility of Licensing Parents."*

THE DEADLY CONSEQUENCES OF "EXPERT" ADVICE ON CHILDREARING

By now, most people know about the 17-year-old Virginia Commonwealth University freshman, Taylor Marie Behl, whose decomposed body was found October 5th in a ravine on a farm owned by one of the primary suspect's former girlfriends. The funeral took place October 14th. The suspect, 38-year-old Benjamin Fawley, confessed while under arrest on unrelated child pornography and firearms possession charges. He told police that Taylor Behl died accidentally during their sexual encounter and that he panicked, according to the Richmond Times-Dispatch. The couple's relationship had been ongoing for an undisclosed length of time.

The victim's mother, Janet Pelasara, commanded national attention with her smiling, upbeat demeanor during the search for her daughter, missing since September, and only in the aftermath of the funeral did she finally lash out against "the sick subhuman that murdered my beautiful daughter." She said she does not believe Fawley's claim of "accidental" death (although, given the popular forms of "kinky sex," who knows?) and has called for the death penalty should he, or anyone else, be convicted of the crime.

Well, who can blame her?

But there is a more troubling aspect of this case, whether or not Miss Behl's autopsy points to an accidental or deliberate act — the elephant in the living room nobody wants to talk about.

Specifically, what was a 17-year-old minor female doing consorting alone with a 38-year-old male, much less having a sexual relationship with him? And why was a 38-year-old man interested in this 17-year-old girl?

So far, none of her friends are talking, publicly at least, about any of her earlier dating relationships. No one has offered anything that is in any way negative about Miss Behl. Everything points to a normal, friendly, cheerful teenager who, according to her mother, had sex with Fawley "once out of curiosity," but then apparently changed her mind about a further relationship. From news accounts, one can assume she had had sexual relationships with other fellows before this incident.

Unfortunately, this is the kind of result we get when children are tasked early on with "making their own decisions" and "discovering their own values" — things the child experts, psychologists — have been trying to "sell" to parents and teachers for decades. And they succeeded — through parents' magazines, childrearing texts and university departments of teacher preparation.

As a young teacher in the late 1960s, on into the 70s and early 80s, I saw history made. I was there when child experts told parents and teachers to "take the screws off" and let toddlers express themselves. I was there when psychologists admonished adults to stop "snooping" in kids' belongings and give them some "space." I was there when educational psychologists scrapped the dress codes, and advised educators and parents to be children's pals instead of their superiors. I was there when school psychologists and counselors started advising adults to stop lecturing and moralizing, because kids wouldn't listen anyway. I was there when schools started sponsoring dances and dating for pre-pubescent youngsters — crushing tender egos and making peer pressure the end-all that it finally became.

I noticed now that the Office of National Drug Control Policy (ONDCP) is sponsoring TV ads telling parents that they "have more influence than they think," that they are the "anti-drug." A little late for that!

Where was the ONDCP in the mid-'80s, when all we heard was that "children have rights" — rights to sexual information and paraphernalia, rights to access porn on the Internet, rights to sue their parents for disciplining them.

But when the fire hit the fan at Littleton, Colorado; Paducah, Kentucky; and Santee, California — guess what? It was parents who got blamed for not doing all those things the "experts" had been lobbying against for some 40 years. By obliterating the lines between right and wrong and advising kids to discover their own values, youngsters like Taylor Behl are now dealing with horrific dangers never previously experienced, not even in the bad old days when students had to stoke the fire to heat up the classroom. Yet experts continue to call early sexual experimentation "normal" — and the resulting atrocities "mental health issues" instead of moral issues.

The logic goes like this: Guilt over supposed "sins" produces neurosis, as opposed to being a civilizing influence. Therefore, redefining "morality" will produce happier, guilt-free, and mentally healthy people. Guilt supposedly begins when youngsters feel forced to take responsibility for things beyond their control.

Eventually, of course, all behaviors have been deemed outside of individual control. If one's genes and hormones predispose them to behave a certain way, then spiritual awareness is delusional; self-discipline unattainable.

Not content with early, graphic sexual training, child experts now are hot to push the rest of their agenda in schools, including exposure to homosexuality, sodomy, oral sex and even self-labeling.

I really do not blame Taylor Behl's mother, Janet Pelasara, for what happened to her daughter. She is a Baby Boomer, after all. She followed the parenting advice doled out stridently and often to her age-group.

But an earlier generation would have recognized that Taylor Behl was not ready for college, that she needed a lot of oversight and guidance. She clearly lacked the maturity and judgment to be on her own.

Today's parents mistake secondary sex characteristics for emotional maturity. The two do not necessarily go together.

I remember my own high school and college freshman experience. Neither was pleasant. In high school, I was not permitted to attend mixed-sex parties unless they were well-chaperoned, or to car date until I was 16 — and even then, not until my parents had met the fellow. I remember my mother complaining bitterly that even at the private school where I was enrolled, some parents in the 1950s and 60s would wait for folks like mine to put their foot down on unchaperoned events like beach parties before stepping up to the plate and saying "no" themselves.

As a 17-year-old college freshman, I started going out with a 25-year-old part-time student living at a nearby air force base. I was flattered, because he was handsome and treated me like an adult — and because he "rescued" me from a truly awful blind date at a college dance. When my parents met him, however, they put a stop to our romance — not because the fellow actually did anything particularly offensive or was unkempt or rude, but simply because he seemed too old for me, and something seemed "off." They nipped our dating in the bud, certainly before it became anything even close to sexual. But they were extremely authoritarian about it and, I thought at the time, downright insulting.

I hated them for being what would be called "over-protective" and "paternalistic" today. But they were right. The fellow turned out to be frequenting strip clubs in his spare time. Had I married him (which we had discussed), it would not have been a year before I would have discovered that I "wasn't enough" for him. My parents knew me well enough to know I was insecure and that I found it difficult to "hurt" someone by ending even a friendship, much less a romance. So they did the hardest thing they ever had to do; they refused ever to let me see him again, at the threat of pulling me out of college. They checked on my whereabouts ("stalking?") from 300 miles away.

Today, I have been married 37 years — to someone else. I've never had to worry about my core values being different from my husband's, or worse, getting some sexually transmitted disease from a philandering mate — thanks to my parents' intervention some 40 years ago. For sure, they had better things to do with their time than deal with my indignation.

Today, it's all the rage to make fun of anyone who applauds the values of the 1940s and 50s, or endorses monogamy within a marital context, or engages in "paternalism." But Taylor Behl's death — and the trauma of hundreds of young people like her — should stand as a lesson to us all. Before psychiatrists were considered childrearing experts, there were parents who took the difficult road. They risked alienating their children out of love for them, even if it meant scrutinizing the friendships, clothing and activities of their youngsters. Today, between Internet stalkers, mainstreamed pornography, vulgar "music" lyrics and "sexploitive" school curricula — not to mention virulent forms of the old sexually transmitted diseases — such oversight is more important than ever.

THE SEVEN DEADLY SINS
OF PARENTAL IRRESPONSIBILITY

Among talk-show hosts who interview on education issues, the topic *du jour* is school violence. Kiddie terrorism has superseded discussions about curriculum, teaching methods and even school choice. Funny how what once was obvious about juvenile misbehavior is bewildering in the "Theraputic Age," when more clinical data on what makes people tick supposedly has been collected than in any previous era. Childhood meanness always has been a part of growing up — taunting other youngsters, playing malicious practical jokes, indulging in gossip and put-downs, and vying for pecking order in snobbish (or rebel) cliques. Adults, especially parents, used to reign in such conduct, being ever vigilant of youthful excesses. They looked around when they changed the beds, paid attention to the company their offspring kept (and idolized), said "No!" to inappropriate apparel and entertainment, quashed disobedience and punished foul language.

Fast-forward 35 years to when our nation's leaders split hairs over the definition of the word "is." One has to ask: Are weapons really so much easier to obtain than they were, say, in 1946? Or have the taboos simply vanished? Or, more sobering: Have our kids suddenly become certifiably nuts? As a former educator who saw the scribbling on the wall in the 1970's, when schools started soliciting rock stars for antidrug-abuse videos (which my eighth-graders, predictably, laughed at), I see today seven factors turning out this nation's first generation of killer kids:

1. Promotion in schools, parenting texts and product advertising of an authoritarian peer subculture which has replaced adults' long-abdicated role in the areas of leadership and guidance (i.e., adults aren't the authority figure any more.)

2. Decision-making based on consensus rather than on principle as a response to important dilemmas and issues.

3. A daily routine that has youngsters spending more time with each other than with adults.

4. Approaches to education and child-rearing that focus on emotional temperature-taking instead of developing conscience or intellect.

5. The tendency to give smaller offenses a free pass, as in "don't sweat the small stuff," especially in areas such as tact, propriety and orderliness, so that a child views life as a constant challenge to test the limits of parents' and society's tolerance.

6. Proliferation of and emphasis on the gruesome, ugly and prurient in all entertainment mediums: music, film and print. Geared toward ever-younger ages, such fare not only desensitizes children to deplorable and demeaning acts, but creates the impression that one's darker nature should be fully explored.

7. A burgeoning legal drug culture which implies that no self-discipline need be applied to behavior, since character is determined by a plethora of syndromes and brain-chemistry imbalances.

Even toddlers recognize that, for the most part, adults today just go through the motions of child-rearing, occasionally mentoring, not wishing to appear unyielding, inflexible, or dogmatic. Having succumbed to counterproductive notions of child management for some 35 years, gullible parents and educators, who no doubt would have apoplexy over the idea of children being seen not heard, are, ironically, settling for compliance at any price, even if it means drugging every kid who squirms.

Would anybody have dreamed 30 years ago that parents would some day be intimidated by school and day-care staff into placing kids, including preschoolers, on prescription stimulants, antidepressants, tranquilizers and other legal mood or mind-altering drugs? Attention-deficit/hyperactivity disorders are just the beginning. New mental-health breakthroughs reveal an evolving pattern of absurdity: for example, a psychotropic drug (a selective serotonin-reuptake-inhibitor) for shopaholics (oniomania) and psychotherapy for nerds. In the wake of the shootings at Columbine High School in Littleton, Colorado, experts now purvey the view that vengeful nerds may belong to the three out of every 100 children who suffer from a mild form of pervasive developmental disorder (i.e., don't fit in).

The same experts who promote drugs for docility still caution parents against lecturing and scolding, advise turning toddlers into decision makers before they have acquired either values or maturity of judgment and admonish parents who complain of messy bedrooms, immodest apparel and coarse language. Carrying an aspirin for a headache, of course, is a serious matter to school officials.

The bomb thrown to postwar parents by psychologists proved to have a longer half-life and greater destructive force than the one that fell on Hiroshima, Japan. Awash in 35 years of moral hypocrisy and therapeutic zealotry, a confused and self-absorbed baby-boom generation today perpetuates the dynamics of violence, even when it purports to do the opposite through a frenzy of legislation, media campaigns and character curriculums.

The violence will continue until we rediscover common sense.

B. K. Eakman

BEHAVIORAL SCIENCE
& MENTAL HEALTH

B. K. Eakman

BUSHWHACKING JOHNNY

At dinner, ten-year-old Johnny is sullen and uncommunicative. It has been a bad day. His parents pass off his ill humor as "going through a phase."

Actually, it was an easy day, taken up with "another stupid school assembly." Johnny had sat there, bored, listening to people drone on about diversity and tolerance. When a lesbian took the stage, Johnny and his soccer buddies had guffawed.

Later, the school counselor cornered him at his locker:

"You're a big boy now, Johnny. Your Mom and Dad are from another generation, you know, so it's not surprising they wouldn't be tolerant of gay people. You can make up your own mind. You wouldn't want someone looking at you and your friends as 'dumb soccer jocks,' would you?"

Johnny has been subjected to cognitive dissonance, a tactic often used to mold public opinion. Not only does the technique neutralize unwanted input, it's a nearly foolproof method of manipulating groups for political ends. An adult subjected to it at least has the benefit of maturity and experience. He may recognize, however belatedly, the cause of his annoyance. Johnny, however, is too young to weigh matters, so he broods. His confusion may fester for months below any conscious level of awareness.

Technically, cognitive dissonance is "a stressful mental or emotional reaction caused by trying to reconcile two opposing, inconsistent, or conflicting beliefs held simultaneously." In practice, it is a form of mental coercion. (I ought to know: I sat through enough workshops as a prospective educator and practicing teacher. We learned how to disrupt logic, how to make it difficult for the uninitiated to sustain a train of thought.)

Creating a disorienting psychological environment doesn't require an expert agitator or professional provocateur if you can get gullible third parties – teachers, factory workers, even parents, who don't realize what they're doing – to do the dirty work. Educators often think that they are using scientific methodology to transmit "thinking skills" or that they are "empowering pupils to be decision-makers." Budding journalism students may believe they are perfecting interviewing techniques. Political-science majors typically encounter it as "negotiating tactics," which is closer to the truth. But the goal of cognitive dissonance, as with all surreptitious opinion-molding, is to get the target to respond to contrived "stimuli" (especially hot-button topics or situations) with knee-jerk, emotional reactions, leaving reason behind. In so doing, the victim "internalizes," briefly or permanently, an alternate view of reality.

In today's politically correct schools, this is sold as intellectual and academic freedom. Take any controversial issue – e.g., homosexuality – and examine the method used to bushwhack ten-year-old Johnny.

As a pre-adolescent, Johnny naturally looks to his parents as the primary source of authority. But they have made it clear that teachers and other school staff are also his superiors, requiring obedience.

Enter the school counselor: In one fell swoop, she shakes Johnny's confidence in his parents and himself. At ten, Johnny is not mature enough to understand what homosexuals do, but judging from the counselor's comment, it's apparent to him that his parents oppose homosexuality. (The counselor is sure of this because Johnny has completed untold numbers of questionnaires revealing details about his family – from what they read to how they worship.)

The counselor blindsides Johnny on five levels. First, she provides a justification for not abiding by his parents' values. ("They're from another generation.") Then, she strokes Johnny's ego by implying he is more mature than he actually is. ("You're a big boy now.") Next, she plants the idea that his parents' ethics are shallow. ("It's not surprising they wouldn't be tolerant.") Then, she forces Johnny to choose between two opposing authorities under the pretext of thinking independently. ("You can make up your own mind.") Finally, she legitimizes a lifestyle his parents probably oppose. ("Would you want someone looking at you as a 'dumb soccer jock'?")

How can Johnny go to his parents with this? He probably won't even remember the context in which this conversation occurred. How will Johnny resolve the conflict? He doesn't have the opportunity to do that, because the counselor's question called for a response on the spot.

When cognitive dissonance is employed against an unsuspecting person – or worse, against a captive audience such as schoolchildren – the short-term objective is to prompt insecure individuals to find company, leading to a group (mob) mentality. This makes it easier to reverse values held by the majority. "Truth" can even be turned against itself – for example, "freedom of speech" is now used to legitimize pornography. The very people freedom of speech was designed to protect are left not only vulnerable but suspicious of the principle itself.

What "new values" are educators trying to instill? Here is a seven-point list, given to educators in North Carolina at an in-service workshop:

- *There is no right or wrong, only conditioned responses.*
- *The collective good is more important than the individual.*
- *Consensus is more important than principle.*
- *Flexibility is more important than accomplishment.*
- *Nothing is permanent except change.*
- *All ethics are situational; there are no moral absolutes.*
- *There are no perpetrators, only victims.*

Notice that all of the items on this list involve no particular issue; rather, they reflect ethical "outcomes" that a child is supposed to "internalize."

So cognitive dissonance is not quite brainwashing, and it's not quite subliminal advertising, either. It's more like setting somebody up for a psychological fall. It plays with the mind by pitting various perceived "authorities" against one another and exacerbating tensions. After a while, intellectual deliberations shut down, and emotions take over.

Classrooms are rife with examples of cognitive dissonance. Take "The Cry of the Marsh," an environmentalist film shown in many seventh-grade science classes. It opens with an idyllic, rustic landscape, birds singing in the trees, mother ducks leading their young on a pleasant excursion down a creek, rabbits scampering over the ground. The scene oozes fresh air, sunshine, and peace.

Suddenly, a tractor-bulldozer appears. The camera zooms in on the word "AMERICAN" on the side of the yellow vehicle, which is actually the name of the company that manufactured the equipment, though young viewers are left to interpret it as "an American bulldozer." Because of the camera angle, the vehicle looks like a tank. It overturns everything in its path – shrubs, grass, plants. Exhaust fills the air.

A man jumps out of the front seat and goes over to the embankment to drain the creek where the ducklings had been following their mother. Another man brings a can of gasoline, pours it over the surrounding area, and ignites it. As the men drive away, flames leap into the air. Trees catch fire. Living creatures run for cover.

Suddenly, the ducklings – which, by that time, have emerged on the other side of the creek – are overcome by encroaching flames and burned alive. Nests of baby birds come crashing to the ground, and the camera zooms in on what is left. In a final close-up, the tractor-bulldozer is shown plowing under the remains of the nest, the ducklings, and some bird eggs.

As the scene fades from the screen, a sentence flashes: "Man cannot foresee or forestall. He will end by destroying the earth." After the film ends, pupils are divided into groups for a canned discussion activity: "Who Shall Populate the Planet?" Note that this was just before "morphing" technology became available to create such special effects.

Why does this exercise meet the definition of cognitive dissonance? First, there is subliminal deception and psychological impact – the way "AMERICAN" is depicted, the camera angle, the carnage. The last frame in the film condemns mankind wholesale – we will kill off our own species and, possibly, the planet itself. There is no issue to debate. The film aims for the gut, not for intellectual discussion. For all the children know, the men were creating mayhem in the forest purely for pleasure.

Finally, the follow-up exercise requires immediate decision-making – by consensus and under pressure. By the time the children get home, they can be counted on to have forgotten the relationship of the activity to the film and, therefore, will have no context to bring to their bewildered parents, who, no doubt, will hear impassioned outbursts over the ensuing weeks and months about grown-ups "destroying our world!" Parents aren't likely either to see the film or to hear any description of the follow-up activity that triggered this reaction.

With this curriculum under their belt, youngsters are deemed prepared to weigh in on such topics as urban sprawl, nuclear waste, and global warming, all of which require considerably more advanced study than seventh-graders possess. But these particular seventh-graders, prepped as they are, will be quite full of politically correct opinions that they cannot articulate.

Cognitive dissonance is not so much about skewing questions, interjecting bias, or censoring information as it is about a controlled-stress approach to precipitating conflict and overwhelming rational thought. The tactic relies largely on obscuring the lines between "authority," "loyalty," and ego.

You didn't "brainwash" your child into believing that a teacher, policeman, or minister is an authority figure. That's much too strong a term. You did, however, transmit the notion. What happens, then, when one of those authority figures forces your child to choose among them or tries to marginalize the others? The answer largely depends on which authority figure the child spends the most time with and which one the child perceives as being the greater threat to his pride.

Thanks to a culture that increasingly keeps children with their peers and away from their parents, most youngsters today view their classmates as the authority figures – as the persons having the greatest effect on their ego. Unethical educators capitalize on this; they use children to punish and report on other youngsters, then call it "peer pressure" or "classroom dynamics."

Herbert Marcuse identified adolescents as the perfect targets – eager, always, to become independent of their parents but still needy of approval. A fan of Germany's Kurt Lewin, who conducted the first groundbreaking experiments to induce neurosis on a mass scale, Marcuse combined the anti-authoritarianism of Erich Fromm with Karl Marx's theory of alienation (people will do almost anything to avoid ostracism or ridicule) and put it to work. If you could get impressionable young people to believe they were thinking independently, even while performing mob-dependent acts, you could start a revolution, he wrote.

Marcuse went on to foment and organize (usually behind the scenes) many of the campus riots of the 1960's. He understood that it was easier to manipulate groups than individuals. In dealing with team players, you reduce the chance of "lone rangers" who attempt to solve problems on their own initiative.

The key was to blur the lines between dependence and loyalty. Marcuse's students confused group loyalty with herd approval. "We're all in this together" became a recruitment slogan. Today, it's a rallying cry for every agitator with a cause, especially in the social sciences, which, increasingly, includes education.

By placing "interdependence" over "rugged individualism" and a herd mentality over personal principle, educators have scuttled American ideals about self-reliance and personal integrity. If it is politically correct to accept promiscuous behavior as "normal" and monogamy as "religious extremism," then anyone who balks is a pariah.

Thus was my generation (the Baby Boomers) educated to "need" our peers more than we needed our principles, making us easy marks for such tactics as cognitive dissonance. Our grandchildren are now sitting ducks, with civilized norms forever under attack.

Consider the following scenario: A pregnant young woman contracts German measles. After a sonogram and an amniocentesis, she is told her unborn child has serious deformities. Two simultaneous and incompatible messages will plague this woman, both bolstered by the media: First, If I go through with the pregnancy and birth, I am a bad person because I am opting, voluntarily, to commit this child to a tortured existence that I could have prevented. Second, If I terminate this pregnancy, I am a bad person because I have murdered my baby. Conclusion: No matter what I do, I am a bad person.

Enter the "third party," an advertisement: "Just do it!" "Take control of your life!" "Be a decision-maker!" "Do what feels right!"

Unless this woman can "default" to firm principles one way or the other, she is a candidate for suicide. She has been given a justification for not abiding by an earlier generation's values; her ego is stroked by implying she has more decision-making power than she really has (she can't undo the German measles); she has been taught that life-and-death dilemmas are inconveniences, not moral decisions; she must choose between two opposing authorities, God and "science," under the pretext of thinking independently; and, finally, all choices are equally legitimized.

Today, cognitive dissonance is an institutionalized method used to force-feed whatever is politically expedient. In a climate where fear of alienation vastly outweighs fear of moral corruption, what has happened to "intellectual freedom"?

B. K. Eakman

ON EPIDEMIC-LEVEL MENTAL ILLNESS IN KIDS

Christopher Stollar's Special Report to the Washington Times, "'It's a hidden epidemic': Diagnoses of bipolar disorder on rise among youngsters" [Wed., March 9, 2005] was itself an epidemic – an outbreak of articles hyping the supposed increase of various mental illnesses among both children and adults.

These commentaries and reports promote the kinds of pseudo-science that will ensure, one day soon, that all the nation's schoolchildren (plus their parents and teachers) are screened for mental illnesses under outrageous pieces of legislation like the one U.S. Congressman Ron Paul (R-TX) has worked so hard, and unsuccessfully, to defeat: the New Freedom Initiative (a.k.a. Universal Mental Health Screening Program). If mass psychological screening succeeds, regardless of what euphemism it goes by ("freedom initiative"?), it will morph into a political litmus test that holds a child's future hostage to whatever viewpoints happen not to be politically or socially correct at that time. Unlike the young man in Stollar's piece, Alex Raeburn, a child will not have the luxury of changing his mind, maturing, and learning to live with his personality quirks. Once a person is labeled "mentally unbalanced," they face great difficulty in being taken seriously, ever again.

There are significant hints in Stollar's article pointing to the ineffectiveness of both psychiatric diagnoses and drugs. One psychiatrist is said to have just dashed off a prescription for Mellaril, "a drug originally used for schizophrenia." Then the boy was treated for depression. The doctor started him on the antidepressant Zoloft, at which point young Alex became suicidal. At length, the doctor opts for "bipolar disorder." I call this "shot-in-the-dark medicine."

Whenever a drug seems to work for psychological ailments, nobody knows why or how, a fact confirmed in Stollar's article. Experts concede that there is no medical test (blood, x-ray, chemical measurement) for bipolar disorder, depression, schizophrenia, mania or, I might add, for virtually any of the

146

mental "illnesses" listed in the entire *Diagnostic and Statistical Manual of Mental Disorders* (DSM), the bible of the mental health profession.

So, just what kind of medicine is this? If we were talking about a painkiller like Vioxx, and it turned out people keeled over after taking it, that drug would be pulled from the market faster than you could say "ouch!" If there is no medical test, then by definition, there can be no diagnosis. All you have left are a bunch of quirky personality traits. Larry Barber, the marriage and family therapist quoted in Stollar's piece, repeats what many dissident psychiatrists, such as Drs. Peter Breggin and David Healy, have already stated: that psychiatric drugs mainly "blunt [the] ability to function." They do not cure anything.

In an article published in the March issue of *Chronicles: A Magazine of the American Culture* "Has America Lost Her Moral Gag Reflex?"), I wrote about Dr. Franz J. Kallmann, who fled to America in the mid-1930's, after having served under Ernst Rüdin, head of Hitler's "racial hygiene" program. It is appropriate here to revisit this man, who somehow received accolades for his ideas in the New York Times. Even after he arrived on American shores to escape the Third Reich's henchmen, he warned of rampant mental illness, exclaiming that if something weren't done soon, schizophrenics would outnumber normal individuals. He went on to argue in favor of mass mental health screening and "psychiatric genetics" (a.k.a. parent licensing),

Stollar's article is treading on some very thin ice, and so are legislators and educators who buy in to increased mental health canvassing in schools and among parents.

Childhood is extremely difficult for some kids, and parenting is more difficult still. I, too, threatened to kill myself, had disconcerting mood swings, talked fast and would pout for hours or days in silence to get my own way. Fortunately, I had wise parents who bit their lips, literally, and said, "Fine, your tough luck, not ours." It was the hardest thing they ever did, but guess what? I decided making wild threats was not a good way to get attention. I grew up. My parents always knew what was going on. They were there. They set limits. I matured. And I learned to live with my idiosyncrasies. As everyone must, sooner or later.

B. K. Eakman

Without our quirks, eccentricities and peculiarities, we no longer are capable of harnessing the genius of human creativity and that precious commodity so revered by the politically correct elites, diversity.

NOT ANOTHER MENTAL ILLNESS

All I needed to see was the headline. A November 12, 2004, piece in the Washington Times read "Warning: Work may be stressful to your health." I knew right away we were in for it – again. Yet another mental illness was about to grace the ever-increasing listings in the *Diagnostic and Statistical Manual of Mental Disorders* (DSM), the bible of the psychiatric profession.

This time the culprit was "work."

Oh, dear...

According to the article by Al Webb, the British have officially included "work" in its arsenal of diseases, with "a tough new code of standards" to deal with the problem. The piece cited everything from "a stressed-out mathematics teacher" to a correctional staffer in a prison as "eligible," apparently, for compensation in the United Kingdom.

Can America be far behind?

Not understanding ones "roles and responsibilities" on the job ranks right up there with breathing toxic fumes when it comes to the burgeoning "stress epidemic" victimizing thousands of British workers – and, no doubt, American employees, too, as soon as the American Psychological Association recognizes the compensation potential. For example, Webb reports that the math teacher, Alan Barber, got $135,000 after Britain's House of Lords reviewed the gentleman's litany of on-the-job complaints, which included "overwork and 'bullying' by ... superiors."

American attorneys and lawmakers surely must be salivating.

That work of every sort was much more harrowing pre-20th century doesn't appear to be a factor. The Times reporter wrote that work-related stress has changed, as British citizens have become more "Americanized," according to Cary Cooper, professor of psychology (what else?) at U.K.'s University of Lancaster. The British government has responded with an apparently mandatory "framework to help employers and employees tackle stress at work."

This, of course, will translate to more paperwork, thus driving up the cost of doing business. Fewer employees will likely be hired to perform some tasks in order to save money – contributing to, guess what? Even more employee stress. So, what's new about government causing the opposite of whatever it was that it originally intended to accomplish with its funding?

Unfortunately, this time the bill will be two-fold for employers: once to compensate complainants, and again for psychiatrists to hold seminars, draft guidelines, and provide therapy to stressed workers. And we won't even factor in how much company time will be wasted on filings, attorneys, and, of course, stress workshops for employees.

What is interesting about all this is that many people actually thrive on stress. Stress, in the context it is being applied here, provides the necessary motivation to accomplish things, and accomplishment is fulfilling, often irrespective of the size of one's paycheck.

Now, of course, if workers are inhaling toxic fumes, that comes under the heading of hazardous, which is another topic entirely. If unions, for example, were advising their members to strike over unsafe and perilous conditions, few would object. But when workers strike over salaries and stress, they lose their credibility with the public – one reason, perhaps, why so many jobs have gone overseas.

Yes, some functions are made unnecessarily stressful. Take the math teacher in Britain. Like the United States, British schools are teetering on the brink of being out-of-control; although if there were a contest, the US would beat the U.K. hands down in the chaos department. The leftists on both continents, however, have ensured that teachers can achieve little; discipline and actual teaching having taken a back seat to psychological calisthenics, social adjustment games, fads, and sports. Educators aren't taught methodologies that actually work; so they have no means of diagnosing or remediating the learning needs of their young charges. Categories like "special education" are misnomers, since nothing "special" occurs at all. In fact, if anyone is "eligible" for compensation, it should be the pupils, who have no option but to sit in a peer-pressure-cooker day after day, while their real educational requirements go un-met.

But teachers can quit, after all. As can the employees of most other professions. Were there not enough teachers to go around, the situation would quickly change. But teachers suffer the same inertia as other workers. And, unfortunately, their so-called "professional associations" (read: unions) incite them to fight, fight, fight instead of quit, quit, quit – in order to keep on getting educators' annual dues.

When I was working for the federal government, there were programs in place for the "stressed," whether that stress came from home, from work, or even from holidays. Every December, in fact, a notice was posted and a brochure distributed advising us of the possibility – make that, the probability – that holidays would not to live up to expectations and that employees would be depressed. An assistance program, paid for with your tax dollars, was always available to provide talk therapy or referral services during this "difficult" period.

No doubt some people are blue around the holidays, for a variety of reasons, such as the death of a loved one or the contrariness of a relative one cannot avoid. But these are issues more appropriately raised with one's minister or rabbi, not one's doctor. Of course, ministers and rabbis these days are busy with issues like gay marriage and lesbian priestesses, which directly involves maybe one percent of their flock, so they have little time for problems that perplex ordinary parishioners.

In any case, most counselors and psychologists are not medical doctors. The emphasis on stress is becoming not just morbid, it is "morphing" into an industry. People are encouraged to shell out big bucks for a variety of psychotropic medications, among other expenses. Worse, they are often labeled with mental "illnesses" codified in the DSM, which are duly reported to their insurance companies, and thus go into their permanent, computerized records.

So, expect to hear a lot more about the stress-free workplace. Expect to see more workers on medication, for better or, more likely, for worse. Expect more employees to suddenly "go berserk" on their medications. Expect more jobs to be dissolved. Expect more psychological surveys in the job application process, and more lawsuits, since psychological assessments are entirely subjective.

And if all this stresses you out, maybe you can just stay home and read something calming, like *Winnie the Pooh*. Oh, wait: I forgot. Piglet has been declared mentally ill, too.

B. K. Eakman

WHAT? ARE YOU CRAZY?

A new nationwide initiative has been quietly in the making since 2002. Conceived in Texas, apparently with President George W. Bush's enthusiastic blessing, there now exist some 27 sites around the country piloting various parts of it. Nationally, however, the proposed legislation earned barely a blip on the radar screen — the project is so hush-hush that two officials were sacked for speaking to the press about it — until mid-July, 2004, when the House Appropriations Committee approved $20 million in new federal monies to begin nationwide implementation.

The New Freedom Initiative is a plan to screen the *entire U. S. population* for mental illness and to provide a cradle-to-grave continuum of services for those identified as mentally ill or at risk of becoming so. Under the plan, schools would become the hub of the screening process — not only for children, but for their parents and teachers. There are even components aimed at senior citizens, pregnant women, and new mothers.

In April 2002, President Bush established the New Freedom Commission on Mental Health to conduct a "comprehensive study of the United States mental health service delivery system. " The commission issued its recommendations in July 2003, chief among them being that schools are in a "key position" to screen the 52 million students and 6 million adults who work at educational facilities. Now they are ready to "go national. "

The precursor endeavor, the Texas Medication Algorithm Project (TMAP), was a trial balloon, not a pilot program. This means a start-up venture (usually confined to one town or state) to assess the amount and type of resistance to an idea. TMAP started in 1995 as an alliance of individuals from the pharmaceutical industry, the University of Texas, and the mental health and corrections systems of Texas. Recently, the New Freedom Commission designated TMAP a "model" medication treatment plan, whereupon President Bush instructed more than 25 federal agencies to develop a nationwide "implementation plan. "

TMAP was funded through a Robert Wood Johnson Foundation grant — and several drug companies that stood to gain billions of dollars. The Robert Wood Johnson Foundation is the philanthropic (*read*: PR) arm of the Johnson & Johnson medical-supply/household-products empire and a major player in promoting controversial prevention curricula in schools.

Here, the plot begins to thicken. TMAP promotes the use of newer, more expensive antidepressants and antipsychotic drugs. For that reason, the commission's nationwide version of the proposal sent up red flags in the Pennsylvania Office of the Inspector General. OIG employee Allen Jones essentially blew the whistle when he revealed that key officials had received money and perks from drug companies with a stake in TMAP. Some members of the New Freedom Commission had served on advisory boards for pharmaceutical companies whose products were being recommended. Other members had indirect ties to TMAP. Jones was sacked in May for speaking to the *British Medical Journal* and the *New York Times*.

"TMAP," said Jones, "arose during a period of decreased FDA oversight and vastly increased sophistication in pharmaceutical industry marketing practices. These practices aggressively pursued favorable public and professional 'opinion' through media promotion and biased reporting of drug trial results. "

Between 1995 and 1999, the use of antidepressants for 7- to 12-year-olds increased 151 percent — and 580 percent for children under six, *with some as young as five committing suicide*. The issue of coercive child-drugging in public schools is so contentious that the U. S. House of Representatives passed the Child Medication Safety Act in May 2003, to prevent schools from intimidating parents into drugging their youngsters as a condition of attending school.

Yet, here comes the New Freedom Commission, linking screening "with state-of-the art treatment and supports. "

At a time when Congress and the FDA are questioning the culpability of many antidepressants in suicide and violent aggression, legislation that would target even more children and adults for unproved, radical psychotropic-drug therapies is highly suspect.

Take, for example, Olanzapine (trade name Zyprexa), one of the newer antipsychotic drugs recommended in the Texas plan.

It is drug manufacturer Eli Lilly's top seller. A 2003 *New York Times* article by Gardiner Harris reported that 70 percent of Olanzapine sales already are paid for by government agencies, such as Medicare and Medicaid.

Eli Lilly has multiple ties to the Bush administration. George Bush, Sr., was a member of Lilly's board of directors. Lilly made $1.6 million in political contributions in 2000 — 82 percent of which went to George W. Bush and the Republican Party. President Bush appointed Lilly's chief executive officer, Sidney Taurel, to a seat on the Homeland Security Council.

During his 2000 presidential campaign, Bush boasted of his support for Texas' TMAP project, without saying exactly how it worked or the role he envisioned for it nationally. Instead, he bragged that the legislation he passed expanded Medicaid coverage of psychotropic drugs.

Leaving aside questions of political profiteering and conflict-of-interest, let us examine the initiative itself.

President Bush appears to agree with the New Freedom Commission's finding that mental illness is pervasive and that aggressive, early screening and intervention are the only means of keeping it at bay. The President's Commission also adds that removal of stigma is key to the success of the initiative, but stigma will, in fact, be heightened as the hapless young "patient" moves into the workforce and the nursing home. He will be permanently classified as "at risk" and tracked for a lifetime by government agencies.

Dr. Darrel Regier, director of research at the American Psychiatric Association, has, of course, lauded the President's initiative. Kevin P. Dwyer, president of the National Association of School Psychologists, and Dr. Graham Emslie, who helped develop the Texas project, are typical defenders of early, mass screening. This "valuable information [is] almost impossible to obtain from any other source...," Dwyer once complained. True, most adults would see right through such attempts. That is why he worries that the flood of lawsuits from parents over invasive, personal test questions under the cover of academic testing (in Virginia, Arizona, Utah, Pennsylvania, among other states) might result in a negative court ruling that would prompt legislators to nix all psychological surveys in schools.

Special interests as well as various social "service" agencies and universities all pitch "prevention" programs (many of them quasi-political, such as those on AIDS awareness), to federal agencies in an effort to get tell-all polls into America's classrooms.

Most are "What-would-you-do-if...?" questionnaires and self-reports that focus on sex, race, depression, drugs, and parents. These surveys are followed by a smorgasbord of nonacademic programs. The rationale is that it is in the best interests of the child and society to "[create] a State-level structure for school-based mental health services to provide consistent State-level leadership and collaboration between education, general health, and mental health systems." The enabling vehicle for the New Freedom Initiative is the No Child Left Behind Act, ostensibly to "fulfill the promise of NCLB...by remov[ing] the emotional, behavioral, and academic barriers that interfere with student success in school."

According to the Commission, large numbers of children are expelled from preschools and childcare facilities for disruptive behaviors and emotional disorders. But are they? Thanks to the Individuals With Disabilities Education Act (IDEA), most are placed right back in the classroom no matter how disruptive or disturbing their behavior. School officials are reluctant to lose precious state funding by showing miscreants the door. As for parents who send their kids to school already disciplined and ready to learn, nobody cares. *Bottom line and core problem: Social policy is geared to the negligent and irresponsible, not to the upstanding and dependable.*

The commission aims not only to assess youngsters, but "to expand school mental health programs and evaluate parents"—through Parts B and C of IDEA.

The commission advocates examining parents and homes for anything that might point to a "physical or mental condition [with] a high probability of resulting in a [child's] developmental delay" — something way beyond the present capabilities of the mental health profession — beginning with a mandatory Nurse-Family Partnership component.

Why the extraordinary emphasis on parents? The Commission and, indeed, most of the mental health community believe that mental "disorders" of parents occurring before children reach the age of six "can interfere with critical emotional, cognitive, and physical development, and portend a lifetime of problems in school, at home, and in the community." Therefore, "treating the parents' mental health problems also benefits the child. "

"Treating parents" means psychotherapy and drugs, and the initiative calls for a mandate to provide "social and emotional check-ups" in all primary health care facilities. This means parents are supposed to be surreptitiously assessed for mental "illness" every time they walk into their physician's office.

Have policymakers learned nothing from the holocaust, the old Soviet Union's "psychiatric hospitals" or, more recently, South Africa's so-called "mental institutions," where political dissidents were routinely "re-educated" and/or tortured?"

Recall that the President appointed drug manufacturer Eli Lilly's chief executive officer to a seat on the Homeland Security Council. Even if one believes that George W. Bush has no intention of abusing the concept of Homeland Security as an instrument of political correctness, who is to say that some future administration will not? Already, the PATRIOT Act is vastly altering the civil rights American citizens previously took for granted.

If you think the "coercion" scenario is too strong, consider: In August 2003, the National Institute of Mental Health and the National Science Foundation announced the results of their $1.2 million, taxpayer-funded study. It stated, essentially, that traditionalists are mentally disturbed. Scholars from the Universities of Maryland, California at Berkeley, and Stanford had determined that social conservatives, in particular, suffer from "mental rigidity," "dogmatism," and "uncertainty avoidance," together with associated indicators for mental illness. Some conservatives and political pundits chortled over the so-called study, but the fact remains that nothing marginalizes a person faster today than a suggestion of being mentally unbalanced. The 20-year-long practice of psychographic (emotional-attitudinal) profiling under the cover of academic testing in schools is already intimidating conservative and Christian students and their parents into silence.

The food stamp program begun under Franklin D. Roosevelt was a temporary response to the Depression. By 1974, every state was required to participate in the program, creating a nationwide mandate. The New Freedom Mental Health Initiative is following the same route, state by state, beginning with Illinois' passage of copycat legislation, the Children's Mental Health Act, requiring (as of August 31, 2004) compulsory mental-health screening for children and pregnant women through Illinois' education system. Between child welfare agencies and schools, government is legislatively usurping more and more of parents' prerogatives — forcing the mental evaluation of all minor children.

Sacked whistleblower Allen Jones estimates that, if the plan were implemented nationwide, the annual costs to Medicaid programs would be approximately $3. 7 billion per year to treat *one psychiatric disorder alone.* That is over ten million dollars per day just in Medicaid expenditures, not to mention the additional burden on teachers and schools.

Do we want our lawmakers even touching this initiative?

B. K. Eakman

ARE WE THERE YET?

Preventive Mental Health Screening's Track Record

With the deadliest school shooting spree in U.S. history at Virginia Tech in Blacksburg has come predictable calls for mental health screening and mandatory intervention—a debate that has been going on, in actuality, for some 20 years.

As early as 1985, some schools were piloting psychological assessments, interspersing personal, opinion-oriented questions among legitimate academic fare. Pennsylvania's Educational Quality Assessment, for example, asked children as young as eight to answer a large number of what-would-you-do-if questions and complete word-association-type exercises that smacked of more sophisticated personality inventories. The Interpretive Literature explaining the tests (when one could get hold of it) detailed what was being assessed: the child's "locus of control," whether a child was "externally or internally motivated," a student's "amenability to change," plus a willingness to "conform to group goals" and "receive stimuli." Another quasi-academic test, the Testing Essential Learning and Literary Skills exam, indicated in a foreword (intended for professionals) that it was looking for "indicators of gullibility," with a caveat further on that the test "also appears to measure knowledge to some extent."

States like Nebraska and Michigan were not far behind, and by the 1990s, nearly all schools were incorporating psychological surveys, especially into their "health" programs.

Eventually, the term "loner" became linked to "misfit" and "sociopath." A person who thought for oneself instead of basing actions on his or her peers was considered out-of-step. This represented a 180-degree turnabout from expectations among the World War I and II generations, when nearly every family owned a gun and youngsters were taught to stand up to bullies on the playground.

Today, everyone from talk show hosts to President George W. Bush and the National Education Association is banking on psychiatric diagnoses to identify, label and treat eccentric behavior before it turns deadly—which is kind of strange in light of sadistic video games, pornographic magazines and how-to bomb-making literature, all easily available to any pedophile, terrorist or nut-case. And then there's the self-esteem issue, which some experts claim turns kids into criminals if it's too low, while other authorities insist high self-esteem results in children becoming delinquents. Indeed, mental health gurus can't seem to agree whether psychopaths and sociopaths have universally low, or high, opinions of themselves.

And therein lays the problem of mental health screening, psychotropic drugging, counseling and therapy, involuntary commitment—and behavioral "science" in general. Put 100 psychiatrists and psychologists in a room and 50 will say the strategies above are the answer to public safety and 50 will claim that the potential for doing harm outweighs any benefit (think Columbine killers on Luvox, and Andrea Yates drowning her five children after imbibing a virtual cocktail of doctor-prescribed antipsychotics and antidepressants). Most assuredly, Americans are excessively self-focused—not a particularly encouraging side-effect among today's non-stop emotional temperature-takers.

Much as we would like to have a magic bullet—better make that "magic diagnosis" or "magic pill"—the behavioral sciences simply don't have the track record to support prediction or prevention of anything. History shows we know just about enough to get into trouble. Psychological profiling seems to come back to bite us (think airport security). Screening seems to follow a predictable pattern of tracking and monitoring innocents. Involuntary commitment schemes have a way of turning nations into political gulags.

Given our computerized, high-tech society, should we expect better this time around? Don't we have quite enough political correctness already, no matter which side tries to use it? Do we really want to homogenize thought—because that is what it really comes down to, eventually, when "experts" start deciding which thoughts are acceptable and which ones are not.

Americans need to stop fixating on so-far unproven theories about chemical imbalances in the brain and trendy mental health labels (attention-deficit disorder, obsessive-compulsive disorder, hyperactivity, oppositional-defiant disorder, etc.) and decide instead how much it is willing to put up with in the way of out-of-control behavior. The bottom line is that too many kids are running amok—at ever younger ages—and too many violent offenders, who have already demonstrated their intentions, are being returned to the streets.

It is average Americans, not "experts," who eventually will draw a line as to what they will tolerate. Until that happens, all the psychologists, medications, counseling services, and screening instruments in the world will not be enough to prevent the "mad" rampages that increasingly define our era.

CRIMES OF OPINION

University student Steve Hinkle was ordered to psychiatric counseling merely for posting a conservative coming-events flier in a predominantly liberal-left environment. Do we really want to institutionalize mental health referrals for those who fail to conform to politically correct thinking?

You may have read a couple of weeks ago about California Polytechnic State University's recent legal settlement with student, Steve Hinkle, who was disciplined last year for posting an announcement concerning a then-upcoming talk, sponsored by the College Republicans. It featured a black social commentator and writer, Mason Weaver, author of the book, *It's OK to Leave the Plantation*. The gist of Mr. Weaver's argument is that dependence on government to solve problems, particularly economic ones, is a mentality that enslaves.

The flier alone was enough to send politically conditioned students, especially those in the campus' "multicultural center," into a spiteful rage. They called campus police to report "a suspicious white male passing out literature of an offensive racial nature."

What readers of that story may have missed in the news reports, however, was the nature of the punishment doled out by Cal Poly's Judicial Affairs Office—letters of apology to all offended students, a meeting to discuss so-called racial healing, and most significantly, counseling with a psychologist to consider "emotional barriers."

Regardless of your opinion on the content—or even the title—of Mr. Weaver's book, it's nothing that other black columnists, commentators, and authors haven't noted in whole or in part, among them Thomas Sowell, Armstrong Williams, Walter Williams, Clarence Page, and most recently actor/comedian Bill Cosby at a formal bash at Constitution Hall in Washington, D.C., commemorating the 50th Anniversary of Brown vs. the Board of Education.

Weaver maintains that while many populations have fallen victim to the dependency trap—socialism's failures being filled with it—in this country it is a rationale disproportionately accepted by blacks, as evidenced by welfare roles and victim-politics, among other things.

The upshot of the brouhaha, reported in several newspapers, is that student Hinkle essentially won his lawsuit against Cal Poly, filed on his behalf by the Center for Individual Rights in California, in conjunction with local counsel, in district court. Attorneys for Cal Poly were permitted a face-saving exit (i.e., not publicly admitting fault) by agreeing to expunge student Hinkle's record, reimburse him for $40,000 in attorney fees, and stop interfering (i.e., censoring) when announcements are posted.

Mr. Hinkle should have added pain and suffering for a year's worth of harassment. For there is a more troubling aspect of the university's attempt at censorship that warrants everybody's attention—mental health referrals of pupils who fail to conform to politically correct thinking. This kind of thing is becoming increasingly frequent at all levels of education.

Whatever is politically correct today can change in a heartbeat. All it takes is one very charismatic person in film, politics or journalism to completely overturn a cause or course people formerly believed was irreversible. One or two images, like the photographs at the Abu Ghraib prison, can undo months or years of public opinion campaigns. And the more uneducated the population, the greater their susceptibility to a turnabout, knee-jerk reaction.

The United States, however, may be at even more risk—because its high school and college graduates are under the impression they are educated when, in fact, the plethora of diplomas and advanced degrees in many cases aren't worth the paper they're written on. Just last week, two newspaper articles (in the *Washington Times* and elsewhere) quoted studies showing the high school diploma to be nearly worthless in the job market, as many graduating students haven't even mastered basic grammar and arithmetic. At the university level, increasing numbers of students major in easy, frivolous nonsense like women's studies, education, and psychology that have little academic value, but plenty of liberal-left orthodoxy.

Suppose the opportunistic diseases associated with AIDS, for example, should suddenly turn up a mutant strain of tuberculosis or pneumonia that is not only incurable, but epidemic. Suddenly homosexuality wouldn't be quite so "gay" anymore. Anyone coming "out of the closet" could well find themselves referred to a psychiatrist for mandatory "adjustment," including sex-drive altering drugs.

Similarly, should a dirty bomb, compliments of any Middle Eastern group—from Hamas to al Qaeda—explode on a subway, expect complaints about ethnic and racial profiling to disappear overnight.

Or how about the generation of young people coming of age that won't remember anything about "the back of the bus." But they do see, and very clearly, a nightly parade of mostly black faces on the TV news committing murder and mayhem. As Bill Cosby so bluntly pointed out in Constitution Hall, educated Americans, black and white, see young black males parading around in ridiculous get-ups and speaking in phrases even Cosby says he can barely understand. Yes, the press misrepresents and overemphasizes these factors, but in the end, that won't matter. The fallout from this nonstop onslaught is apt to mean that, in another ten years, the "leg-up" advantages currently being offered to minorities in the form of affirmative action, mortgage breaks, and Head Start programs will generate a backlash. Tomorrow's Jesse Jacksons and Johnny Cochrans could wind up being referred to mental health specialists for being "delusional."

One could go on—the list of potential scenarios, racial and otherwise, is endless—but you get the point. No matter how carefully people are nurtured, conditioned, indoctrinated, or brainwashed to accept certain beliefs, especially on hot-button issues, all it takes is the correct "stimulus" (as psychologists would say) to topple what currently is politically correct. Today the Gay Lobby, tomorrow the Skinheads.

Do we really want to institutionalize mandatory psychiatric counseling? Because if we do, it won't stop with just a mandatory "referral" like Mr. Hinkle got. Already, something called "universal behavioral screening" and "outpatient commitment" are creeping into the American legal system and lexicon.

Let's look at both: Universal in the context above means mandatory. "Behavioral screening" means someone you don't know checks whatever perceived behaviors or reactions you may demonstrate against a list of controversial (and decidedly negative) categories like "inflexible," "dogmatic," "intolerant," "individualist," and "loner."

This information is often collected by teachers without degrees in psychiatry at the behest of state and federal grant recipients such as the Institute on Violence and Destructive Behavior at the University of Oregon's College of Education. This is just one among a large cottage industry of child development centers pitching psychiatric screening instruments to schools. Teachers are taught by the Institute's educational psychologists to match the classroom and playground conduct of pupils against a list of behavior patterns. This means that "recess" is no longer about playtime. Certain "markers" (or "red flags") signal a child's need for professional help. These youngsters are referred to a school psychologist, counselor or other "mental health professional," who makes a determination about each kid's "counterproductive behaviors." The child is taught alternative, "adaptive" behaviors to use as "coping mechanisms." Parents are expected to reinforce these alternatives.

So a teacher might check off a red-flag term like "loner" to describe a child who is merely more "reserved." The ensuing psychological snooping may reveal that the parents are rather "private people," not given to showy, public displays of emotion. But psychologists interpret such modesty as "coldness," even "inhibition," so the counselor (usually, a school psychologist) teaches the child so-called adaptive behaviors that result in bizarre ideas about openness and tolerance.

The child (even his or her parents) rarely sees what all is contained in a student's "electronic portfolio." Loopholes in privacy laws make it difficult to stop your child's file from landing on the desktops of college admissions officers, executives, security officers, credit bureaus, or anybody with an ax to grind. If your child falls into one of the above shadowy categories, how will he fare in the job market—or as an airline security risk, for that matter?

"Outpatient commitment," which is gaining adherents in the legal circles, the medical profession and government, can be defined as coercion to take psychiatric drugs or face lock-up. This means you, the patient, are no longer allowed to determine whether a medication is right for you. As eminent author and psychologist, Dr. Thomas Szasz, explains, if a doctor prescribes glasses for you, it is your business whether you wear them or not—unless of course you cause a car accident and it can be proved you cannot see to drive. Other than that, you can put the glasses in a drawer for all the State cares. But if a mental health referral results in a determination that you should have a powerful, mood-altering drug, then even if it makes you physically ill, an official will come around and check to see that you take it anyway—and punish you if you don't.

Countless parents nationwide—in Florida, Michigan, and Colorado, for example—already are reporting being harassed and intimidated by school personnel and the child protective services to give their children these medications even in the face of adverse reactions and faulty diagnoses. This has resulted in several lawsuits, many of which parents have won, but not before they have nearly spent themselves into bankruptcy and/or had their kids taken away.

This is the road we are going down when a person with an unpopular opinion can be ordered—not asked—to see a psychiatrist.

No matter what your politics, your religion, or your viewpoint on the hot-button issues of the day, mandatory counseling requires our full attention. The so-called psychiatric prison is one of the easiest ways to get rid of opponents, by declaring such individuals a danger to society. Psychiatric prisons in Nazi Germany, the Soviet Union, Cuba, and, more recently, South Africa are now legendary. And if we think it can't happen here, better think again.

Mr. Hinkle was ordered to counseling merely for putting up a coming-events flier—sponsored by Republicans (i.e., conservatives) in a predominantly liberal-left environment. But he is not the first to be caught up in this kind of situation. Think of the numerous phony hate-speech accusations that have been hurled at individuals over the past decade for spouting only controversial opinions—some of them, like baseball star John Rocker's, admittedly less tactful than others.

The question is: Where does that leave the First Amendment rights for the rest of us? And how long before the tables are turned?

B. K. Eakman

IS UNCIVIL BEHAVIOR
A MARKER OF MENTAL ILLNESS?

About three years ago, a rash of articles started appearing nationwide asking, essentially, why everyone seemed so angry and depressed. Of course, a variety of psychiatrists were consulted but, tellingly, hardly any philosophers or clergymen. Reasons for our collective angst ran the gamut from "a transient society," "lack of familial ties/support," and "too much to do" to "increased mental illness."

So I suppose it was just a matter of time before one of the justifications given by mental health specialists for screening schoolchildren—and, more recently, the population at large—would be: increasing anger and depression. It mostly starts, say psychiatrists, in childhood, where the first signs of sociopathy, psychosis, and anti-social tendencies can be spotted even by alert nonprofessionals trained to notice the red flags. One of those "red flags" is uncivil behavior—usually by parents. Frequently, these lapses are reported by youngsters themselves, via such comments as "mommy is screaming at the telephone" or "daddy is yelling at the cars on the road." Of course, such "reports" leave to the imagination whether anybody was actually on the other end of the phone when mommy yelled, or whether daddy was just venting in his own car with the window rolled up and not at other drivers.

Since 1935, "behavioral eugenicists" (a branch of psychiatry specializing in eugenic, or hereditary, illnesses and abnormalities) have been warning of rampant mental illness. Dr. Franz J. Kallmann, who came to America in the mid-1930s, after having served under Ernst Rüdin, head of Hitler's "racial hygiene" program, argued in favor of "psychiatric genetics" even after he arrived on American shores to escape the Third Reich's henchmen. He claimed that if something weren't done soon, the number of schizophrenics would outnumber normal individuals.

Amazingly, accolades surrounded his outlandish pronouncements and solutions, even in such publications as the *New York Times*. Fortunately, wiser heads prevailed as Nazi atrocities increasingly came to light after the war, and both "psychiatric genetics" and mass psychiatric screening got a black eye for most of the post-war period.

Until now. The recent prominence in the news of so-called mental health issues like depression, anger and its close cousin, school violence, dovetails with the increasing emphasis on parents in screening instruments disseminated among students, not to mention the new, controversial parent component of the New Freedom Initiative—a nationwide project to screen the entire U.S. population for mental illness and provide a cradle-to-grave continuum of quasi-mandatory therapeutic "services" for those identified as mentally ill or even at risk of becoming so. Under this plan, reported at length by Dr. Dennis L. Cuddy in NewsWithViews, Dr. Karen Effrem through Minnesota's EDWATCH, myself in *CHRONICLES: A Magazine of American Culture*, as well as by other authors, the school will become the hub of this legislated, psychological screening process. But parents, new mothers, teachers, senior citizens and even pregnant women are prominently included, too. Similar pieces of legislation are being crafted in various states, such as Illinois and Pennsylvania.

Ignoring for the moment the question of whether it is our society here in America, or even those societies throughout the free, industrialized nations, which are spewing forth the lion's share of certifiably berserk people (recent events in Afghanistan and Haiti come to mind), as a former teacher I wonder if the cause of mental "health" might not be better served by building a little context around certain signs-of-the-times that appear to be chipping away at our progressive, collective sanity. Instead of concentrating on heredity and predisposition, maybe we should be focusing our attention on certain critical factors of contemporary life in the industrialized world for which there exist no counterparts in primitive societies.

Whereas in the 1940s, Johnny might have written an essay on whether the pen was indeed "mightier than the sword," today he might write one (assuming, that is, he can write at all) centering on whether human beings were meant to drive on virtual obstacle courses at 55 miles per hour no less than twice per day—"flight-or-fight" response, and all that. Or, instead of

167

having sixth-grade science classes writing snotty letters to President George Bush accusing him of ruining the planet and destroying the environment (that sort of thing was popular after the President refused to sign on to the Kyoto Protocol), we might have them composing polite queries to the Department of Transportation asking whether anyone there had considered conducting a study on the number of accidents over a particular period involving a driver attempting to read a road sign that was too small or half hidden from view.

Or, here's an item for debate (assuming youngsters still actually deliberate): Billions of dollars are being spent on rebuilding Iraq's infrastructure. Why isn't a comparable sum being targeted to America's deteriorating utility and transportation networks, especially in the cities and metropolises, where gridlock is pervasive, power lines are some 60 years old and the lights go out every time someone spits on the sidewalk?

Yes, I'm sure there are some people for whom road rage is a way of life, replacing the old gun-slinger of Dodge City vintage who came to town with a chip on his shoulder and itching for a fight. But how many so-called "Road Ragers" are simply poor saps scared half out of their wits for the fourth time that week or day, having just made another instant life-or-death decision on a thoroughfare strewn with orange barrels and concrete barriers, negotiated a series of undecipherable lane shifts, and dodged a wading-pool-sized pothole along with other equally befuddled drivers?

How many of those kids standing in their dining rooms watching their mothers screaming into telephones or their fathers picking up the pieces of their computer keyboard off the floor have the remotest inkling what life was like when one actually got through to a live human being on the other end of the line the first time around to ask a question? When did the level of complexity in instructions to, say, install a spam filter on a computer become so onerous as to completely outstrip the relative ease with which one could follow assembly directions for Junior's Christmas bicycle in 1965?

So let's examine this "uncivil behavior" and see what alternatives, other than "mental health" solutions, might be available.

A colleague quipped to me last year in his office: "No wonder they lock and seal the office windows!" Be that as it may, I suppose humans do somehow adapt, over time. Take Bill Gates; he has made billions figuring out how to give intricate, step-by-step instructions to machines to perform the tiniest function. But is he the oddball, or am I? I have no clue. Is the person who somehow maintains his sanity holed up in a windowless room with digitized equipment, which he must instruct for hours on end in mini-bytes to compose the word "c-r-a-z-y," the well-adjusted one, or is the guy who chafes every time he has to "listen to each of the 9 options on your touch-tone phone" the fellow who is nuts?

Is the nitwit who happily careens down the freeway dodging orange barrels, pretending every day he's on a NASCAR course, with rap music turned way up in his vehicle to help get him "in the groove," the rational one? Yes, I know it's supposedly illegal to do that. But maybe this guy actually is saner than my coworker friend in Houston who once told me that, well, she no longer had a problem driving the freeway: She just took two Valium some 20 minutes beforehand and had at it! (Which, no doubt, is illegal as well).

Issues like these have no equivalent in the non-industrialized world, and they have all come about in an amazingly short period. It occurs to me that human adaptations tend to be taking one of three routes—resistance (i.e., anger, sometimes escalating to violence, at least against inanimate objects), acquiescence (utter passivity, up to and including the use of tranquilizers), or "vegging out" (doing whatever you have to, then forgetting everything—your proverbial "couch potato").

The prominent conservative organizations are no better than their liberal brethren when it comes to topics tangential to issues surrounding these problems; perhaps that is why they have nothing to offer to counter behavioral "scientists" who come up with dangerous ideas like mass mental health screening, a process which, once institutionalized, will inevitably take a precarious political turn, compromising freedom of thought and conscience for everyone. For example, at least two conservative think-tanks here in the Nation's Capitol have determined that funding for public transportation, particularly for subways in major metropolitan areas, is unwarranted. They want the money devoted to roads instead. Their liberal counterparts, on the other hand, are against roads, citing environmental factors, and want everyone forced into public transportation systems.

Both camps are asking the wrong questions. Here's what political activists should be asking:

Are human beings actually built for having the living you-know-what scared out of them at least twice a day, five days a week, for 25 years or more? If not, what can be done about it, other than, or in addition to, building roads and public transportation systems? Might not the Department of Transportation do something really useful, like attaching monetary incentives for states/cities that construct individual street signs large enough for a normal person to read at night without a spotlight attached? Would the cause of traffic surveillance be better served by exchanging speed detectors (and reallocating manpower) to unmarked reckless driving patrols that comb congested freeways in real-time for cars weaving in an out of traffic, tailgating, and cutting off other drivers? If computerized tracking devices can be assigned to the task of hunting down money launderers, white collar criminals and terrorists, might not a similar effort be directed toward apprehending and shutting down spammers and hackers who cost private taxpayers and businesses billions of dollars and countless hours of time by sending viruses, pornography and salacious solicitations? Isn't it time to replace 60-year-old utility infrastructures that no county or municipality can afford, given the mobile nature of today's population which perceives no stake in any particular "neighborhood" per se? Doesn't a national infrastructure improvement program logically coincide with the spirit of the old railroad projects, because they crisscross state lines?"

Moreover, isn't it time for those campaigning for public office to start considering the needs of the backbone of society—the folks who foot most of the bills—instead of tailoring their primary messages, for the most part, to the most negligent and irresponsible elements of society?"

Or is the problem more systemic in nature? Is it that, to aspire to the level of a serious candidate, one has to be so wealthy, so out of touch, with mainstream Americans, as to be capable of hiring, for most of one's lifetime, someone else to do everything from standing in a grocery line, to picking up the dry cleaning, to punching all those options on the phone, to driving your car or limo, to dealing with the idiosyncrasies of computer upgrades?

CHILDREN OF THE THERAPEUTIC SOCIETY

Some 35 years ago, social scientists began unveiling unworkable philosophies of child management, characterized by a lack of adult guidance and punctuated with heavy doses of pop psychology. For openers, they told parents to lay off the discipline and let kids express themselves. Professors at university departments of education joined in with admonishments to prospective teachers against putting red markings on pupils papers and criticizing youngsters' work, manner of dress, and speech. School counselors took up the cause and levied a cease and desist order against adults who persisted in "shoving" their outdated moral and religious values on children.

Eventually, the suggestion that parents had the right to direct the upbringing of their children became synonymous with overprotective-ness, then with child abuse, while tolerance of bad manners and obscenities was viewed as "being flexible."

By 1987, what kids wanted at any given moment had become more important than their knowledge base. Children were made drunk on their own importance. Teacher training was taken up with courses in behavioral psychology ("ed psych") instead of academic subject matter.

Standardized tests started looking more like opinion surveys than cognitive assessments. By 1996, even math courses had started placing correct world views and teamwork (read: "peer pressure") over correct answers.

Soon the cumulative effect of therapeutic/socialization-style education hit critical mass. Parents in Littleton, Colorado, got a good jolt of the "mental hygiene" approach to schooling, up close and personal.

Psychologized education, which first came to Littleton in 1991 under the name "outcome-based education," changed labels when it came under attack from parents and the public. But in typical fashion, curricular "standards" and the thrust of

171

programs remained the same. Rocky Mountain News reported in June 1994 that the Jefferson County Education Board voted to continue funding the renamed outcome-based – i.e., psychology-based – education to the tune of $1 million, over parent protests. Drug education, refusal skills, self-esteem, and relationships became centerpieces of the curriculum, pushing academics to the back burner. Yet, in the aftermath of the Littleton tragedy, the President and pundits are calling for more of the same.

Only a few seem to connect the sudden surge of high-profile student violence with the progressive undermining of adult leadership, denigration of religiously based moral values, lurid media entertainment, and lack of substantive tasks to occupy the child's mind and time.

Today, we have human warehouses, not institutions of learning. The peer pressure approach to teaching has unleashed a "Lord of the Flies" mentality which even police, stationed in school hallways and on rooftops, can no longer be expected to control. This result should have been predictable, especially among those calling themselves "child experts" – psychologists.

"Trench-coat Mafia"? Heavy eye makeup? Black hats and knee boots? What on earth did we expect when we started allowing kids to come to school permanently decked out in Halloween costumes? When we stopped giving youngsters more to do than primp, preen, strut, intimidate, and spout filthy song lyrics, what we reaped was swastikas and vampire cults.

Curriculums and activities that revolve around psychological calisthenics instead of serious learning fuel a morbid preoccupation with self. They don't increase self-esteem or instill self-respect. It doesn't take a psychiatrist – or, for that matter, a priest – to figure out that youngsters who are allowed to spend the largest part of their days acting out fantasies, who are drilled with "antiauthoritarian" theology, who can get easy A's under phony "standards" are eventually going to unleash an environment of social chaos that in 10 years will transform even a United States of America into a Haiti, Iraq, or Bosnia.

The Littleton incident, added to those in Jonesboro, Arkansas; West Paducah, Kentucky; Springfield, Oregon; and Edinboro, Pennsylvania, among others, signals that the public school system is about to implode. More importantly, it indicates that schooling isn't about literacy, basics, or proficiency at anything, no matter what educators pretend. It's time for Americans to send an unequivocal message to legislators and school boards to pull the plug on psychology-based education programs and practices.

B. K. Eakman

THE CELEBRITY "ANTIDEPRESSANT WARS"

"Smear over substance" is, once again, the order of the day in an important controversy. I'm talking about the brouhaha surrounding actor Tom Cruise and his Hollywood colleague, Brooke Shields, regarding their respective views on antidepressant drugs. Inevitably, psychotherapies in general became intertwined with the topic of mind-altering substances – and so did Scientology, the bête noire of the psychiatric profession.

First, to clarify matters: I am a conservative Episcopalian (no, that is not an oxymoron, quite yet), not a Scientologist. Until Scientology's spin-off organization, the Citizens Commission on Human Rights, contacted me in 1996 concerning two of my books on education, I had only heard of it in passing and had never heard of CCHR. Long ago and quite independently, I had come to certain conclusions, the primary one being that psychology had compromised the educating process. That was why I left the teaching profession. The new emphasis on emotions meant that academics took a back seat. It inaugurated what I felt was a phony and counterproductive self-esteem movement. Finally, psychologized education brought in a counseling industry that undermined the moral authority of adults, with the consequence that teachers were handling little "mob-ocracies" instead of kiddy cliques.

Not only was real, scientific research on learning methods being scuttled, but I couldn't find any hard, statistical validity behind the claims for psychiatric drugs that were being prescribed for behavioral problems. Eventually, renowned experts in government and on the boards of major pharmaceutical companies were blowing the whistle on unreported side-effects, unsubstantiated claims, and outright fraud – and they weren't Scientologists. Experts and authors like Drs. Peter Breggin, David Healy, Charles Medawar, and (more recently) former Pennsylvania Inspector General Allen Jones were, in many cases, actually hostile toward Scientology.

174

Today, reports that many antidepressants have no more effect than a placebo are ubiquitous. Which brings up the question: Is the aggressive marketing of psychotropic drugs creating a market based on the power of suggestion?

That is the crux of the argument between Tom Cruise and Brooke Shields. If Ms. Shields believes she had a real disease after the birth of her child as opposed to feeling unsettled in her new role of "mother" over "actress" – no doubt an enormous change of pace – well, it is her privilege. But that antidepressant she thinks brought her out of the doldrums may be a time bomb in her system, robbing her first of sexual enjoyment, then impulse control, and a whole bunch of other side-effects she may not have noticed yet.

Should she experience additional "symptoms," she will no doubt be offered another drug, on top of the one she might still be taking, and then another, and another, until she winds up like Houston murderess Andrea Yates: totally delusional – this time, perhaps, with a bona fide disease that is both verifiable and permanent.

Like many people, I take most of what Hollywood stars say with a grain of salt, and Tom Cruise's June 24th interview on NBC's "Today Show" may not have been the most articulate discussion about drugs or that whole field technically known as "behavioral science." Mr. Cruise was particularly blasted for suggesting that vitamins and exercise could serve as solutions for emotional and mental problems.

But we must remember that such interviews revolve around sound bites. That's all television journalists really want: short sentences that explain little but are easily merged into a 7-minute topic segment that TV executives believe will keep viewers from changing channels. Hollywood's stars know whatever they say must be condensed down to a sentence.

Experts increasingly are learning how to do that, too. For example, in testifying on a proposed bill before the Florida legislature, one legislator erroneously lumped narcolepsy with "conduct disorder" in an attempt to illustrate that many so-called psychiatric "diseases" are not diseases at all, but rather, subjective phenomena.

Nobody else caught it, but I winced, because I knew that narcolepsy was a real illness, provable via medical tests, whereas "conduct disorder" is not. The legislator probably knew it, too, but that's what happens when hammering home a point and maintaining eye contact supersedes reference to notes.

The fact is, there is nothing in the medical, scientific literature that confirms objective abnormality ("objective abnormality" equates to disease) in Attention-Deficit and Hyperactivity Disorder (ADHD), Conduct Disorder (CD), Oppositional Defiant Disorder (ODD), Post-partum Depression, "math disorder" or hundreds of other "diseases" that psychiatrists swear up and down are "biological." If they were biological, scientists would be able to see evidence in blood workups, x-rays, urinalyses, taps of spinal fluid, or something. But they can't. No one knows, for example, how much serotonin (the chemical associated with depression) is normal, or how much is too much or not enough. But medical doctors can tell for sure if you have a vitamin deficiency, and they can tell you which vitamin, too. Vitamin deficiencies, allergies and sedentary lifestyles frequently do contribute adversely to mental function.

As much as we would all prefer to jettison unwanted emotions, along with those behaviors we feel compelled to perform, even when they clearly are bad for us; as much as we would like to chalk up our character faults, lack of self-control, impatience and social foibles to bad biology, our chemical makeup and our brains are usually very much intact. Until something is found amiss, no pill in the world is going to fix us up – except, perhaps, in our dreams.

There are reasons why experts have suddenly found their voice regarding antidepressants and other psychotropic drugs. These can be summed up in the massacres at Littleton (CO), Santee (CA), Paducah (KY), and Red Lake (MN). Every one of the perpetrators was on a psychotropic cocktail that started with an antidepressant.

Today, it's not uncommon to see youngsters taking anti-depressants like Prozac, stimulants like Ritalin, tranquilizers like Valium, and anti-anxiety drugs like Xanax at different hours of the day. Schools literally disseminate substance-abuse surveys with one hand and dangerous drugs with the other. The effort to turn morality, personality quirks, and now even political incorrectness (like racial bias) into diseases has backfired.

And here's the thing: Even if you like the political landscape today – i.e., the boundaries of acceptable opinion and taste –

what is the guarantee that you will like it in 10 years when personality inventories come back to bite you? Forced drugging and therapy can cut both ways.

School psychiatrists have been loath to describe fully the side-effects of the psychotropic substances – much less predict the statistical chances of a healthy outcome. Well, they can't predict, actually, because no such statistics exist. Indeed, the track record of psychotherapy has not yet matched its promise.

The Drug Enforcement Administration reported in 1995 that the U.S. consumed some 80 percent of the total world supply of methylphenidate (Ritalin, Concerta, Adderal, etc.), to treat ADD-ADHD – a drug with enormous potential for abuse because it mimics cocaine-like highs and lows. But psychotropic drugs send a more disturbing message to young people – that all emotional turmoil throughout their lifetime can be solved by medicating themselves.

By the time youngsters are job-hunting, they frequently find themselves shut out if they were ever prescribed a psychotropic drug – information now easily accessible by computer. The military, for example, screens out for individuals who have ever taken Ritalin. Why? Psychotropic drugs affect judgment – and no one knows for how long.

This issue, then, is not liberal-versus-conservative, or even theological, except insofar as we have unwittingly replaced religious ethics with psychiatric dogma.

As for the Scientology, I am not qualified to speak for or against it. However, any philosophy or organization that can channel Hollywood stars away from lives of drugs and therapy must be doing something right, as entertainers are disproportionately at risk of falling victim to the siren songs of drugs and expensive, long-term psychotherapy.

Actors must have, above all else, a thick skin and a high energy level. Reputations are made and broken mostly on the basis of individual persona – as well as on their ability to pretend they are somebody else.

Once a superstar, there are the tabloids, the paparazzi, the parties, the shmoozing, the memorizing of lines, which together can take up most of every night. Actors get up while everyone else is asleep for an early morning "shoot," which ends maybe some 17 hours later.

So, they can't sleep. And when they finally do, they can't wake up. They can't eat, because the camera adds 10 pounds.

And they certainly can't age – well, at least the women can't. Public humiliation comes with the territory. Superstars must project the image of perky, happy, hip, and adorable.

Can you imagine a better recipe for depression? Pretty soon, it's pills to get to sleep, pills to stay awake, pills to be perky, pills for irritability, diet pills, anti-nausea pills for that audition, and maybe steroids, too.

Unless a star's ego and principles are strong, it would be difficult to imagine a career more destabilizing. Mel Gibson – a Catholic who owed his life and his marriage to some re-adjusted priorities – is among those who have negotiated that precarious path, according to his TV interview with Diane Sawyer.

So maybe we ought to cut Tom Cruise and the Scientologists a little slack. They may be in the right place after all: Hollywood.

WHEN SEX CONQUERS LOVE

Much as I hated to admit it, former AIDS czarina Kristine Gebbie, under the Clinton Administration, actually got it right. She claimed that the message to youngsters these days gives the impression that sex is ugly, dirty, and a more perverse than pleasurable experience. Mizz Gebbie bungled only when she took on the role of anti-Victorian-moralizer/crusader.

In the space of a few months, I read about public school teachers who "have sex with" (not merely "seduce") their students; priests who sexually abuse little boys; naval officers who apparently make orgies an annual, celebrated event [the Tailhook scandal]; and movie stars who, like "Madonna," take on the names of solemn religious figures to promote videos and books portraying kinky sex. Then there was the ongoing debate over gays in the military, which meant that newspaper and magazine readers were treated to ever more graphic descriptions concerning the sexual gymnastics performed by homosexuals. Rap music lyricists got accolades for their latest achievement in moving the term 'hos into the mainstream of American lexicon. The Whitney Museum of American Art launched its exhibit, "Abject Art: Repulsion and Desire," which managed to outdo even Robert Mapplethorpe, Annie Sprinkle, and Madonna. And in August of 1993, South Florida installed a "public service" hotline for teenagers (377-TEEN) called "The Link," which promoted sex as a means of getting rid of tension, abortion on demand without parental consent, and homosexuality as a lifestyle as opposed to a handicap.

All this doesn't begin to include the multifarious accounts of rape-torture murders; the endless articles exploring the DNA analysis of semen found on some poor, dead girl's panties; the demands of the Man-Boy Love Association; the aborted fetuses in our faces; and new horrors on the sexually transmitted diseases front, such as cytomegalovirus (CMV), which is causing birth defects in pregnant women. At a subway station entrance, my husband and I were shocked by a billboard as

179

stunningly tasteless as the sexual message it sought to rebut. The billboard was designed to appear spattered with blood. The caption read: "*Virgin* is not a dirty word."

By last summer's end, I was glad I wasn't a kid anymore. Somehow such an introduction to the world of sexuality would have failed to inspire passion, raging hormones or no. Indeed, if one observed the admonitions of then-Surgeon General Jocelyn Elders and deposed New York School Chancellor Joseph Fernandez, we shouldn't wait until youngsters' hormones are raging. We should assault their sensibilities in kindergarten with a panoply of condoms, sex toys (no kidding!), and legitimized pornography.

The National Guidelines for Comprehensive Sexual Education, produced two years ago by the Sex Information and Education Council of the United States, recommended teaching kindergartners to "feel comfortable with their genitals" by having them holler "penis" and "vulva." By fourth grade, the sex education curriculum had youngsters performing the now-familiar ritual of unrolling condoms on bananas and discussing the benefits of "mutual masturbation." In seventh grade, children advanced to discussing oral and anal sex, role-playing sexual situations, and learning the street names for a variety of sexual acts. In high school, young students were awash in bisexuality, transvestitism, sadomasochism, and bestiality. Teachers were supposed to pass around "finger cots," which are condoms for the fingers, and "dental dams," a kind of condom for oral sex, and discuss "brachiopractic penetration," which the curious may look up. The idea, supposedly, was to make youngsters hygiene-conscious at dating time. This was sold in catchy phrases like "safe sex" and "no glove, no love!"

Love, indeed. What happened to it?

Somewhere between the bluegrass-country ("rockabilly") ballads that groups like the Everly Brothers and the Kingston Trio interpreted for their teenage audiences—songs that expressed an amorous sentimentality, incorporated complex harmonies, evoked an entreating innocence and connected sex with affection—and the heavy metal-rap era, music moved from seduction to sadism, from beautiful to brutal, from romantic to repulsive. Today it is difficult to find a mainstream station to wake up to in the morning that isn't riddled with squealing and shrieking and a what's-love-got-to-do-with-it attitude. Talented new instrumental composers like John Nilsen, Danny Wright,

Tom Barabas, Karunesh, Gary Sills, and Clifford White are ignored by disc jockeys and can be located only through independent music distributors, the new and expensive satellite radio networks, and word of mouth, as increasing numbers of individuals seek to escape the cacophony of pulsating commercials and "sexploitive" song lyrics for more uplifting and romantic fields.

Meanwhile, television languishes in the language of abuse—nonstop sexual innuendos, putdowns, and lascivious cat-calls from the audience. Youngsters cut their teeth on the putrid squalor of *Beavis and Butt-head*. Media moguls say these and other shows are successful because they attract a large share of the "viewing audience."

But what about the non-viewing, non-listening audience? How about those who rarely turn on the tube or listen to mainstream radio anymore? Where are the statistics on us?

More to the point, when did sex become a mere animalistic instinct? When did "flirting" and "courtship" become synonyms for "sexual harassment"?

As a final indignity, the Ann Landers column, after 58 years of preaching commitment and caring, offered a commentary on a piece reprinted from the *Los Angeles Times* by a Dr. Steven Sainsbury of San Luis Obispo, California. He had written to comment on a 15-year-old girl he was treating for "a rip-roaring case of gonorrhea"—a typical occurrence in his practice, apparently. It was bad enough that he criticized experts who equate condoms with "safe sex," saying the high breakage rate during normal, vaginal intercourse did not support such a claim. But Dr. Sainsbury committed the ultimate blasphemy when he maintained that the only safe sex is no sex, until one is ready "to commit to a monogamous relationship." The key words, he reiterated, were "abstinence and monogamy."

The good doctor didn't mention marriage, but no matter. Ann Landers took on the heretic, declaring that she was going to "stick her neck out" and "suggest a more realistic solution than abstinence." Her recommendation? "Self-gratification or mutual masturbation, whatever it takes to release sexual energy."

"This is a sane and safe alternative to intercourse," she wrote, "not only for teenagers, but for older men and women who have lost their partners." Her rationale was that "the sex drive is the strongest human drive after hunger."

It was this sanctimonious diatribe that brought me to the word processor. Well, I'm going to stick my neck out and say: No. The sex drive is *not* the strongest *human* drive after hunger. It may be the strongest *animal* drive after hunger, but it is not the strongest human drive. Love is. Love is what separates animals from humans. Animals may exhibit loyalty, trust, and affection, but these are not the equivalents of compassion and commitment, which comprise the key elements we know as romantic love.

Certainly there's physical attraction, or "chemistry." But after the 25th wedding anniversary, I can tell you it's commitment and compassion that keep the "chemistry" intact decades after the wedding march is over. Conversely, as any separated or divorced couple will tell you, when there is no love left in a relationship, sex is the first thing to go.

Down through the centuries, music from popular to opera has revolved around love. Love lost. Love gained. Endless love. Falling in love. Unrequited love. Sometimes naive, sometimes corny or sentimental. Occasionally erotic in an amorous, lighthearted way. But love, nevertheless. Until recently, song lyrics were never mean, grotesque or disrespectful. The music did not remind you of a *grand mal* seizure. Certainly love was not reduced to crotch-grabbing, cruel images of caged, raped or battered women and of even ripped genitalia (à la "2 Live Crew").

How ironic that the 60's generation—*my* generation—which once proselytized "make love, not war" now admonishes its young to "have sex, not love" and to equate love with a glove, sex toys and condoms. These are the "ugly" images, Mizz Gebbie; these, Mizz Elders, are the "dirty" messages.

Too many psychologists, too many grownups in general, have forgotten what it was like to be a child. Never mind whether it was the 1950's, 60's or even the 30's. Just a child. We all had hormones, you know. Today's kids didn't invent them. But that first exposure to sexual topics, as I remember it, was not about hormones.

Before I knew where babies came from, before I knew about menstruation, before I knew about the sex act or needed a bra, my little friends and I fantasized about love. Paul Newman was handsome; we weren't all that interested in his groin. And from the teenage years on, flirting was fun; conversation was the means of exploring the first exhilarating feelings of attraction;

and those initial, fleeting moments of physical intimacy were exciting. We were in love with being in love. An off-color joke, if it was clever, drew a smile. The details of people's sex lives did not. Those were private. A person's virginity intensely so. A girl's first sexual experience generated a serious emotional bond, which was hard-wired, not merely "learned." Even the evolutionists admit that primitive women looked for men who would help them raise children and fend for them.

Because of my books, I receive of all kinds of adolescent tests and surveys in the mail—some anonymously, some not. One, from Nebraska, asked youngsters, among a long list of provocative questions, what they thought **about** when they thought of sex. Ignoring the inappropriateness of such a question for a moment, I wonder how many wrote "love." Or "caring." Or "warmth." Or "tenderness."

I was not raised a Fundamentalist-style Christian. But ever since my first two books were published—they apparently struck a particularly sensitive chord among the orthodox Christian community, as well as with other religious groups—I think I better understand why those sneeringly referred to by the mainstream media as "religious" get bent out of shape when the topic of teaching evolution comes up. It's not merely that humankind may have at some point had a close relative among the simian family, although no direct proof of that theory has ever been confirmed. What really gets under the skin of serious Christians and other religious parents is the suggestion, frequently passed along *with* this theory, that humans really are just advanced animals.

Now don't get me wrong. Anyone who knows me will tell you that, left to my own devices, I would take home the entire contents of the animal shelter. But humans are not animals. Despite some similarities to humans, including the rudimentary ability to think, plan, make decisions and understand language, animals are not humans with fur. Humans are not at the mercy of their instincts; animals are. Animals, including species that mate for life, do not contemplate their own existence.

At the heart of the resistance by orthodox religious people to today's government-mandated, sex-training programs is that children are being encouraged to consider themselves as animals, with slightly more advanced brain functions, of course —i.e., animals cannot be trained to use a condom. But the fact is that animals don't *need* condoms. Nature did not construct animals in such a way that "promiscuous," or indiscriminate, sex is going to hurt them. The purpose of sex in the animal kingdom is reproduction—period. To animals, procreation is of serious interest only when the female is in heat. In humans, procreation is of serious interest mainly when a man and a woman are in love. How does one explain—I have never heard it broached by any biological expert—how humans, if they were descended from animals, could have made the huge genetic leap from viable pregnancy occurring *only* in heat to pregnancy *prevented* during the menses?

Love is at its most fulfilling to humans when it involves loss of self to another person. For that reason, sex tends to fall short of expectations if its sole purpose is self- (much less group-) gratification—turning it into a kind of sporting event. It is this point that is at the core of what is called the "sanctity of the family." Sex, the most intimate way possible for humans to express love on a physical level, is an intensely private matter.

Which brings up the other source of objection among orthodox religious parents to currently voguish sexual teachings: the rejection of a "privacy ethic" by sex educators. Look at the surveys and the distribution of sex paraphernalia to young, impressionable children. What is the message?

It is that they won't have any problem with this unless they have something to hide. And also, that nothing is private. Not even "what you think about when you think of sex." Not your bowels and other bodily functions, either, if you really examine the sex surveys. And when you move on to some of the drug and alcohol questionnaires (incorporated into even so-called academic tests like the Metropolitan Achievement Test put out by the Psychological Corporation), it is clear that the details of your family life are not private—and shouldn't be! Do your parents do such-and-such? Do your parents have this or that in their homes? If you believe the professional literature on such tests, the purpose of this information-gathering is to construct a curriculum that will instill ethical "values."

Isn't it ironic that we once had social sanctions that worked in this country. That kept behavior within tolerable limits and the libido in check. When adults, not adolescents, held cultural authority, young men were actually taught that certain behaviors are unacceptable around women. They were taught attentiveness and courtesy and to avoid foul language. They weren't given lame excuses about their sexuality peaking at the age of 17.

Similar codes of conduct were taught to young girls. You didn't go alone to a man's room or bar-hopping at all hours of the night and expect no consequences. You were taught what it meant to conduct yourself in a dignified fashion. You didn't even consider going to bed with a fellow on a first, second or even third date. Today it is expected. You didn't go around braless in tank-tops, wear skin-tight skirts, fishnet hose and three-inch heels, get your legs shaved by a bunch of drunken sailors, and then turn around (as in the infamous Tailhook incident) and complain about sexual harassment. Bearing a child out of wedlock was disgraceful and showed a lack of self-discipline and character.

Then a cadre of countercultural mental "health" experts and the courts came along, and in just 30 years they managed to remove the stigma from behaviors that, today, are completely out of control. No law against "sexual harassment," no sex-ed course, no deadbeat dads legislation is going to bring back the kind of morality, the sense of privacy-in-intimacy that once was passed from one generation to the next—values like modesty and chastity, *which parents are no longer **permitted** to pass along*, because the schools and the media—backed up (unwittingly, perhaps) by the courts—continually undermine the efforts of responsible parents who comprised the backbone of society.

Thus has sexuality become the stuff of billboards and bumper stickers, each vying for attention, each more shocking than the last. Oh, yes. Today's teachings about sex are negative, all right, just as AIDS czarina Kristine Gebbie said. But no more so than allusions to, and discussions about, the subject in entertainment and the nightly news. As a result, the allure of physical attraction and the rituals of courtship are no longer cute, fun, flirtatious, titillating, or even risqué; they're just plain gross. Sex and love have been granted a divorce.

Sex is now defined as "release of tension." Art, music, and much of literature focus not on romance, but on genitals, multiple orgasms, and little-understood chromosomal mix-ups that result in unfortunate genetic mix-ups like homosexuality and the penchant for pedophilia.

What have we done to love? We have debased it. Defiled it. Desensitized it. Depersonalized it. Disparaged it. We've even

185

urinated on it. And, judging from our drug and crime statistics, society is paying the heaviest possible price.

Published in June 1994 by CHRONICLES: A Magazine of American Culture, under the title "When Sex Conquers Love, reprinted in Opposing Viewpoints Series: Human Sexuality *(college textbook), 1995, Greenhaven Press, as "Sex Is Becoming More Casual and Less Intimate." Both are adapted from the author's speech entitled "What They Did To Love," 1993. A few sentences have been edited for this anthology.*

PRIVACY

(DATA-MINING, PSYCH PROFILING, COMPUTERIZATION)

B. K. Eakman

IMPLANTED IDS: *CLICK HERE!*

Applied Digital Solutions (ADS) announced in March that it had filed for FDA approval of its tiny ID implant, VeriChip, and the Florida-based company performed its first commercial implant on three local children on May 10, promising "easy access of medical records."

While both announcements were greeted with surprise, ADS had already revealed that it had received the patent rights for VeriChip's prototype, Digital Angel — a miniature digital transceiver designed for implantation in the human body and powered electromechanically through muscle movement. Unlike other experimental implants created by competitors, ADS's was intended not merely to identify but to send and receive data and, eventually, to be able to track the implantee using Global Positioning Satellite (GPS) technology. For now, the sales hooks are "medical emergencies" and "identifying missing persons," including soldiers in the field and corpses — particularly effective, given the nation's post-September 11 mentality.

There have been many indications for years that "technology creep" would someday revolutionize our conceptions of what is personal and private, but legislators, in this information-based society, have been slow to sense the dangers of microchipping people.

Most of us probably can tick off a long list of programs that started out as voluntary, temporary, or "pilot projects" but eventually morphed into permanent mandates, sometimes with draconian ramifications: the income tax, Social Security numbers, annual auto-emissions tests, psychological screening for school-children. Both the national ID card and various universal health-care schemes were rejected over just such fears of arbitrary and dehumanizing applications, but both are about to sneak through the back door via the ID implant.

By the time ADS mass markets VeriChip, bureaucrats will likely have scared young parents into microchipping their babies — right now, today, before your child gets swapped, stolen, kidnapped, into an accident, or lost! Will an "adult microchip," like today's beginners' driver's license, then become a rite of passage for teenagers?

Shortly before Christmas 1993, a program to identify pets through chip implants was launched nationwide. Veterinarians and humane societies promoted the new devices, which were (and still are) implanted by means of a painless injection under the animal's skin. The pet chips provide only the basics — pet's name, owner's address, vaccination dates, and vet — all readable with hand-held scanners. But if your pet is gone, so is your microchip. How exactly does this chip improve on a collar or dog tag?

The pet program may have been less about finding Fido than about getting the bugs out of ID-implant technology. While data-collection techniques, consolidation, and cross-matching capabilities were exponentially expanding, the door was opened for the next logical step.

In a 1993 speech entitled "Microchipped" (published as part of a book in 1994), I predicted the first human ID implant incorporating tracking and cross-matching capability to be a mere decade away.

Nine years later, Digital Angel is suddenly a big winner on the stock market. To attract investors, ADS has a website that hypes a variety of potential uses, from tamper-proof identifications to enhanced e-business security and the monitoring of serious medical conditions. ADS notes that the device can "be activated either by the 'wearer' or by the monitoring facility."

Every news story missed that little fact. Most people would assume that the wearer and the purchaser are a "team," working on the same side. But who will really have control, not only over your whereabouts but of your privileged information? Whether it is school, airport, and building security; "red flagging" your banking transactions; facial-recognition systems in public places; e-mail intercept/recovery capability; laser scanners picking up cell-phone conversations; cameras mounted on the roadway; or computers logging everything from your urinary-tract infection to your rock-concert tickets, we are being acclimated to believe that, if we have nothing to hide, privacy is no big deal.

Meanwhile, ever-increasing advances in computer cross-matching dog us wherever we go — from census, motor-vehicle, tax, title, and insurance databases to school records. The result is a burgeoning information industry of data traffickers and "brokers," licit and otherwise, all linking information to accommodate the needs of employers, credit bureaus, universities, police, corporate spies — and government. Not surprisingly, data-laundering has become a lucrative spin-off industry.

The student who divulges on a school questionnaire which magazines, modern conveniences, and medications are in his home, or the vacation spots most frequented by family members, has no idea that this "lifestyle data" can be cross-matched with responses relating to social attitudes, worldviews, religion, and politics.

At first, most analysts were interested in aggregate data to determine public-policy trends or to assess the results of advertising strategies aimed at specific demographic groups. But with government-mandated database consolidations, uniform codes, standardized definitions, and compulsory compatibility among local, state, and federal computers — ostensibly "to facilitate information-sharing" — it was only a matter of time before this technology targeted the individual.

The new generation of ID implants holds a sizable paragraph of information. That one paragraph, however, is also capable of being linked with other information systems, and search-engine technology is outstripping the best expectations of even the experts. More ominous, information thought to be anonymous is readily identifiable. The term "confidential," in a legal context, has come to mean "need to know."

A statistical model can be created from computerized information to predict, sometimes with stunning accuracy, future reactions and behaviors using information from a person's past activities, ranging from responses on a survey to frequency of toll-free telephone usage to recurring trends in discretionary spending.

As Larry Ellison, chief executive officer of the software giant, Oracle, explained in an interview on The News Hour with Jim Lehrer, there are thousands of compatible databases that track and cross-reference generic information about people — their beliefs, family ties, friends' and associates' names, addresses, phone numbers, and aliases; political/civic clubs and associations joined; magazine and newspaper subscriptions; frequent shopping places; political campaigns and causes contributed to; how important a person is by region, state, or city; and criminal and medical histories, including potentially embarrassing information from long ago. Together, these can forecast a person's future actions.

So where's the abuse?

In 1995, the National Institutes of Health quietly provided a grant to the Western Psychiatric Institute and Clinic for a "Multi-site Multimodal Treatment Study of Children With ADHD." Among the significant aspects of the ensuing legal case was that kids who had not been labeled with any disorder were discovered to have been given a battery of psychological tests without informed consent from parents, and, worse, the collected data had been mixed not only with students' education records but with their medical records. Once caught, Western Psychiatric refused to share the information it had collected with parents, yet it was unable to prove that data on a particular child could not be retrieved at a later time, causing "compensable harm." Might not insurance companies, potential employers, or even a political opponent find such information useful down the road (e.g., a child having once been referred to a psychologist)?

DNA microchipping and other implant technology have progressed in a similarly quiet manner, save a few occasional tidbits. For example, the Times of London reported in October 1998 that "film stars and the children of millionaires [were] among 45 people, including several Britons . . . [who] have been fitted with chips (called the Sky Eye) in secret tests."

Meanwhile, a barrage of mixed messages erodes our concept of privacy. Beepers, cell phones, key ("swipe") cards, and passwords all make us aware of the need for personal security. Security, however, is not privacy. A person's body and what one does with it (abortion, homosexuality, etc.) supposedly are sacrosanct and inviolable. On the other hand, if other people's money and health are compromised by someone's private behavior (say, smoking or drunk driving), then we are told that a person's bodily functions are everybody's business.

Insurance companies certainly think so. The Maryland Insurance Group (part of a Switzerland-based conglomerate in Zurich) sent policyholders a notice in 1994 announcing that it would henceforth collect information on "your character, habits, hobbies, finances, occupation, general reputation, health and other personal characteristics"; that it would, at its discretion, talk or write to "neighbors, friends, insurance agent and others who know you" as well as access "motor vehicle reports, court records, or photographs" and anything else that "may pertain to your mode of living, character . . . and personal characteristics."

Today, such globally accessible dossier-building is standard operating procedure.

More recently, the cloning debate has put a spotlight on geneticists, who are hot on the DNA/gene-mapping trail to head off genetic "mistakes" and diseases. The criminal-justice system wants biometric identifiers for both employees and criminals (apparently interchangeable distinctions since September 11). International proponents of biometric implant chips — Interpol, for example — use "global cooperation" to justify mass identification and tracking techniques.

The common thread, of course, is a compelling worldwide interest in collecting, tracking, and cross-referencing information on private citizens. Janlori Goldman, deputy director for the Center for Democracy and Technology, saw the handwriting on the wall in 1991 when she commented that there is "barely a piece of information about people that isn't used for far different purposes than it was initially gathered for [sic], and always without approval."

Among the cybertech pioneers is Professor Kevin Warwick of Reading University, working with Blackbaud Inc. (another American software giant) and a renowned British subsidiary software company. Warwick made the headlines in the summer of 1999 when he had a silicon chip transponder surgically implanted in his forearm. For a bemused media, he demonstrated his ability to switch lights on and off and to start and shut down computers and thermostats as he entered or left a room. A computer monitored his every move as he made his way among detectors scattered throughout his building. There was only one problem: The chip was unstable and had to be removed every few weeks, then re-implanted.

Warwick admitted that he missed the chip when it was removed. The Warwick experiments were short-range. The chip emitted radio waves through a mobile-phone network and beamed its location to a computer. A person could be located on a computer map from a few blocks away.

Short range, however, was good enough for what Warwick had in mind for tomorrow's workers: He touted the business possibilities, particularly for companies with high labor costs.

The implant, he said, was a relatively cheap means of keeping tabs on employees. "You can tell when people clock into work and when they leave the building," he beamed. "You would know at all times exactly where they were and who they were with."

Although Warwick acknowledged that most people would be "shocked" if companies asked their employees to submit to implants, he pointed out that many employees already carry swipe cards, which can serve as tracking devices. Warwick also suggested that submitting to an implant might be made a condition of being granted a gun license, since computerized background checks amount to virtually the same thing.

Anyone who owns an automobile or boat with GPS knows that satellite tracking is not short-range. The reason Warwick's chip had to be removed frequently is that a GPS enhancement required two penlight batteries to power it for approximately 40 hours. This chip was postage-stamp-sized instead of near-microscopic and had to be made compatible with specific kinds of antennas.

By the time ADS was ready to go commercial with VeriChip in May, human chip implants were not science fiction anymore. In light of recently well-publicized, horrific child abduction-murders, there was, predictably, no shortage of volunteers. Who cared whether the chip was invisible or not? Improvements could be expected.

More portentous suggestions than Warwick's have been made. The Fetal Treatment Center at the University of California, San Francisco, has connected implantable biotelemetry devices to unborn babies. Other specialists, such as Dr. Roy Bakay of Emory University are ready to install chip-to-brain implants.

Charles Ostman, a senior fellow at the Institute for Global Futures and science editor of Mondo 2000, believes implanting chips will become a routine process. "Neuroprosthetics are. . . inevitable," he says. "Biochip implants may become part of a rote medical procedure. Interface with outside systems is a logical next step."

Today, the products of permissive childrearing make up the largest population of individuals labeled "mentally inferior" — learning disabled, emotionally disturbed, hyperactive, ADHD, etc. People holding politically inconvenient opinions and world views, but who have committed no crime, also are frequently saddled with psychiatric labels that suggest "unfitness." Now here come "cybertechies" promoting biochip implants and GPS tracking as a part of "rote medical procedure."

The ID implant also will impact the impending issue of baby licensing.

Under a new computerized initiative called the Program Information Management System" (PIMS), social workers nationwide are encouraging expectant parents to sign a permission form at the hospital that allows agents to go into private homes to provide parenting training — up to 50 visits annually per family While they are at it, these "experts" will also collect medical and psychological information that can be merged with future written observations about family relationships — in effect, tracking each newborn's development (as well as any attitudes) from infancy into their school and college years. But make no mistake: Their primary mission is to assess parental "fitness."

When we place the PIMS project alongside such parent-unfriendly projects as Western Psychiatric Institute and Clinic's "Multi-site Multimodal Treatment Study of Children With ADHD," we find some very troubling prospects. With the recent increase in crime among juveniles, computerized dossier-building, and the concurrent war on parents waged by schools and various government programs, we have a recipe for technological abuse. Microchip implants, used to track, monitor, and cross-match information, could greatly enhance political screening in the name of "parental fitness." Even those who feel comfortable with the political and social winds today may not feel so warm and fuzzy tomorrow when they stop to think how fast society's mores and priorities can change in just a few years with the right promotional packages and enough surveys.

Forget, however, about banning ID implants: They are already in the pipeline. In June 1998, the U.S. Department of Energy's Argonne National Laboratory revealed its joint project with Motorola and Packard Instrument Company to commercialize, market, and mass-produce advanced biochips "and related analytical technologies."

All that remains is selling people on the idea, perhaps with an ad like this:

How'd you like to avoid waiting in lines for the rest of your life? Breeze through a checkout line like you owned the place?

B. K. Eakman

Watch lights snap on, open doors automatically, never have to show an ID, remember a password? You wouldn't have to carry a wallet. Ever. Family and friends could find you if you were sick or unconscious. Click here!

THE SLIPPERY SLOPE OF SAFETY

Keeping up with technology is tricky. Sometimes, you find information in a press release; other times, you ascertain the full measure of what is going on through obscure legal and scientific papers, last-minute legislative "riders," and seemingly inconsequential blurbs in the foreign press. Even as my piece on implantable identification tags was going to press ["Implanted IDs: Click Here!" Vital Signs, Oct. 2002], rumors were emerging from Great Britain.

Applied Digital Solution's primary human guinea pig and proselytizer, cybernetics researcher Kevin Warwick of the United Kingdom's Reading University, fell into hot water. Electronics expert Bernard Albrecht called the General Medical Council, various social-service agencies, two district councils, and eventually the police to file assault charges against Warwick for conducting unethical medical and surgical procedures on volunteers. His favorite targets were the children of parents seeking peace of mind, for reasons of health or security. When the authorities failed to bring charges, Albrecht appealed to the university's guidelines on research, alleging misrepresentation of a technological device. In the ensuing uproar, the press dubbed Professor Warwick "Captain Cyborg." None of the charges against Warwick have yet been pursued.

A plethora of details emerged that revealed a great deal more about the stake that various corporations—and government— have in making human monitoring and tracking succeed. In addition, there are clearly aspects of ADS's "research initiative" that had yet to be revealed to the public.

In at least one of its products, ADS was rumored to have rigged something that required neither a ground-based network nor triangulation and to have reduced cell-phone components to such a size that they could be implanted under the skin or in muscle tissue. The point of the journalists crying "fraud" was to extract an explanation.

The answer came in the form of sales. Dr. Peter Zhou, the chief scientist who developed the ADS implant and president of

DigitalAngel.net, an ADS subsidiary, boasted: "Your doctor will know [about a health] problem before you do.... We have received requests daily from around the world for the product."

One interested party was the U.S. Department of Defense, which apparently made inquiries through a contractor.

Journalists, commentators, and lawyers began to uncover fascinating projects, all incorporating aspects of people-tracking and monitoring, including the use of the jawbone as an antenna and the adaptation of a silicone gel as a protective covering for implants and as an injection-delivery agent. They also noted developments in "nanotechnology," the integration of micro-electronics and molecular biology to create organic systems literally capable of "breeding"—i.e., reproducing biologically— complex solutions to problems. The Clinton administration provided $227 million in fiscal year 2001 alone for research under the National Nanotechnology Initiative.

Journalists also reported on the development of a smorgasbord of implantable and external monitoring/tracking gear, either already, or nearly, on the market, including: "the Babysitter," a jelly-bean-sized microchip implant that is placed under a child's collar bone so parents can track his location; "the Constant Companion," a tracking device for senior citizens; and "the Invisible Bodyguard," to protect you from kidnappers when you are out of town. The "Micro-Manager," the "Personal Private Eye," the "Maximum Security Guard," and the "Border Patroller" require no explanation. Then there is the coming "decoder ring," an implant placed into the human eye that is read by a retinal scanner, and the "genegg," designed for implantation in the belly button.

The rationalizations offered for these invasive products are even more fascinating than the technology itself. Tom Turner, senior vice president of marketing and business development for WhereNet, believes the benefits to "a parent looking for a child at a theme park" or to "a student [needing to feel] safe as he walks across campus far outweigh privacy" and abuse concerns. WhereNet has already licensed its technology to companies that make pager-like devices worn as bracelets or carried in a pocket or purse. Customers include a water park in Denver and the Universities of South Florida (Tampa) and South Alabama (Mobile). Turner's target markets include cruise ships, gated communities, and shopping malls.

Brendan Fitzgerald, the president of Microgistics (which makes WalkMate, a device used by college students to contact campus police), argues: "If you were working in a hazardous industrial environment, you would want to know that you could push a button and have someone help you if you need help."

"Safety First" is a slogan that is difficult to argue with. But carrying a panic button is considerably different from "transparent surveillance." As pacemakers, artificial knees and hips, and implants (temporary and permanent) for the delivery of pain medications and other drugs become more common, many Americans increasingly view I.D. implants as similar advances. Just as automated, multitechnology readers like Smart Cards claim to offer freedom from toll booths and long lines, Digital Angel and similar implant devices promise peace of mind. "Ideally," the ADS patent states, "the device will bring... an increased quality of life for those who use it, and for their families, loved ones, and associates who depend on them critically.

In an interview with WorldNetDaily two years ago, Dr. Zhou dismissed religious and ethical objections to implant research:

"I am a Christian, but...the purpose of the device is to save your life and improve the quality of life. There's no connection to the Bible. There are different interpretations of the Bible. My interpretation is, anything to improve the quality of life is from God. The Bible says, 'I am the God of living people.' We not only live, we live well."

ADS has sunk millions into the Digital Angel project and understandably does not want bad press now. Zhou explained that, just like the cell phone, Digital Angel "will be a connection from yourself to the electronic world. It will be your guardian, protector. It will bring good things to you.... We will be a hybrid of electronic intelligence and our own soul."

Which brings us to the real question: Who will be able to demand that a chip be implanted in another person? Parents? The criminal-justice system? Immigration authorities? Employers? Katharine Mieszkowski, in an article entitled "Microchip Children" in the November 2000 issue of the online magazine, Salon, states the obvious: "The potential for abuse is so ludicrously high that it's almost impossible to overstate." She cites George Getz, communications director for the Libertarian Party, who noted that:

"No government has ever forced anyone to have a drivers license, [but now] try getting along without one, when everyone from your local banker to the hotel operator to the grocery store requires one in order for you to take advantage of their services; that amounts to a de facto mandate. If the government can force you to surrender your fingerprints to get a drivers license, why can't it force you to get a computer chip implant?"

ADS opened the floodgates when it acquired, as part of its patent rights to Digital Angel in 1999, the right to sublicense the development of specific applications to other entities and to seek out joint-venture partners to develop, expand, and market the technologies. This changed the original focus of Digital Angel from banking and electronic purchases to emergency-location and medical monitoring. ADS's "joint venture" with Professor Warwick moved the device into the realm of tracking and monitoring employees, criminals, and whomever else might be deemed in need of monitoring. ADS anticipates a "potential global market . . . exceeding $100 billion." ADS even received a special "Technology Pioneers" award from the World Economic Forum for its contributions to "worldwide economic development and social progress through technology advancements."

Mieszkowski also quotes Chris Hables Gray, a professor, self-proclaimed "cyborgologist," and the author of Cyborg Citizen, who observes that "Technology is continually trumping [our] constitutional guarantees." He calls for legal protections against the misuse of chips before they become commercially available:

"Citizens could ask for a law that makes it a crime to put these into a person without their permission, and to forbid, under any conditions, the government to put these into . . . citizens. . . . [W]e do not have to accept every new technology."

Increasingly, however, we simply accept new technologies by default. Scientists, inventors, and investors can scarcely resist the temptation to push the boundaries of possibility—often, of course, with the best of intentions. Understandably, men desire technologies that will save time or improve quality of life. But knowledge, once obtained, cannot simply be unlearned—a lesson as old as Adam and Eve.

CATCH IT IF YOU CAN

In a way, it galls me. Except for the little voice deep down—the one that keeps smirking.

In 2003, it was the Terrorism (formerly "Total") Information Awareness Office. Then "Super-Snoops." Mid-January 2004, it was news concerning a collusion between a prominent government agency giving an airline some 90 days' worth of private information on some 440,000 US citizens—to assess terrorist risks. The same month we learned that 2000 census data had been used in a data-mining effort to cross-match so-called "anomalies" with passenger lists. Then, Cendent Corporation's "massive database" on customers, with more than 200 pieces of cross-referenceable information. Not to mention, potential of arrest for "crimes of opinion."

All this dovetails with a culture of political correctness run so completely amok, that one's views can be known—and dealt with—even before a person has had a chance to give them voice.

And our legislators, journalists and commentators are outraged. Shocked!

Since 1990 a plethora of award-winning books and articles (my own and others') have outlined the breadth and scope of data-trafficking, cross-referencing and information-sharing in the U.S. and abroad. PBS's NOVA series featured a special, "We Know Where You Live." Business Week writer/analyst, Jeffrey Rothfeder, wrote *Privacy for Sale*, which revealed, among other things, just how much unauthorized information the author was able to dig up, on a lark, about a certain Vice President Dan Quayle, of whom he was not particularly fond. Until, one day it wasn't so funny, and Rothfeder started writing his watershed book. Earl R. MacCormac, science advisor to the then-Governor of North Carolina, penned a lengthy document for his boss warning of a technological and legal nightmare. MacCormac started with a scrap of paper and explained just how much personal information he could locate about someone via computerized cross-matching in just 24 hours.

The bottom line? Your privacy's toast.

My own particular emphasis was the unethical use of schools and children, an angle none of the other writers up to that time had looked into. I focused on a little-known technique (outside of advertising and marketing circles) known as "psychographic surveying" with a view to altering attitudes. Then I traced the evolution of automatic transfer capability to federal and international databases from 1969 onward. A definition of psychographics is found in Webster's New World Communication and Media Dictionary: "the study of social class based upon the demographics income, race, color, religion, and personality traits." These characteristics, says the dictionary, "can be measured to predict behavior"—prediction being the point of the exercise.

How? By collecting personal information, especially "lifestyle data," which includes opinions and preferences, via surveys, tests, and questionnaires; cross-matching the responses with various public and private records; and then applying a mathematical model (a) to predict individual and group reactions to future, hypothetical scenarios, and (b) to find areas of commonality among socioeconomic, demographic, political and religious groups.

As early as 1989, evidence started accumulating concerning questions falling under the rubric of psychographics which, inexplicably, were being included in standardized school achievement tests. The first what-would-you-do-if queries and word-association games passed off as vocabulary questions I saw were test items from Pennsylvania's Educational Quality Assessment in 1985. As time went on, test creators got better at devising questions in such a way that the "target subjects," as it was termed, would be unaware just how much they were divulging.

Soon, technical papers detailing state and nationwide plans for compiling and storing computerized, private information were uncovered—the U.S. Department of Education's "Measuring the Quality of Education" (1981) and "A Plan for the Redesign of the Elementary and Secondary Data Collection Program" (1986). The next shocker featured justifications concerning "the permissibility of deception" in school testing based on "the rights of an institution to obtain information necessary to achieve its goals," set out by behavioral scientists Richard Wolf and Ralph Tyler.

Wolf pointed out in "Crucial Issues in Testing," that privacy implications aside, there "are occasions in which the test constructor [finds it necessary] to outwit the subject so that he cannot guess what information he is revealing." Wolf and Tyler both emanated from the Educational Testing Service (ETS). Tyler was also a former Commissioner of Education under the US Department of Health, Education and Welfare—which seemed rather a conflict of interest at the time, but apparently nobody cared. He was largely responsible for creating our nationwide test, the National Assessment of Educational Progress (NAEP). Under separate contract he wrote, or weighed in heavily, on at least 12 state tests—called "assessments" to hedge the legal definition of testing.

So offended were citizens when news of attitudinal questions incorporated into achievement tests hit the presses with my first book in 1991 that lines to the Department were temporarily jammed with irate callers.

"Rubbish," howled Robert J. Coldiron, head of Pennsylvania's Chief of Testing and Evaluation at the State Education Agency in Harrisburg in a Letter to the Editor in Education Week.

"Nonsense," insisted Ohio's then-chief of testing when I was invited to Columbus to speak at a state board meeting at the insistence of parents there.

With my second book in 1994, officials from various agencies —among them, the National Center for Education Statistics— were asking for a meeting with me to "prove" none of this was happening. Emerson Elliott, then-head of NCES, urged: "Come see the new National Assessment tests for yourself. Oh, by the way, that computer you named—the Elementary and Secondary Integrated Data System—it doesn't exist."

And so on, in one state after another on my lecture circuit— New Hampshire, Nebraska, Indiana, Maryland. Meanwhile, I was amassing enough proof from informants, anonymous and otherwise, to wallpaper the entire Department with phony test questions.

Then there was the House and Senate. The then-legislative assistant for education to Senator Charles E. Grassley — the same fellow later demanding congressional review of the huge profiling database about to be brought online to snoop for potential terrorists via the Pentagon's Defense Advanced

Research Projects Agency (DARPA)—huffed that my allegations were "alarmist" and could never happen here. (The former assistant, Shannon Royce, surprised me with an apology when I saw her at an event some years later.)

By the time my third and final book, *Cloning of the American Mind*, hit the street in 1998, the official tune had changed. Well, they said, there were "a few demographic" as well as "noncognitive" questions included on state and national tests. Then, testing companies admitted that "some" questions were aimed at assessing "extenuating factors" (including home life, parents' habits, worldviews, magazines, financial status, etc.) which might affect a child's learning. Finally, curriculums in subjects like health and sex required some method, after all, of estimating and predicting their impact, above and beyond "mere" right or wrong answers.

All this was passed off as part of an increased emphasis on accountability. As for my earlier allusions to the Department of Education's Elementary and Secondary Integrated Data System, taken from Appendix E in the 1988 Nation's Report Card: Well, heh, heh, you see, there were ongoing technical difficulties in computer compatibility at the state and local levels; so the Department of Education, through the Council of Chief State School Officers, launched a series of "incentives" to improve matters until there emerged a bigger and better version of the system, the SPEEDE/ExPRESS, into which all student, teacher, and school records have flowed since the mid-1990s. So many computer experts were there on the project that Florida's Associate Commissioner of Education, Cecil Golden, was once prompted to remark (prophetically, as it turned out): "[L]ike those assembling an atom bomb, very few of them understand what they're building, and won't until we put all the parts together."

For the past decade students have had to plow through not only quasi-tests called "assessments," featuring all sorts of questions about their parents and home life, but a multitude of intimate and personal surveys, nearly all of them computerized, as part of their class work. Where do you think newspapers get statistics like "12% of students say they have had intercourse by age 15," or smoked a joint in the last 6 months, or dislike their parents?

But, of course, these responses are anonymous, you say.

Dream on. Surreptitious "slugging," "bar-coding," "sticky-labeling," and "embedding identifiers": All these techniques, and more, are described at length in the testing contracts and literature, should anyone bother to read them.

Children have always been the consummate sources of data, notoriously undiscerning about the kinds of information they disclose. Like all computerized facts and figures, youngsters' responses can be cross-matched with everything from medical and health insurance records to credit card transactions. But no legislation or guidelines have emerged from our hallowed regulative bodies to sufficiently put the brakes on the tremendous upswing of such activity over the past two decades. The 80s and 90s were spent largely in denial. If anything, our leaders made it worse by swallowing malarkey about the supposed benefits of mental health profiling, personality inventories and behavioral screening—to identify potential troublemakers and ensure public safety. Society's reward? More Columbine-like atrocities—and a near-perfect political weapon, now neatly in place.

I used to be asked on talk shows: Who would ever use such a thing? What kind of democracy would amass information, and snoop on its own citizens?

None, of course—unless national security were at stake, unless there were a dire threat, some trigger. September 11 was that trigger. Sleeper cells of terrorists are that threat. We can argue all day about porous borders, lax immigration control, permissive childrearing and bleeding-heart responses to crime as contributing factors to our public and private security woes. None of that matters anymore. The Family Educational Rights and Privacy Act—like the 1970 Fair Credit Reporting Act, the 1974 Privacy Act, the 1978 Right to Financial Privacy Act, the 1988 Cross-Matching and Privacy Protection Act, the Gramm-Leach-Bliley Act, and all the various other incarnations—are virtually meaningless. They're so filled with loopholes they look like Swiss cheese. Not only is every scintilla of your personal information available to government agencies (both national and international), but incorporated is a capability to assess anything from parental fitness and tax fraud to a child's state of mind. Not only that, so-called "directory" information—including a youngster's name, address, phone number, picture, and e-mail address—can be released without consent to predators.

B. K. Eakman

So now our revered legislators and media moguls are worried about amassing dossiers, covert cross-matching, government prying, and freedom of conscience.

Well, it's a tad late, Suckers. The horse has busted out the barn door and is galloping down the street. Go catch it if you can.

[Author's note: This piece was first published in Media Bypass Magazine in January 2003. In light of recent events, it is more true now than it was then, and the second and third paragraphs reflect recent news updates.]

THE DARK SIDE OF NATIONWIDE TESTS

President Bush's education initiative calls for the testing of every student in the nation, but these 'assessments' in the past involved Big Brother-style psychological profiling.

The proponents of President George W. Bush's education initiative, called "No Child Left Behind," believe that they can make schools accountable to parents as well as taxpayers. The centerpiece of this, as it appears in the amendments to the Elementary and Secondary School Act, is a massive nationwide program designed to test every student in grades three to eight in reading and math. Both the House and Senate bills propose some $400 million in federal funds to be sent to the states to devise and administer the tests on a state-by-state basis.

By giving tax money to each state to devise its own tests, supporters hope to mollify conservatives on the one hand, who fear national indoctrination by the U.S. Department of Education, and liberals on the other, who dread the consequences of holding educators personally accountable for whether the children they teach actually learn. The language of the 2001 House bill, HR1, for example, stated in an unresolved contradiction that each state shall demonstrate that it adopted "challenging academic standards and challenging academic-achievement standards." In the same breath, the bill said that "a state shall not be required to submit such standards to the Secretary."

The problem is that "academic standards" as defined by common sense and by lawmakers tend to be meaningless when defined by educators. The bill calls for "challenging academic-content standards in academic subjects that specify what children are expected to know and be able to do" and contain "coherent and rigorous content ... and encourage the teaching of advanced skills." Yet both House and Senate bills shy away from using the term "tests" and substitute the edu-speak word "assessments."

The reason is that public education during the last 30 years has tended against testing for knowledge of content, instead emphasizing a psychological assessment of a child's needs, background and ability to conform to the group. A "test" is an objective measure of a child's ability to solve a problem; an "assessment" is a social scientist's speculation about the environmental conditioning of the child.

Thus the "assessment" of a child's ability to read or to do math in the current testing already in use has more to do with probing the child's psyche and teaching him or her to conform to group values than with testing ability to add two plus two. The leading educational experts will read the bill's language as a license to invade the privacy of every child in the country rather than hold failing schools accountable. And since the bill necessarily honors the principle of local control, it is likely the local educational bureaucracies doing the controlling will welcome the bill as a $400 million slush fund to do exactly what they have been doing to thwart educational reform.

The trouble with school tests begins with the increasing inclusion of sophisticated "behavioral" components that encompass a wide variety of lifestyle and opinion data, nailing down student proclivities, social attitudes and parent-inculcated worldviews. Combined with the plethora of "health" (sex and drug) surveys, mental-health screenings, diary/journal-keeping and other miscellaneous questionnaires — mostly taking place in the classroom under cover of academics — testing has become more equated with personality inventories than proficiency exams. In that context, what passes for testing even may undermine the accountability President Bush advocates.

The case against standardized tests hinges on the quantum leap in data-gathering, cross-matching and information-sharing capabilities, with all the accompanying problems associated with data-trafficking, invasion of privacy and consumer profiling. Barely a week goes by that a publication somewhere doesn't carry a story detailing a new affront to what used to be considered "nobody's business."

One of the earliest examples of psychological data-gathering under the cover of academics occurred in the pivotal 1980s, when enormous breakthroughs in computer technology were being piloted with federal funds in selected localities. One of those was in Allegheny County, Pa., initiated under the eight-state Cooperative Accountability Project. A handful of parents — among them, Gen Yvette Sutton, Anita Hoge and Francine D'Alonzo — got wind of a standardized academic test "no one could possibly study for" being disseminated in the McGuffey School District: the Educational Quality Assessment (EQA). After several unsuccessful attempts to gain access, a trip to the state education agency in Harrisburg finally yielded the facts. Not only did more than one-half the questions not relate to factual knowledge, but numerical codes next to the questions as printed on the administrative version of the test turned out to correlate with specific "remediating" curricula. It included questions such as:

"I get upset easily at home: [a] very true of me; [b] mostly true of me; [c] mostly untrue of me; [d] very untrue of me.

"You are asked to dinner at the home of a classmate having a religion much different from yours. In this situation I would feel: [a] very comfortable; [b] comfortable; [c] slightly uncomfortable; [d] very uncomfortable.

"There is a secret club at school called the Midnight Artists. They go out late at night and paint funny sayings and pictures on buildings. I would JOIN THE CLUB when I knew ... [a] my best friend had asked me to join; [b] most of the popular students in school were in the club; [c] my parents would ground me if they found out I joined."

This last question, in particular, got parents' attention. It presumes that the child will join the club under some circumstances, including the desire to provoke parents. They thought the question more or less asked: "How can we get this kid to vandalize property?"

The EQA had 375 questions covering attitudes, worldviews and opinions — mostly hypothetical situations and self-reports. There were 30 questions on math and another 30 covering verbal analogies — just enough academic questions to appear credible.

Every such test is distributed with professional literature for the educators — which is strictly off-limits to the parents. The EQA told educators it was testing for: the student's "locus of control," his "willingness to receive stimuli," his "amenability to change" and whether he would "conform to group goals." In lay terms, these translate to: Where's the child coming from? Is he easily influenced? Are his views firm or flexible? Is he a team player who will accede to group consensus? Choice "b," then, was the preferred response to the Midnight Artists question because it reflects a willingness to "conform to group goals."

Today, such testing is more sophisticated. A fascinating aspect of a recent Michigan Assessment, for example, was that regardless of the section — reading, science, geography — the questions all sounded like social studies. For example, there was nothing about topography in the geography section; it covered "global issues" — overpopulation, colonial victimization and redistribution of resources to Third World countries. The writing-sample topic? "Coping With Change."

Five science questions for fifth-graders concerned universal child fingerprinting, but involved no science. The multiple choices, even the "incorrect" ones, seemed more like endorsements than questions: "fingerprinting doesn't hurt," "lost children can be identified," etc. Not a single "down side" was offered. The one question that sounded like a question was so simple that one could reasonably have asked whether this was the reading or the science section: "Fingerprinting is MOST useful in which of the following jobs: [a] police work, to help in crime fighting; [b] window washing, to help clean windows; [c] auto mechanics, to help cars run better; [d] teaching, to help kids learn to multiply."

Task I from the history section — on women in combat — was "Interpreting Information." Prefaced in small print was, "Directions: Read the following hypothetical information about a public policy issue. Use it with what you already know to complete the tasks that follow."

Parent activists Deborah DeBacker of Troy, Mich., and Joan Grindel of Bloomfield, Mich., say it's doubtful fifth-graders either understood or acted upon the term "hypothetical." In any case, the only interpretation one could draw from the data provided is that women should be in combat. Despite assurances in the essay instructions that the student's views per se don't matter, it's clear that any view not supported by those "hypothetical facts" in the data section will be judged insufficient to warrant a top grade. In the example, testers actually begin the paragraph for the pupil: "I think that women members of the military should definitely be allowed to participate ...."

Questionnaires, curricula and activities that target the belief system are called "affective devices." Psychology texts describe the belief system as made up of attitudes, values and worldviews existing below the level of conscious awareness. Affective means "noncognitive," "dealing with emotions and feelings" rather than the intellect. Using affective-questioning techniques makes it easier to test the subject's belief system. Some go so far as to test for "psychological threshold." The teacher's guide to Pennsylvania's 1986 citizenship curriculum defined this threshold as "the severity of stimulus tolerated before a change of behavior occurs." The manual explained that "it is possible to assess not only the students' predisposition [toward certain reactions] … but also to provide some measure of the intensity of that predisposition across a wide spectrum of situations."

Some profiling instruments are explicit and blatant, such as Pennsylvania's and Michigan's, while others are more subtle. Most states label them "assessments" rather than "tests," further confusing the issue for parents. Regardless of the label, opponents claim that personality testing in the context of an academic setting, and the psychotherapeutic sales packages (curricula) that typically ensue, portend a high-tech threat not only to privacy but to a child's future employability and freedom of conscience.

Then there are the student-identification methods applied to "confidential" tests and surveys the testers say are not "individually identifiable." This doesn't mean, however, that students are not "individually identified." Confused? The National Center for Education Statistics 1993 Field Restricted Use Data Procedures Manual explains this semantic sleight of hand. Techniques range from simple bar-coding and "slugging" to more-complicated exercises such as "sticky-labeling" and inserting "embedded identifiers."

To the testers, however, the term "confidential" means "need to know." The "confidential" label casually applied by officials to modern testing and survey devices invariably is taken for anonymity, thereby masking the fact that: (l) higher scores are accorded "preferred" viewpoints, (2) curriculum is modified and targeted to specific groups of children to correct "inappropriate" attitudes and, more ominously, (3) certain views that once were considered "principled" now are deemed "rigid" and associated with mental illness or psychological defects.

Among the at-risk "indicators" are viewpoints and behaviors deemed by the testers to be what they call "indicative of a rigid or underdeveloped belief system." Pupils are referred to psychologists for "remediation" to render their attitudes and responses more "realistic." Several professional papers, beginning with the acclaimed 1969 Behavioral Science Teacher Education Project (BSTEP), place "firm religious belief" in the "rigid/inflexible" category. BSTEP also projected a world "so saturated with ideas and information [by the 1990s that] few will be able to maintain control over their opinions."

So far from confidential is all this testing and evaluation that today's burgeoning computer cross-matching capability of public and private records has launched an information industry of data traffickers and information brokers. Some are licit and others black-market, but they cater to the needs of employers, credit bureaus, universities, corporate spies and government agencies.

Of course, evidence of serious peril to our American presumption of "personal affairs" was being debated among high-ranking educators as far back as 1969, when Wolcott Beatty wrote his seminal work, "Improving Educational Assessment and an Inventory of Measures of Affective Behavior." Dozens of related publications followed, documenting a slippery slope from conceptual design of a test that would evaluate and compare effectiveness of learning programs to a federal-funding carrot that would ensure massive personal-data collection with automatic-transfer capability to federal and international databases.

In 1970, L.J. Chronbach's *Essentials of Scientific Testing* sounded the first alarm: "Coding of records is not a full safeguard. Identity can be detected by matching facts from the coded questionnaire with other facts that are openly recorded."

By that time Dustin Heuston of the renowned World Institute of Computer-Assisted Technology (WICAT) in Utah uttered his prophetic assertion: "We've been staggered by realizing that the computer has the capability to act as if it were 10 of the top psychologists working with one student. ... Won't it be wonderful when no one can get between that child and that curriculum?" Behavioral-science gurus Richard Wolf (Teachers College, Columbia University) and his colleague, Ralph Tyler, openly were advocating a need for surreptitious methods of data collection and student identification as early as 1974 in their coedited book, *Crucial Issues in Testing*. They called for unified coding and standardized definitions to enhance cross-matching and data-sharing — from elementary schools on into the workplace.

Wolf supported "the permissibility of deception" in school-testing based on "the rights of an institution to obtain information necessary to achieve its goals." He stated that, danger or not, there "are occasions in which the test constructor [finds it necessary] to outwit the subject so that he cannot guess what information he is revealing. From the constructor's point of view this is necessary since he wishes to ascertain information that the individual might not ... furnish if it were sought directly. A number of personality tests fall into this category."

Despite admonitions, the lure of computerized cross-matching proved too enticing. In 1981, the first education databanks were launched: the Common Core of Data, the Universe Files and the Longitudinal Studies. In what is perhaps the most evidential document on the subject, "Measuring the Quality of Education" by Willard Wirtz and Archie LaPointe, the writers outline the U.S. Education Department's (ED's) intention to ignore the legal and ethical warnings against privacy invasion:

"Getting into the students' personal characteristics and situations invariably prompts warnings that the NAEP [National Assessment of Educational Progress] purpose is not to analyze human development, and injunctions against confusing the measurement of educational results (outcomes) and the analysis of cause (inputs). But it is being recognized increasingly that the measurement of achievement is incomplete without the accompanying identification of whatever educational circumstances may affect these results."

More prophetically, Wirtz and LaPointe wrote: "A different kind of assessment would help correct the tilt in the educational-standards concept toward functional literacy and away from excellence."

Direct education away from excellence? That's right. The authors detailed how a clearinghouse-style database incorporating demographic and psychological-profiling data would help steer schools toward what these "experts" deemed a more realistic ideal: mere functional literacy.

Policymakers at the ED quickly moved to shelve concerns about student and family privacy. For example, James P. Shaver wrote a detailed monograph, "National Assessment of

Values and Attitudes for Social Studies," published through the Office of Educational Research and Instruction (OERI), a division of the U.S. Department of Education. But by then there was no need to hide intent because OERI already had brought in four computer experts from Utah's WICAT to prepare a working paper for the first consolidated education database.

In 1986, "A Plan for the Redesign of the Elementary and Secondary Data Collection Program" was finalized, incorporating attitudinal, lifestyle and value information. It fell to the federally funded Council of Chief State School Officers (CCSSO) to ensure state/federal compatibility of computer systems and promote collection of data at the local level. In a 1985 speech, CCSSO Director Ramsey Seldon placed "coordination of educational assessment and evaluation" on the highest priority, promoting the exchange of information about private citizens and their children in the name of comparing educational achievement.

Today, the three original education databases are part of a mammoth data-tracking/sharing system called the SPEEDE/ExPRESS. Among other capabilities, data can be transmitted to universities and prospective employers via WORKLINK, a system set up by the Educational Testing Service.

In 1988, the National Center for Education Statistics named 29 organizations, some with no clear ties to education, that were given automatic access to national assessment data — among them the Census Bureau, the office of the Montana State Attorney General, the Rand Corp. and the Economic Policy Institute. Then technology took another quantum leap — more storage capability in less space, ultrasophisticated search engines, intricate cross-matching methods.

And critics of all this are saying that puts President Bush's national-testing initiative in a different light. And it cuts left and right. After all, if one faction can target a child's belief system and keep records, so can another.

The basic dilemmas remain: If the use of psychographic instruments is legal and ethical, without informed, written, parental consent; if behavior-modification curricula can be brought into the classroom as legitimate learning material; if teachers, or even bona fide mental-health workers, can use the schools to "treat" youngsters for real or imagined psychological problems — then are schools really educational institutions or day-care clinics?

PSYCHOANALYZING THE PUBLIC

It had to happen. A taxpayer-funded study by the National Institute of Mental Health and the National Science Foundation (NIMH-NSF) announced in August 2003 that adherents to conventional moral principles and limited government are mentally disturbed.

NIMH-NSF scholars from the Universities of Maryland, California at Berkeley, and Stanford attribute notions about morality and individualism to "dogmatism" and "uncertainty avoidance." Social conservatives, in particular, were said to suffer from "mental rigidity," a condition that, researchers assert, is probably hard-wired, condemning traditionalists to a lifelong, cognitive hell, with all the associated indicators for mental illness: "decreased cognitive function, lowered self-esteem, fear, anger, pessimism, disgust, and contempt."

Most journalists and political watchdog groups chuckled over the NIMH-NSF's study, "Political Conservatism as Motivated Social Cognition" – especially conservatives themselves. Rep. Tom Feeney (R-Fla.) was a bit more testy, though, when he called it "left-wing rhetoric ... dressed up as a scientific study" and said taxpayers shouldn't be paying for such nonsense. But allegations of mental illness have become the trump card in the cultural usurpers' arsenal of strategies to ostracize traditionalists. Professional change agents then do their best to mold public opinion to fit their own employers' totalitarian designs, thereby reducing the number of supposedly mentally challenged traditionalists. And molding opinion requires learning what the public already thinks and how best to beguile people into accepting a new morality.

Data Mining

For years, market research firms have aggressively collected value and lifestyle (VALS) data on children and adults from any source capable of generating quick feedback – popular magazines; Internet, telephone, and household surveys; news polls; school health questionnaires; behavioral screening instruments; census forms; market and consumer research; and even academic tests. Some are polling instruments, pure and simple; others incorporate VALS data to a lesser extent. Either way, the common goal is to find out what makes certain groups and individuals tick – and then to see if they can be made to tick differently.

The Terrorism (formerly "Total") Information Awareness (TIA) program, designed by the Pentagon's Defense Advanced Research Projects Agency (DARPA) to track down terrorists, homegrown and foreign, is taking advantage of the latest technology. Spokesmen at the Department of Defense now admit they are amassing behavioral dossiers on American citizens. DARPA is combing multiple databases, cross-matching computerized sources of information such as magazine subscriptions; political, religious and other charitable giving; medical records from insurance and physicians' databases; and even clothing sizes. Meanwhile, the federally funded, $12 million Matrix database project has been quietly amassing information in the offices of a private company (Seisint Inc.) in Boca Raton, Florida, paralleling the contentious TIA project. And DARPA's planned "Lifelog program" will track and "trace the 'threads' of an individual's life."

No single response on a survey or questionnaire is likely to make or break anyone. It is the totality of the responses – the identifiable trends – that produces a behavioral profile. Cross-matching responses with other computerized records about a group or individual is what is meant by the term "data mining." A dossier is an individual case file built around the "mined" information.

Long-term tracking and monitoring usually are based on individualized variables among the mined data points, such as what political party you affiliate with or which magazines you subscribe to. The U.S. government obtains such information with the help of database companies like ChoicePoint Inc., which resell personal data to the U.S. government. At press time for this article, federal and state governments had paid some $50 million a year to examine ChoicePoint's many databases.

This tracking, coupled to survey and other computerized records, is what enables probability experts to predict via a mathematical model what you will do in politically charged situations five years or so down the road. In a computerized world where most major systems are compatible for information sharing, if somebody wants a name matched with a response, all they have to do is grease the palm of a person who can access the coded identifiers on the questionnaire or survey. Thus the brave new world of data-trafficking and information brokers – businesses that buy, sell, and occasionally doctor information.

All that was ever needed to turn databank information into a political weapon was some national crisis or emergency. That crisis came on September 11, 2001. Virtually no legislation since that time has emerged to put serious brakes on the tremendous upswing in data-trafficking over the past two decades. Indeed, since 9-11 our leaders have craved even more!

Predicting Behavior

The technique of fusing social, economic, demographic and psychological information is termed psychographic surveying. The method became a staple of marketing firms and advertisers in the mid-1980s, once cross-matching computerized data became practicable. Webster's *New World Communication and Media Dictionary* defines the method as "the study of social class based upon the demographics ... income, race, color, religion, and personality traits." These characteristics, says the dictionary, "can be measured to predict behavior."

Today, experts have become so adept at phrasing their questions that the "target subjects," as we ordinary people are called, generally are unaware just how much they are divulging. The result is a behavioral baseline – retained in databases for posterity.

All that remains is the spin some entity wishes to inflict on the data collected. That's what behavioral researchers did with their NIMH-NSF study. Although the researchers' conclusions may be outrageous, their data doubtless contain kernels of truth. Spin is all about interpretation, how various data points are juxtaposed to reflect whatever substantiates the position of those funding the study.

If you are the National Education Association, for example, and you want to get AIDS education mandated for grade-schoolers, you must create the illusion that most parents actually want their pre-adolescents involved in such a class.

Your first step is market research, just as if you were determining receptivity for a new line of soft drinks, or for a day-care center in a particular section of town. Putting the question to people directly is often less productive than surreptitiously gathering data about your target audience. The down-side is that the latter takes more time and requires high-paid analysts (usually behavioral scientists – psychologists and sociologists – with specialties in statistics and computer science).

Any marketing campaign, of course, is only as good as the data and analysis behind it. Therefore, accurate, hard data and unflawed analysis must exist somewhere no matter how distorted the publicized conclusions or how misleading the spin advertisers put on them. That is why survey questions typically are phrased several different ways, and with no obvious right or wrong answers – to nail down the true views of the respondent. Pinpointing attitudes, including temperament and disposition, are key to predicting – and controlling – the future.

Marginalizing the Opposition

There aren't many stigmas anymore. Or so we are told. But nothing gets a person quarantined from mainstream thought faster than a suggestion that he or she is mentally ill. Thus the term "homophobic." It's a virtual conversation stopper. Ditto for "intolerant," "inhibited," "rigid" and "dogmatic." No one knows better than leftist strategists that anyone linked with a code out of the premier psychiatrists' bible, the *Diagnostic and Statistical Manual*, is guilty by association. Thus, individuals who opposed the Episcopal Church's consecration of homosexual Gene Robinson as a bishop in New Hampshire never had a prayer of swaying the radical church leadership. The opposition was simply designated "homophobic."

Which brings us back to the scientific finding by NIMH-NSF researchers – that conservatives carry markers for mental illness. This wide-brush smear is a sure-fire way to defuse any controversial issue – abortion rights, racial preferences, banning the Ten Commandments, etc.

Once a suggestion of mental illness is planted, activists can move on to the final exam phase of the operation: determining the extent to which they have impacted public perceptions.

Using the homosexual issue again as our example, consider the Bravo Channel's TV hit "Queer Eye for the Straight Guy." Some excellent psychographic surveying went into selling a TV show featuring homosexuals in such a way that it would be accepted by a mass audience, including those who may not like homosexuals. This strategy has been used before in the 1970s and '80s. Archie Bunker of "All in the Family" renown tested perceptions about bigotry among a population still largely resistant to busing and feminist goals. Maude's abortion assessed the circumstances under which the general public might accept taking the life of an unborn child. So, high ratings for Bravo Channel's "Queer Eye," or good sales for a "Gay Billy" doll, a take-off on the familiar "Barbie" and "Ken," will earn "A"s for homosexual activists. Mediocre ratings and sales would mean that either the early data gathering or its analysis was flawed.

Schools and Mental Health Fraud

Comparing the proverbial school test and dolls to scandalous television fare may seem something of a stretch. But, in fact, advertising executives took their cue from behaviorist educators like the late Ralph Tyler.

Tyler was the former commissioner of education under the old Department of Health, Education and Welfare. More significantly, he was past president of the Carnegie Foundation for the Advancement of Teaching, and its multi-million-dollar spin-off, the Educational Testing Service, the source for most of this nation's school tests.

It was Tyler who pioneered the psychological test questions that have become staples of educational testing. He created almost single-handedly the National Assessment of Educational Progress (NAEP), America's nationwide test, as well as some eight state assessments, under separate contract. The NAEP, in which random samples of 4th, 8th and 12th graders are tested, has since served as the model for nearly all state assessments, for which pupils are tested on alternate years, such as 5th, 9th and 11th grades.

Tyler and his colleague Richard Wolf (Teachers College, Columbia University), were openly advocating surreptitious methods of data collection and student identification as early as 1969. In their co-edited work *Crucial Issues in Testing*, they responded to this 1967 passage from Bernard Berelson in the Journal for Educational Measurement:

"... there are recent indications that the involvement of public funds evokes a special public concern for privacy ... greatly heightened by the advent of computer technology.... The danger lies in the gradual erosion of the individual's right to decide to whom he wishes to disclose personal information."

However, Wolf did admit that:

"... if the results of a testing situation in which deception was employed are used in making a decision which the individual considers adverse, such as denial of admission to a particular program or institution, there are serious legal and ethical questions. Entrapment is an explicitly illegal procedure in the United States. To what extent the use of deception in testing can be considered a form of entrapment has yet to be determined."

One attorney after another subsequently took a negative legal view of personality/opinion testing in schools, especially under the cover of academics. But the entrapment problem was never tested in a court of law, and Tyler and Wolf's determination prevailed. The federally funded Council of Chief State School Officers was saddled with ensuring that all local, state and regional education databases were compatible with federal ones – in preparation for the enormous national database known as the SPEEDE/ExPRESS (Standardization of Postsecondary Education Electronic Data Exchange/Exchange of Permanent Records Electronically for Students and Schools), which stemmed from two earlier attempts. Information from these systems can be automatically transmitted to university admissions officers and potential employers.

Most of the time, political "fishing expeditions" are at least subtle. Occasionally, a blatant one will surface. For example, one question on the civics section of the NAEP wants to know the "percentage of 9th-grade U.S. students who think economy-related actions 'probably' or 'should definitely be' the government's responsibility."

B. K. Eakman

Freedom at Risk

In the process of improving computer compatibility and questioning techniques, a bonfire of insanities is being lit under our freedom of conscience, using mental health as the ostensible handle. Today, we know what will happen to anyone caught uttering a comment even remotely perceived as critical of hot-button issues like affirmative action, welfare, illegitimacy or immigration (think of Trent Lott and baseball star John Rocker). What need is there for logical debate or a reasoned exchange of ideas, after all, with the mentally unbalanced?

Of course, the same strategies could be applied in reverse; the leftists' opposite number just hasn't quite caught onto the game yet.

That's where the Law of Unintended Consequences kicks in for Americans already on the wrong side of a behavioral dossier. With the passage of data-collection initiatives that are international in scope, like the National Education Sciences Reform Act of 2002, the federal government may join with any other agency or bureau, including international entities, to compare your personal information. International organizations, of course, are not subject to U.S. laws. As with the United Nations' International Criminal Court (ICC), over-zealous and pretentious coalitions in far-flung countries can use data-collection as a cover to interfere with and impede the legitimate actions and beliefs of private American citizens.

By cross-matching VALS data with medical, credit card, title, motor vehicle, court and thousands of other computerized records, and then applying a mathematical model to the results, the National Education Sciences Reform Act categorically admits that almost any factual information about a person can he linked to the individual's "emotional, attitudinal, or behavioral condition."

That is psychological profiling – with a foot in the door for world-government advocates.

For now, the critical question is only whether somebody wants your name. But should you run for school board, become an activist, or seek a job involving leadership and influence, then the "whether" becomes "when." Even the best and brightest already are finding they've been screened out of their university of choice, or diverted from a career path, based on personal and political beliefs. Increasingly, a young person's fate is sealed by forces far more threatening than a grade-point average. A cottage industry of mental health *apparatchiks*, under the cover of sniffing out violent kids, learning problems, dysfunctional families and terrorists, is making judgments that go beyond knowledge–assessment and into the realm of world views and values.

Today, political correctness is running so completely amok that one's views are punished almost before a person has a chance to give them voice. Just look around. Already, if a child is difficult to teach; if he's a nuisance to somebody important; if he's a class clown or quirky; if he makes politically indiscreet remarks – his parents are intimidated into seeking counseling and psychiatric drugs (for the child's own good and that of society, of course). Mind-controlling drugs are well-known to break down resistance and augment suggestibility.

With judges forcing accused criminals to undergo forced psychiatric evaluations and to take medications prior to trial, the handwriting is on the wall for the rest of us. At the very least, one's reputation and position will be irrevocably tarnished by a mental illness accusation.

Can forced placement in a psychiatric facility be far behind? Most will insist that it can't happen here. But who, even 20 years ago, would have imagined courts forcibly removing the Ten Commandments from public places, including schools, or public school students being forced to read homosexual literature?

The National Institute of Mental Health/National Science Foundation finding that traditionalists are mentally disturbed is not an aberration; it is instead symptomatic of how – under the false flags of political correctness, tolerance, etc. – once-mainstream thoughts are now being dismissed as abnormal, hateful and dangerous.

B. K. Eakman

POLITICAL CORRECTNESS & DECEPTION

B. K. Eakman

CRIME, CHAOS AND CONTROL:
THE LEGACIES OF LIBERALISM

The list of child kidnappings and sexual assaults grows, endlessly it seems. Eight-year-old Shasta Groene of Coeur D'Alene, Idaho, was finally found. Her brother is dead following six weeks during which the two children were continually raped and tortured. Their mother, a friend and other family members were bludgeoned to death. While the perpetrator, Joseph E. Duncan III, had an ongoing history as a violent sexual predator of children dating to the 1970s, he was inexplicably set free. Little Shasta, no matter how wonderful her future care, will "serve" a life sentence.

Such is the scenario in countless cases — violent culprits released or pronounced "cured" by psychiatrists, only to repeat their crimes. Expecting a child rapist to register as a sex offender is about as realistic as a field agent asking an illegal alien to show up for a court hearing in ten days. It ain't gonna happen.

But the patent illogic of liberal theology still reigns, in the face of common sense. In the liberal worldview, sexual freedom has transformed rape from the equivalent of torture to an unremarkable crime on the order of petty theft (read, "nonconsensual sex"); all criminals can be rehabilitated (i.e., "cured" with therapy); and the first duty of government is to "understand" the root causes of delinquent behavior, up to and including terrorism.

Such a mind-set exemplifies what is wrong with instilling in schoolchildren a liberal world view without benefit of the alternatives. It illustrates what is unethical about testing students on the degree to which they have "internalized" (read: "mastered") liberal world views and rejected Judeo-Christian values.

Initially sold as "value-neutral" education, ostensibly to avoid having teachers injecting their own political and moral attitudes into a curriculum, the transmission of "humanistic" ethics was anything but neutral – or humane, for that matter. "Humanistic education" was the euphemism given to the old "progressivism" of the 1930's and 40's.

The term "humanism" eventually was absorbed into the American lexicon in the late 1960's and early 70's. But humanistic education was liberal dogma straight out of Karl Marx's writings and psychology textbooks. It was agnostic at best, atheistic at worst.

Conflict resolution, nuclear-free (or drug-free) zones, peace studies, self-esteem classes, collaborative learning, sex-drenched "health" curricula, school psychologists as replacements for now-forgotten academic counselors, mass mental health screening: all these and more have been part and parcel of an aggressive timetable aimed at assuring that America's youngsters grow up to be socialistic, left-leaning adults.

Closet Communists got part of what they wanted. While an ego-centered "me-first" mentality reigned on the economic front – managing somehow to perpetuate most aspects of a free economy – this, too, is shifting as private property rights are slowly eradicated, both by Supreme Court edict and by individual, massive credit card debt, which transfers ownership to lending organizations and to the government that insures them. Future generations will find themselves progressively less able to afford property, send their kids to private schools, or to purchase things our grandparents took for granted. Those who do have money – particularly sports celebrities and entertainers – will tend not to care so much about schools or savings accounts. They will be more inclined to spend, and lose, their money as fast as they earn it.

The singer-superstar-sexpot, the one who insults Christians by using the moniker "Madonna," recently gave her 10-year-old daughter a credit card with a purchasing cap that would stun most people. The purpose, supposedly, was "to teach [the child] about the value of money." Yet, there she was, simultaneously plugging the liberal line at the Live Aid concert, reminding those considerably less monetarily endowed than she or her daughter that they should spend their money on African poverty despite the massive, albeit unproductive, aide American taxpayers have already dumped into that continent.

Thus has liberalism bequeathed to a new generation crime on a scale inconceivable to parents of the 1950's; cultural chaos on a level unthinkable when the now-grown officials who attend summits like G-8 were children; and arbitrary controls that restrict all citizens' basic rights.

Whereas we should have been focusing on sensible, constitutional limits to free speech in areas like pornography and violent rap lyrics, we now find ourselves subject to censorship of religious references instead. Whereas parents once worried about their children shoving in cafeteria lines, chewing gum, and running in the school halls, now modern mothers and fathers have to deal with drug addiction, bulimia and sexually transmitted diseases. Whereas Americans once trusted that government, for all its faults, would put protection of its citizens first, today's neighborhoods find career criminals running amok on their streets, terrorists threatening to blow up restaurants and subways, and the borders wide open, all the while, to those intent on taking unprecedented advantage of American largesse, overwhelming emergency rooms, schools, and social safety nets intended to benefit taxpaying citizens alone.

The result is draconian controls on a law-abiding populace, which they increasingly accept in the name of keeping order. It will get worse, as the nation's young people become accustomed to being tracked and monitored, assessed and regimented, with scant memory as to the historical roots of the Republic we once knew. Instead they are inundated with the root "causes" of crime, which of course always boils down to more money to fund the liberal agenda.

Will the American electorate ever say "Enough!"? Maybe. Will it reject liberalism and its close cousin, socialism? Doubtful. This will put Americans on a collision course.

The liberal dogma is entrenched and has found respectability. Today's 10-year-olds have no institutional memory of anything but an entitlement society combined with increasing doses of surveillance. Unless something completely unexpected happens, the American response to an inevitable increase in crime and chaos will be to launch ever more radical control measures.

B. K. Eakman

THE ACCIDENTAL SATIRE

At first I thought it was a spoof, spurred perhaps by the acerbic jibes of talk-show hosts like Rush Limbaugh or conservative firebrand Ann Coulter. But on closer examination, Nissan's "Pathfinder" automotive commercial—tag line: "Suppose you could only make left turns..."—appeared oblivious to the fact that their slogan was the stuff of political slapstick. I mean, if they had given this opener to a comedy troupe like "The Capitol Steps," the cast would have had a field day.

The past 40 years have produced little else but left turns—be the topic entitlement programs, criminal justice, foreign policy, marriage, religion, lobbying scandals or last November's "midterm" election.

Just for fun, I started constructing a mental list of left turns, dating from 1966—the height of my "Baby Boomer" college experience. I came up with the following: a rock ensemble, using a dopey moniker, "the Beatles," was sporting hairdos reminiscent of the Three Stooges and changing the face of popular music. Marxist provocateurs started moving onto American campuses, instigating riots and sit-ins among students who understood practically nothing about the issues they were demonstrating against. Left-leaning professors, like many of their journalistic counterparts—too sanctimonious and spineless to fight for freedom themselves—passed up no opportunity to censure and ridicule those who served their country. God was declared "dead," and Judeo-Christian became a pseudonym for "bourgeoisie" values, which were suddenly in the cross-hairs. Free love, feminism, recreational drugs, and enviro-extremism were "blowin' in the wind"; they wouldn't really come into their own for another 20 years.

For all that, our lives were relatively innocent in 1966. By 1986, we woke up to discover we "could only make left turns."

As the first wave of us hits age 60 this year (yikes!), perhaps it is appropriate to reflect upon our legacy:

• Most people no longer recognize the difference between a republic and a democracy; the terms are used interchangeably.

• Untarnished citizens are routinely harassed, searched and divested of their personal property without probable cause. Schoolchildren (as well as visitors to events and museums) are patted down and inspected. Only a few "fringe groups" bother to bring up the phrase "unreasonable search and seizure."

• Crime is out of control. Thanks to a judicial system dominated by the likes of the American Civil Liberties Union, not to mention legal one-upmanship and psychobabble, dangerous criminals rarely serve out their sentences and are freed on frivolous technicalities. Trials for violent offenders, even those caught in the act, take years and cost taxpayers a fortune. The middle class spends thousands of dollars on high-tech locks and duplicitous gadgets aimed at thwarting every kind of criminal from robbers to rapists, pornographers and spammers.

• Local police, once called "pigs" by Boomers, are now reduced to trolling for seat-belt violators. Armed with radar "guns," they labor to catch violent criminals—one speeder at a time. When they do manage to foil a criminal act, the media—drunk since the Watergate era on its own importance—quickly divulges the tactics used to thwart it.

• In a Supreme Court decision reminiscent of Marxist dictatorships (Kilo v. New London), the U.S. government now dictates ("assesses") what private property is worth, rather than leaving it to the consumer market. A citizen may be evicted from his/her home should a property be deemed of greater taxable value to the State via more "accommodating" parties.

• Although the Berlin Wall fell and communism was consigned "to the ash bin of history," the year 2007 finds the U.S. surrounded by hostile Marxist regimes in Argentina, Bolivia, Brazil, Chile, Cuba, and Venezuela. We go it virtually alone against global terrorists and anarchists with whom it is impossible to negotiate. North Korea and Iran give new meaning to the old "nuclear nightmare." An appeasement-focused, left-leaning Europe learned nothing from their near-destruction by the Nazis; its leaders ridiculously accuse the U.S., not knife-wielding sadists who videotape beheadings, of being a threat to world peace. Even as the U.S. rushes about rescuing hapless populations from every conceivable global catastrophe, natural or otherwise, stalwarts of journalism like the Financial Times blames America for compromising global stability.

• Having forgotten the expression "barbarians at the gate," our nation was easily attacked by not-so-well-armed foreign hostiles with an 8th-century mentality on September 11, 2001, killing and wounding more people than died at Pearl Harbor in 1941. Our government's response? Virtual amnesty to existing illegal immigrants, prosecution of our own border patrol agents merely doing their job, and a welcome mat encouraging trucks to come across the Mexican border.

• Some 14 million illegals help themselves to American entitlements. Immigrants no longer are required to have a skill, a sponsor, a job, or even to learn English. Such immigrants, of course, are fodder for votes—the less educated the better.

• As the hassle factor is turned up on good citizens, the once-dreaded ID card, featuring biometric data and microchips, is gaining acceptance. The same Baby Boomers who protested rules, supervision and oversight, are purchasing implants with tracking features for their grandchildren and elderly parents. Devices come with names like "the Babysitter" and "the Bodyguard."

• Environmental leftists like Greenpeace, rooted in the Marxist-inspired "peace" movement, have been allowed to control the debate over energy and natural resources. Unbalanced publicity-seekers like Jane Fonda and third-rate science students like Al Gore control the scientific debate. Although as early as the 1970s, scientific drawing boards were awash in forward-looking concepts that actually allowed for increases in consumer energy demand even as they ensured the nation's autonomy—e.g., space-based solar arrays that beam energy via microwave to massive Earth-based grids headquartered in non-habitable localities—in 2007, political correctness foils any serious attempt at long-term solutions. For the foreseeable future, the U.S. is stuck with ineffectual, high-dollar vehicular concepts and low-tech management of resources—recycling, crop-based fuels, "conservation" and rolling brown-outs.

• Despite valiant efforts to curtail the welfare state after the Johnson era fiasco of the 1970s, today it grows more entrenched with each election cycle. Whereas wealth-redistribution schemes were viewed in 1966 with alarm, modern legislators and the media compete to outdo each other, using slogans like "compassionate conservatism" and "free-market socialism" to appeal to their clueless audiences.

• Black illegitimacy has reached 70 percent from its civil-rights-era 30-percent mark, despite massive entitlement and sex education programs and all manner of "incentives." In 2007, the euphemism "single parent" de-stigmatizes unwed motherhood, equating it with widowhood, even as hordes of fatherless youths decimate our cities.

• Abortion-on-demand, in-vitro fertilization and cloning are either acceptable or in the offing, cheapening life even as the last Holocaust survivors futilely chant: "Never again!"

• Boomer adults remain fixated on their youth, spending exorbitant sums on cosmetics, liposuction, fad diets, fitness clubs, and sexual-enhancement products. Whereas Boomers once bellowed "make love, not war," their children and grandchildren are content to just "have sex."

• Babies are viewed as trophies—or worse, as nuisances. Most youth today possess neither the guidance nor the resources to negotiate a path to maturity. Many parents have no idea what goes on in their children's lives or even in their rooms, such as whether lethal weapons might be stored there.

• Adolescence is prolonged indefinitely; 30- and 40-year-old "boomerang kids" wend their way back to Mom and Dad, unable (or unwilling) to come to terms with the responsibilities of adulthood.

• Pornography and smut are legally protected while God is marginalized in public places, including schools. The church—indeed the entire religious establishment—is now so infiltrated with leftist leaders that scriptural wording and doctrine are either watered down or excised. Judeo-Christian ethics face non-stop legal scrutiny and scandals.

• Surges in crime, sexual predators and violence have spawned calls for universal mental health screening. Such bills as the one passed by the U.S. House of Representatives on June 13, 2006, drive states to produce copycat legislation, affecting thousands of schoolchildren, prospective parents, and even infants. Prescriptions for dangerous psychotropic drugs are pervasive—prescribed for everything from attention "deficits" to shyness.

• "Mental "illness" has become fodder for political opportunism. Crimes of opinion are on the rise. Psychotropic drugs are morphing into mandated antidotes for politically incorrect viewpoints. (George Orwell must be turning over in his grave.)

• Youth role models are primarily entertainers and sports figures of disreputable character—glorified strippers, rapists and drug-abusers. Celebrity criminals are only rarely punished. Gifted, upstanding individuals of genuine ability find it increasingly difficult to obtain an agent or an audition in 2007.

• Public schools (and some private ones) are predominantly day-care facilities. Gangs and police eye each other in the hallways, daring each other to hurl the first taunt. Spelling, grammar, geography, mathematics and penmanship are deemed inconsequential as computers become more sophisticated. Harvard is revamping its curriculum because too much time purportedly is spent on academics. Political indoctrination masquerades as scholarship. What used to be called "common knowledge" and "cultural assimilation" are anachronisms.

• American youth so love the modern school's casual "learning" environment that drop-out rates have skyrocketed to about 30 percent generally, 40 percent for Blacks and 50 percent for Hispanics.

• Whereas in the 1970s, a TV concoction called The Gong Show was summarily rejected by the public as dehumanizing, in 2007 the top-rated show is American Idol—an updated, more tasteless replica of The Gong Show—which alternately derides, demoralizes, and devastates young contestants. Schools, meanwhile, spend countless hours on anti-bullying curricula, anger-management and conflict resolution. Go figure...

Thus do the Baby Boomer's grandchildren negotiate their way in a bizarre era of contradictions and lost principles—a kind of Twilight Zone in which only "left turns" are allowed.

RONALD REAGAN,
INDIVIDUALISM AND LEADERSHIP

With the death of former President Ronald Reagan and another election season upon us, it is appropriate to recall a favorite election-year campaign theme of commentators and journalists: the lack of leadership among the various political contenders. As far back as 1960, one can find a flood of articles, speeches and books bemoaning America's loss of leadership, the rising tide of moral decay, and a general lack of vision, or mission.

Yet, however hard they tried, the chattering classes never could make that charge stick when it came to Ronald Reagan. His would-be critics knew they were trumped when he gave his first televised address to the nation—on behalf of presidential nominee Barry Goldwater in 1964. In what has come to be known as the "rendezvous with destiny speech" (or simply "The Speech"), he challenged his audience with such blunt remarks as: "**If ... you fear taking a stand because you are afraid of reprisals from customers, clients, or even government, recognize that you are just feeding the crocodile hoping he'll eat you last.**" Clearly, Ronald Reagan didn't concern himself about whom he might "offend" with his rhetoric—and as a consequence, he rarely did. He might have made those on the left who disagreed with him angry, as with his "Evil Empire" characterization of communism. But "offended"? No, nobody tried to level that charge.

Ronald Reagan was atypical for the years covering his administration. Americans had largely forgotten by the 1980s what leadership was about. The late author and president emeritus of Brown University, Henry M. Wriston, observed in a lecture to Bowdoin College in 1960, that "the individual once was at the core of our political, religious and economic thought." This meant, he said, that "initiative is decentralized [while] responsibility is personalized." Wriston noted that somewhere in the 1930s, individualism had become associated

B. K. Eakman

with exploitation of one's fellow citizens, whereupon the term individualism became, well, a dirty word.

Of course, leadership is a quality of individuals, not of society. The era that produced Reagan, Churchill, Truman, and Gandhi did not look to others to make the hard choices of life. They knew that real leaders do not hide in a social group.

Unlike Bill Clinton, who dithered "while Rome burned" following the first attack on the World Trade Center in 1993, and again after the bombing of our soldiers in Saudi Arabia in 1995, the Khobar Towers bombing in 1996, the attack on U.S. embassies in Africa in 1998, and the USS Cole incident in 2000, Ronald Reagan sent bombers to strike Libya as soon as it became clear that Colonel Muammar Gadhafi was behind in the attack on American soldiers in a West Berlin nightclub. The Libyan dictator didn't bother us again.

Mr. Reagan was decisive in sending troops to Grenada in 1983 to save the island from Cuban soldiers. The materials confiscated following that conflict sent an unmistakable message that Grenada was targeted for takeover. Fidel Castro didn't try the same stunt twice, either.

Then there was President Reagan's proposed missile-defense concept, facetiously dubbed "Star Wars" by his left-leaning critics. But the idea not only helped put the final nail in the coffin on Soviet weapons-buildup, but was ahead of its time in anticipating the threat from rogue nations. Today, a missile-defense shield is back on the front burner.

Besides President Reagan, people today can point to Rudolph Giuliani as a leader. He took an ailing New York City by the horns, put teeth back into laws already on the books regarding public decency and ethical conduct by officials. He brought down crime, cracked down on welfare fraud and nearly eradicated the open-air drug trade, even in the face of rabid criticism by the liberal-leftists in the media and among the special interest groups. After the 9/11 attacks, Mr. Giuliani was the fellow everyone looked up to—and not just in New York City. Even today, in the shadow of the highly politicized—and phony—9/11 Commission, which has worked tirelessly to blame any available conservative for the terror attacks while conveniently ignoring all five separate warning incidents by al Qaeda terrorists under Clinton-Gore, Mr. Giuliani, in Reaganesque fashion, put the blame for the attacks squarely on

236

the terrorists, instead of wasting time lashing out at his political enemies on the Commission.

With the 60th anniversary of D-Day, the opening of the Memorial to the Greatest Generation in Washington, D.C., and renewed interest everything World War II, it is fitting to note how in pre-War Britain, Winston Churchill was sidelined because he was viewed as overly opinionated and difficult to work with. Parliament and the public changed their minds, of course, once British society was faced with a make-or-break confrontation against Adolf Hitler. At that point, Britain could hardly instate Churchill fast enough to guide that nation through its darkest hours. They recognized, quite correctly, that what they really needed was a leader, not a consensus-builder or an intermediary. Important principles about freedom and justice were at stake. Arbitration was not an option.

The measure of a leader has three parts. It entails one part risk-taking, one part vision, and one part self-assurance. There is no room for security-worship if one is going to be a leader.

The belittling of leadership qualities in America and, indeed, the free world, has come about slowly. The first tell-tale signs surfaced in the usual place—the schools. In the 1950s, this nation's guidance counselors (back when they actually were concerned with academics) started advising students to put security before everything else, to aim for certain jobs because there were plenty of vacancies, or because the pay was good, or because there was less chance of unemployment. It became rare for a counselor to urge students to pursue a career for its intellectual, spiritual, or emotional satisfaction, especially if that choice involved risks.

Such defensive counsel, of course, did not help produce a leadership mind-set—and we started paying for it in the 1960s and 70s, when then-college-age Baby Boomers (including, sadly, the Reagans' own children, Patti and Ron) began responding to world problems with a pack-mentality instead of approaching issues on a rational, principled basis. Their protests and demonstrations were more about bonding with their friends and blowing off steam than any expression of well-considered thought.

That turned out to be only the beginning. Simultaneous with the idolization of security was the tendency, also beginning in the mid-1950s, to level down requirements so that the "slowest" wouldn't have their personalities warped (today called "loss of self-esteem"). This lowering of standards was the first step in a disastrous march toward mandated mediocrity. What 60s-era youth needed was a little humility; instead their heads were so swelled that they were emboldened to think they knew everything, without the benefit of facts or experience.

Then, the very term democracy was redefined. The leftist takeover of, first, our education system and, after that, the media finally succeeded in refashioning democracy to mean "total equality of results and outcomes," which of course was pure Marxism—on the order of "from each according to his ability, to each according to his need." This superficial interpretation of democracy was increasingly served up to students until by the 1980s it was an article of faith.

Young people are never very good with subtleties, but in the 1950s and 60s their teachers made sure they would miss the point that the Declaration of Independence says that we are created free and equal, not that we are born free and equal— which is altogether different. Obviously, not everyone has a great singing voice, or a model's physique, or Einstein's intellect. It is equality of opportunity that matters, and that is what the Constitution was written to accomplish. In order to take advantage of that kind of equality, however, it requires individual effort, self-reliance, sacrifice, vision and self-discipline. Those who excel in all these departments, like Ronald Reagan, become leaders. Wealth and luck alone will not suffice.

But the mental-health-oriented school counselors who emerged in the late 70s actually took pains to discourage individualism, calling it "romantic" and "outmoded." They emphasized teamwork over individual effort, indulgence over initiative, and accommodation over confrontation—even if it meant relinquishing one's principles and core beliefs. "Going along to get along"—the heart and soul of progressive education's socialization movement—wound up valuing consensus over what used to be called "thinking for oneself." Even individual desks were exchanged for long tables, where every pupil could compare notes and work with all the other students. This became known as "cooperative learning."

Once youngsters succumbed to the groupie mode of thinking, however, concepts about self-reliance, self-sufficiency, and sacrifice were compromised. More importantly, these concepts tended not to be passed along to Generation X. Today, it is not unusual for the adult children of the Boomers to come back to live with their parents. They can't make it on their own—and don't want to.

Today, even if a child's personality profile (to which school officials have copious access) indicates the student to be a self-starter and self-motivated, the pupil is channeled into activities that demand collaboration, cooperation, conformity and consensus. While lip-service is given to individuality, imagination and ingenuity, in reality these traits are suppressed. One can be imaginative only in the context of the group—for example, in a group science project. Too often, individual creativity and resourcefulness are equated with egotism, eccentricity and self-centeredness.

Anyone who feels it necessary to "shine" can pursue sports or entertainment. These are the only venues, apparently, in which drive, boldness and determination are deemed appropriate.

All this, of course, amounts to an utter denial of the American dream. How many, under such an indoctrination process, are going to become leaders—or even recognize a leader should they encounter one? A "leadership" personality today viewed as egocentric, arrogant, or—worst of all—"not a team player."

But men like Ronald Reagan, Winston Churchill, Rudolph Giuliani, and Mahatma Gandhi were not "team players"—unless it suited them. They called the shots, not the other way around, and today's imitators find it difficult to measure up.

Amid all the noisy chatter in the 1950s and 60s about resistance to communism, Americans silently surrendered to two of its central principles: economic interest, or security ("It's about the economy, Stupid..."), and moral relativity, the idea that "right and wrong" are dependent on culture, place and time.

No wonder that by election year 1992, polls were finding that the public had largely turned a blind eye to Bill Clinton's personal behavior, as long as the economy seemed to remain intact. Of course, by then, most were so uneducated they didn't realize it takes roughly seven years before any new economic policy is felt by the man-in-the-street; that President Clinton was, in fact, capitalizing on the gains made under Reaganomics —essentially by leaving the economy alone.

In an ironic twist, it is no longer religion that can be called "the opium of the people"; it is security that has become America's narcotic of choice. Henry M. Wriston rightly insisted that we will not get boldness, or dedication, or responsible behavior from those who choose as much popularity as possible as a way of life. Populations that sell individualism short cease to be masters of the State, they become instead its wards, Wriston said. Once individuals start deferring to special interest groups to articulate their causes for big bucks, government stops listening to mere individuals. When that happens, government defaults to guardianship, as is increasingly the case in every aspect of American life. Democracy, such as the Founding Fathers envisioned it, is on the way out.

Those with even a little sophistication always knew that winning elections is often more about special-interest hobnobbing than leadership. The turning point came when candidates began to actually fear taking a definitive stand on the issues. Two smart-aleck journalists, Bob Woodward and Carl Bernstein proved, through the Watergate fiasco—in reality, payback for Richard Nixon's having uncovered the traitor, Alger Hiss—proved that the leftist press finally had amassed enough power to tell the American people what they were going to think about and for how long. About the same time, a massive consolidation scheme occurred in the largest teachers' union, the National Education Association (NEA), under the cover of promising educators more pay. With larger annual dues the union was able to front leftist causes and candidates and bring in counterculture curriculums.

Suddenly, it required legions of public relations "handlers" to script a candidate's every speech, interview and "photo opportunity." Carrying an identical message to all audiences, regardless of whom it might "offend," was a virtual death wish. It required a huge leap of confidence, risk-taking, and vision for individuals like Ronald Reagan and Rudolph Giuliani to flout convention and actually mean what they said and say what they meant—every time. And on those rare occasions when that didn't happen, such as the Iran-Contra incident—brought about when then-President Reagan was sent a video showing the torture-killing of prisoner William Buckley—Mr. Reagan regretted he hadn't remained true to his instincts.

What Mr. Reagan's instincts told him was to act in the spirit of the Framers of our Constitution. They thought "outside the box," as we say, and created something unique. But to make it "stick," they knew that education was key. Every generation would have to develop a mind-set of self-reliance, self-determination, principle and individualism, be taught to take the long view and to value the precarious adventure of freedom over limiting notions like tenure, security, and guarantees.

Possibly it is because, in America, poverty is regarded as the ultimate evil that security has come to be worshiped. For this reason, it is often charged by Third World nations that democracy can only flourish among the relatively wealthy. But those who wrote the blueprint for our democratic pattern were not leaders of a wealthy nation. As Henry Wriston noted, we would have to describe this country and its people as predominantly poor in the 1700s, although with great natural resources. Indeed, Ronald Reagan was born into a poor family, the son of an alcoholic father. If ever there was a "common man," it was Ronald Reagan.

But born as he was in 1912, he had the benefit of an era which still recognized that nothing in the Bill of Rights promises the freedoms outlined there can be enjoyed in comfort. He knew that speaking out on controversial matters would be uncomfortable. It is all well and good to combine energies, as he did as a member (and later, head) of the Screen Actors Guild. But along the way, when many colleagues were drawn into communist and socialist doctrines, he decided that leadership required him to step out. He could not, in good conscience, voice only those opinions or ideas favored by the group—even if it meant his career.

George Romney, a Reagan appointee in California, warned Americans back in 1959, in an address to the Commonwealth Club, that unless individuals started fighting for their citizenship, we would find ourselves enslaved, first by power groups, and then by an all-powerful State that exercises our inalienable rights for us, supposedly to protect us from the excesses of other power groups.

George Romney was right. I was there in the 1970s when teachers believed they would make more money and be assured of ongoing job security if they had a super-strong collective bargaining agent. The glorified scam artists at NEA played on fears about lower-paid, younger teachers taking over the jobs of more experienced ones by creating an "us-against-them" mentality. The union, which at that time still operated separate local, state, and national membership options, shoved a continuous stream of inflammatory flyers in teachers' mailboxes that vastly exaggerated the divide between administrators and teachers, parents and teachers. Once they had incited teachers to fever pitch, the union demanded mandatory membership at all three levels—and instituted an equally mandatory leftist political agenda that in the end hurt both the students and teachers themselves.

Today, many teachers are reportedly outraged that they are involuntarily bankrolling candidates they don't like, and subsidizing rallies for causes like abortion and gay rights. But the die was cast long ago when teachers stopped thinking for themselves in the 1970s and allowed power brokers to dictate viewpoints. Today, the NEA management exercises all their members' inalienable rights for them.

Ronald Reagan's insight about the relationship between individualism and leadership has been proved correct over and over. Even as more rules and regulations are continuously generated at the behest of power-hungry interest groups bent on keeping the hand of government firmly planted on the backs of the average taxpayer—in direct opposition to the tenets of Reaganism, which centered on getting government "off people's backs"—Mr. Reagan's political friends and enemies alike praise him for his sincerity, integrity and commitment to principle.

Whether it's property rights over environmental extremism, or something as basic as safeguarding marriage, today's political process has morphed into an impediment to autonomy and majority self-rule. Yet, praise for Mr. Reagan pours in from all quarters. I suspect that is because somewhere, deep in the American collective memory, resides an understanding that this was not the way things were supposed to be in a democratic republic.

May the Gipper rest in peace.

FLORIDA STATE LEGISLATORS
STEP UP TO THE PLATE

In April 2005, I was asked to testify, as a former teacher, at a legislative hearing in Tallahassee, Florida, concerning two pivotal pieces of legislation, one in the House (primary co-sponsor: State Rep. Gus Barreiro) and one in the Senate (sponsored by Victor D. Crist).   Both related to mandatory psychiatric referrals and psychotropic drugging of children as a condition of attending school. The bills were remarkably well-written, concise and to the point.   Both hinged on (1) "full disclosure" notices to parents concerning the subjective nature of psychiatric labels listed in the ever-expanding bible of the profession (the Diagnostic and Statistical Manual of Mental Disorders, or DSM), and (2) the right of parents to refuse both psychiatric referral and/or psychotropic drugging for their children.

On the face of it, there didn't seem to be anything to debate. Parents were being given credit for average intelligence—enough to make a determination as to whether a mental health referral or psychotropic drug is appropriate, and full disclosure attesting to the lack of medical validity behind psychiatric labels (i.e., virtually none can be validated via a blood test, x-ray, chemical analysis, or other visible diagnostic measure), including a warning that DSM labels may result in adverse repercussions when a child applies to a college or for a job.

Many of those fighting the bills were, of course, themselves parents, yet the mental health and psychopharmaceutical lobbies were apoplectic, school officials were furious, and spokespersons for various school-related professional organizations seethed. Debate on both bills drew standing-room-only crowds.

And for good reason. After some 40 years of lousy teacher training, lax discipline, deteriorating academic focus, ineffective fads, and federal legislation that mainstreamed belligerent juveniles, producing a recklessly endangered educational

243

environment, Florida schools had become mostly unmanageable. From a public school official's, or even a teacher's, perspective, about the only recourse left for getting miscreants and children who weren't learning out of the room was to refer them to a mental health worker, who too often intimidated parents unto drugging their youngsters into submission.

The sticking point on the bills was "full disclosure," with "right of refusal" running a close second. On the Senate side, one legislator refused to support the bill because, he said, it would leave an opening for the state's Department of Children and Families (a typical child protective services agency which receives state funding and, indirectly, federal funding as well) to come in and charge a parent with "medical neglect" if he or she refused the recommendation of a psychotropic drug—a "Catch-22" featuring your tax dollars at work. Another legislator complained that it would have a "chilling effect" on confidentiality between the school psychologists and the child.

How about the "chilling effect" on the family? Oh, well...

And we won't even discuss the Individuals With Disabilities Education (IDEA) Act, which has morphed into a psychiatric "disabilities" behemoth that keeps unruly kids in the classroom instead of showing them the door so others can learn. Or the pending effort to screen the entire U.S. population through the schools, via the so-called "New Freedom Initiative," utilizing the No Child Left Behind Act and IDEA as the enabling vehicles.

Professionals from around the country were flown to Tallahassee, including a pediatric neurologist, Dr. Fred A. Baughman—a frequent face at such hearings nationwide. He outlined the faulty science contained in the DSM. Like the other experts, he had just three minutes to make his case. Afterward, he made an extraordinary observation to me worth repeating here: "You see, at hearings like these," Dr. Baughman said, "they might fly experts in from all over the world and avail themselves of some of the finest minds. But legislators increasingly find themselves debating literally dozens of unrelated bills in a single day. That means they are making truly momentous and life-altering decisions based on what amounts to a sound bite from people who have spent their entire lives researching and studying one issue."

This time around was no different. Parents patiently awaited their turns, along with the various experts and the obligatory celebrities, while legislators in both the House and Senate scrambled through a dizzying array of non-education-related bills, amendments, riders and briefings.

I was the token classroom teacher—a profession I once loved, but escaped after nine years to pursue fairer fields as a technical editor, science writer, speechwriter, and finally author in the Washington, DC metropolitan area.

How does one go about defending (in three minutes) a highly credible piece of legislation that would restore some measure of control to parents—knowing that various "gotcha's" at the state and federal levels will inevitably tie the whole effort up in knots?

After listening to all the experts, including parents whose children had been hurt or killed due to side-effects from psychotropic medications, I really didn't know where to begin. So I started with myself.

I explained how I was a "natural" for teaching and for this debate, because I was once one of those quirky, pain-in-the-derrière kids who drive their elders nuts. "If the term 'hyperactive' had been 'in' in the 1950s, I'd have found my niche," I told the assembled legislators and the crowd. My mom might even have been able to indulge in pursuits more satisfying than disciplining me, I added, if she could just have found some justification to explain away my behavior—like "a chemical imbalance in the brain," perhaps.

"But ... alas", I quipped, "I was born too soon—too soon to be labeled with a code out of the DSM. "

Happily, I said, I had the luxury of altering my conduct the old-fashioned way. I didn't have to worry about somebody accessing a computer file 20 years down the road and trudging up some label like Attention-Deficit-Hyperactivity Disorder or Oppositional Defiant Disorder. I never had to worry about losing out on a career choice, based on a DSM label I acquired in the 4th grade. I didn't have to sit by and watch my mother being intimidated with innuendos pointing to what various government agencies might do to her if she didn't refer me to a psychiatrist or, worse, "drug me for, well, behaving like a child."

What I didn't have time to tell the legislators and packed forum was what I actually did in school that would have, no doubt, earned me a DSM label, and probably a drug cocktail, too. Like the cartoon character, Calvin, I fantasized glorious deeds and made myself the hero.

I suppose the worst of the lot was "The Medical School." The polio scare was all over the news in those days and a vaccine, hopefully, was on the way. Well, I had one of those Playskool doctor's kits. I replaced the make-believe plastic syringe needles—which looked kind of phony, I thought—with Mother's hatpins and threatened to inoculate the 3rd-graders with a mixture of Vicks Vaporub and salt water, until some spoilsport called my mother.

Then there was the classmate who handed me a pair of scissors and dared me to cut just a snip of her dress. Well, you can imagine who got in trouble for that one—me, the "cutt-ee." I fell for it. Now, if we'd just had school psychiatrists around, they would no doubt have written that I "failed to pick up on social cues," which today is associated with "mildly autistic behavior."

But back then, we weren't so "enlightened." My mother never had to wonder what was going on, because she always got an unsolicited report at 4:30 p.m. Had I thrown my sandwich in the trash can again? Had I excused myself from study hall to giggle in the bathroom with my best friend? Worn lipstick to class? Well ... it would all come out at 4:30 when she came to pick me up. That was the kind of "behavior modification" teachers and parents employed to keep us youngsters in line— frequent interface between our parents and teachers— not mind-altering drugs and encounter sessions.

We got in trouble for the small things, before they could escalate—like for telling a classmate to "shut up." Well, if we were going to get read the riot act for saying "shut up," we sure weren't going to be using the other four-letter "s"-word anytime soon! I recall my 6th-grade teacher: She confiscated all the girls' purses because we were spending class time "showing off with them." By the time I was teaching, however, such a teacher would be fired for "disrespecting a pupil's legitimate property without cause."

But I couldn't cover these things in the time allotted, so I explained instead to the legislators why I left the education field; how it really began during my four years of teacher training, when I discovered that school was no longer about "basics," or literacy, or proficiency but, rather, "mental health."

I produced a laundry list of courses I endured as a prospective teacher: education psychology, child psychology, adolescent psychology, and so on. I described how nobody cared whether we, as future educators, had a grasp of our chosen subject areas.

The justification for emphasizing psychology, as I eventually understood it, was to produce happier, freer, more inquisitive minds: mentally healthy kids who would be less inclined toward conflict. We collegiates were encouraged to apply the same philosophy to parenthood, should that event occur sooner rather than later.

Well, at 19 years old all this seemed a flash of insight! It was a pivotal moment.

Even parents' magazines suddenly were filled with articles by child experts advising moms and pops to lay off the discipline and "moralizing," to let kids express themselves and give children their "space." Remember that? Don't snoop around, they said. Remember, a child has a right to privacy, too.

Oh, man! I thought. To have been raised like that! Imagine what I could have done with my Vicks Vaporub-salt water concoction if my parents and teachers had just had a little better attitude!

How I wished I could have said that to the mental health lobbies at the Florida hearings! Here they all would have been, trying not to laugh, because they were going to have to get up and testify to the benefits of drugging "challenging" kids like me —the same folks who would have had me labeled, on Ritalin, and in therapy faster than the FDA could recall Vioxx! I mean, a 4th-grader, for Heaven's sakes, trotting around with a hatpin!

And my conduct wasn't the only problem. Every time my mother got a report card—which came in the mail, by the way, not in my devious little hands—there would always be that irritating note typed on the bottom that said "Beverly would do better if she paid more attention in class and did not daydream." Aha! Proof positive of attention-deficit/hyperactivity disorder! A perfect candidate for Ritalin!

In my school, they graded us not merely on our subjects, like history and reading and arithmetic, but there was this whole other list of stuff like oral expression, and written expression, and abstract reasoning. I kept getting this big, fat "D" in oral expression. For the life of me I couldn't figure out why I kept getting a "D" in oral expression, seeing as how I had so much to say, and how much I participated in class and all! Until one semester it was explained to me by my teacher that my mouth and my brain were out of sync! My mouth, you see, was two miles down the road but my brain was still in the garage. Now, if I could just get the two together, the problem with those D's might get resolved.

Well, this was a blow to my already low self-esteem. I mean, I was a poster-child for ego-challenged youth! I was so skinny that even my friends told me I looked like I had two pipe cleaners hanging down from my gym shorts, frizzy-hair, Coke-bottle-thick eyeglasses, zits, and, well, let's just say my body gave new meaning to the term topless.

My mother, on the other hand, was this auburn-haired knockout, a former concert violinist and, later, vice-president of a bank. Not only that, she could fix an entire Thanksgiving dinner dressed in this long, green velvet hostess gown WITHOUT EVER DONNING AN APRON. Every year, I'd wait for some crafty cranberry to make an inauspicious detour onto the sleeves. But, every year, she'd put the dress back in the closet, completely unsoiled, and bring it out again at Christmas.

I was completely dumbfounded. And so was my mother, because she couldn't figure out how she could possibly have produced such a klutz!

Well, that clinches the case for drugs! Obviously, I was "acting out" because of my low self-esteem and my gifted mother, so you might as well add a little Prozac to my Ritalin cocktail, and first thing you know, I might have been slopping cranberry sauce all over Mother's lovely dress, just for meanness—not unlike some of the kids on psychotropic drugs "act out" today. Or, I might well have died as a result of drug interactions and side-effects, like so many other children whose names and photographs were presented at the Florida hearings.

Most parents probably do not remember it today, but it was educational psychologists, in the early 1970s, who came up with the bright idea of doing away with dress codes. That was also when school counselors stopped advising students academically and started "intervening," as they called it—looking for signs of supposed maladjustment in that DSM.

"We have endured one fiasco after another for 40 years in the name of 'mental health'," I told the legislators. "Let me ask you," I said, "are your schools any the better for this intervention? Does this sound like a track record for more? We do indeed have kids today who are totally out-of-control, but it's thanks to the advice an entire generation got about childrearing and "socializing" education. We're warehousing kids, not educating them!" I chastised.

Somewhere along the way, we lost out priorities. Good parents and serious teachers started being treated like well-intentioned dummies because they didn't have advanced degrees in clinical psychology.

"We are teaching our children to approach their studies and their lives as a series of psychological calisthenics, while they flit from one activity to another. We don't teach them to research and examine the meticulous deliberations of philosophers and great thinkers. That's why I left teaching," I said.

"We need full disclosure," I advised, "because young parents hear psychologists throw around terms like obsessive-compulsive disorder, attention-deficits, and hyperactivity and erroneously believe a medical test has shown their child to be sick. What kind of heartless parent is going to discipline a sick child?" I asked. "Parents stop right there, without ever thinking to seek medical confirmation through an MRI, CAT scan, or blood test. They don't know these DSM markers are subjective, based on transient observations, or that the labels easily change—one category after another. One drug on top of the next."

You could have heard a pin drop in the crowded room.

The bottom line is that the mental "health" cartel has had its chance. Their "free-to-be" brainstorm didn't work. Their "Schools Without Failure" plan didn't succeed. Their admonitions against lecturing and moralizing flopped. And the killings at Columbine and now Red Lake, Minnesota, don't exactly sound like promotionals for their drugs, either. "Why should a kid have his brains turned into scrambled eggs, until he can't tell what part of his personality is really him and what part is 'the drug'?" I asked.

Like the proverbial frog in the pot, parents and serious teachers have been treated as "amateurs"—unfit to make judgments concerning a child's welfare or curriculum.

On April 19, 2005, Florida State legislators got an opportunity to do the right thing, to codify parental consent and full disclosure notices into law so that child "experts" can't hide behind their bastardized version of "science" anymore.

The war (and, for that matter, the battle) were far from over, but guess what?

B. K. Eakman

For a moment in time, Florida's legislators stepped up to the plate.

UPDATE:

Despite positive signs from the April 2005 vote, a full disclosure and right-of-refusal parental-rights bill predictably got delayed and waylaid. Despite a mighty effort in 2006 by the Florida Coalition for Protection of Parental Rights, which again proposed a bill requiring fully informed consent to a parent prior to sending a child for any mental evaluation (including under the cover of a "learning disability"), a bill still had not won final passage in Florida by 2007.

Worse, another bill was introduced asking the Legislature to provide $600,000 for a Signs of Suicide program (developed and promoted by Screening for Mental Health, Inc.: http://www.signsofsuicide.org). House Bill 999 (SB 1876) would have screened the entire student body in high schools in Brevard, Orange, Osceola, and Seminole counties. But a groundswell from voters against the measures ensured their timely demise in April 2006—one year exactly after the bill discussed in the article above was tentatively approved by Florida legislators. The good news was that the effort in Florida did lead to promising parental-rights bills that passed in Arizona, Alaska, and Connecticut.

But mental health screening proponents are never idle. For example, an item appeared mysteriously in Senate budget bill 2800 (http://tinyurl.com/2e5p9l). Some $400,000 was tucked away on page 81 of the 401-page budget for a Statewide Suicide Prevention Program.

On April 24, 2007, Florida Senate Bill 224 was heard in the Senate Health and Human Services Appropriations committee. It would have created a "Statewide Office of Suicide Prevention" within the Florida Office of Drug Control (http://tinyurl.com/yrt6pk). Such an office is, of course, a precursor to all kinds of surveys and mental health intrusions into school and home.

The Office of Drug Control—a state clone of the U.S. Office of Drug Control Policy—is located in the Governor's Office. It is tasked with halting substance abuse in Florida. Ironically, this Office has vigorously pushed TeenScreen, a questionnaire-style suicide prevention program (http://www.flgov.com/drug_prevention) that again collects psychological assessments on schoolchildren, with a view to labeling kids and sending as many as possible for mental health "counseling" (and inevitably legal drugging, with antidepressants, so-called concentration-enhancers like Ritalin, and so forth)—intimidating parents who balk in the process.

The bill also calls for the creation of a "Coordinating Council." Among the key members is the National Alliance on Mental Illness (NAMI), a front group for the pharmaceutical industry that gets millions in pharmaceutical funding from government.

Wherever mass screening is pushed, NAMI (www. namipharma.org) is helping to organize it!

(For tax records on Signs of Suicide program, for example, see http://www.signsofsuicide.org/tax_records.htm).

The same bill died over three legislative sessions. But like the Energizer Bunny, a look-alike bill keeps returning.

The following summary of Senate Bill 2286 on Informed Parental Consent, provides a good overview of what parental-rights bills are all about:

Before a public school student may be evaluated for a mental disorder, the parent shall be fully informed concerning:

a) the risks associated with psychotropic drugs (well-established by health agencies world-wide);

b) the possible physical roots of a perceived mental and behavioral disorder (such as allergies, toxins or thyroid conditions), which are diagnosed according to objective standards by medical doctors;

c) alternative treatment options available for their child which do not include psychotropic drugs;

d) legal restrictions on forcing parents to give their child psychotropic drugs—in particular, any charge of "medical neglect" if they refuse to treat their child with psychotropic drugs; and

e) the availability of special education services in public schools regardless of a parent's choice of intervention for a specific behavioral, emotional or mental disorder.

Moreover, parents should be the ones making decisions about their children's health and have a right to be fully informed.

Complicating matters further is the fact that federal initiatives keep providing incentives to states to create their own copycat laws institutionalizing mass psychological profiling of children. The following is a sampling of come-ons that entice state legislatures to get onboard:

1.)   State Incentive Transformation Grants (SITGs - $19,796,000).

These grants allow states to put in place the recommendations of the highly controversial "New Freedom Commission" (NFC) Report on Mental Health, now passed as the New Freedom Initiative. Universal mental health screening, starting from a very early age, is a primary goal of the NFC. Early mental health screening, assessment and referral to services are to be incorporated into school programs and doctors' offices nationwide as common practice.

SITGs provide so-called "technical assistance" money to non-governmental organizations (NGOs) like the National Association for State Mental Health Program Directors, whose members include NFC Chairman Michael Hogan. Hogan brought the controversial Texas drug-treatment/psychological assessment program called TMAP to Ohio—while being paid by the pharmaceutical industry. Many proponents of screening are part of organizations having a vested interest in expanding the mental health system. Sometimes that interest is political—something many legislators just don't "get."

2.) Suicide Prevention ($26,730,000), also called Garrett Lee Smith Suicide Prevention Act enacted in 2004.

Among the activities funded are mental health screening programs, particularly TeenScreen. Specific problems associated with TeenScreen include the use of passive consent. Some experts cite an 84% false-positive rate of the questionnaire for mental illness. Programs like these are bankrupting already overburdened public programs like Medicaid and foster care.

3.) State Early Childhood Comprehensive System (SECCS)

SECCS funds grants for states to develop "mental health early intervention services targeted to infants, toddlers, preschool, and school-aged children." These grants are steering states to establish universal infant mental health screening. Inasmuch as it is virtually impossible to assess an infant's mental health, such an initiative will necessarily morph into a political whip that is held over a parent who resists some popularized cause or government policy.

Minnesota's Road Map for Mental Health System Transformation (an example of an SECCS, as applied to one state) affirms on p. 165 that its purpose is "to coordinate and integrate early childhood screening systems to assure that all children ages birth to five are screened early **and continuously** for the presence of health, socioemotional [mental health] or developmental needs." (Emphasis added)

According to the Center on the Emotional and Social Foundations for Early Learning, South Dakota's strategic plan for infant mental health lists this Orwellian vision:

"All children in South Dakota are supported by the community through a comprehensive system of care that meets their social, emotional, physical, and spiritual needs."

4.)   Foundations for Learning Grants ($1,000,000)

This is a mental health program funded through No Child Left Behind for children ages birth through age seven. It provides "mental health," among other services, in order "to deliver services to eligible children and their families" to foster "emotional, behavioral, and social development." These services are based on such vague eligibility criteria as: "the child has been exposed to violence"; "the child has been removed from child care, Head Start, or preschool for behavioral reasons or is at risk of being so removed"; "the child has been exposed to parental depression or other mental illness."   The federal government has no proper role or constitutional authority to be involved in or setting norms for anyone's mental health, much less for very young children. NOTE: President George W. Bush has (thankfully) recommended this odious program for elimination.

5.)   Violence Prevention Grants – Safe Schools/Healthy Students ($75,710,000)

These grants involve mental health screening programs for both infants and TeenScreen with all of their invasiveness and lack of scientific merit. In addition, they use a subprogram funded under the NCLB Safe and Drug Free Schools Program that labels children as potentially violent and or mentally unstable based on attitudes, values and beliefs. This subprogram is called Early Warning, Timely Response. Among the purported warning signs of violence is "intolerance for others and prejudicial attitudes."   The US Department of Education (DOE) website for this program states:

"All children have likes and dislikes. However, an intense prejudice toward others based on racial, ethnic, religious, language, gender, sexual orientation, ability, and physical appearance when coupled with other factors may lead to violent assaults against those who are perceived to be different."

Given the multiple problems with the mental health screening and psychiatric drug treatment for children already mentioned, as well as the politically correct, thought-control aspects of this program, it is a dangerous piece of legislation. Students who demonstrate intense prejudice or who bully others, irrespective of the reason, should be disciplined, as such conduct historically has been, but opinions per se do not call for mental health referrals and/or psychotropic drugs.

6.)   Mental Health Integration in Schools ($4,900,000)

This is yet another vehicle for mental health screening to be implemented in schools. Due to government and private insurance reimbursement patterns, treatment almost always means with psychotropic medications, very few of which are actually approved for children and carry black box warnings for serious, if not fatal, side effects.

B. K. Eakman

HOW INDEPENDENT ARE WE?

There was the Stone Age, the Bronze Age, the Iron Age, the Industrial Age, the Space Age, the Information Age, and now the Surveillance Age – an era in which phone calls and keystrokes may be monitored; the comings and goings of individuals can be tracked; and a person's private thoughts, like his purchases, are open to inspection.

Three recent legislative decisions, seen from the perspective of 240 years of American history, show just how far we have come from the Founding Fathers' ideals about self-determination and independence as crafted into our nation's Constitution.

Consider first the passage of H.R. 3010 on Friday, June 24, 2005 – the universal mental health screening and drug treatment bill, without even the meager safeguard offered in Senator Ron Paul's amendment, which might have bought Americans a little extra time to reconsider this horrendous affront to their rights. The Departments of Labor, Health and Human Services, and Education passed the appropriations measure with $26 million for "state incentive transformation grants" to fund implementation of the New Freedom Commission's psycho-pharmacological recommendations, thereby giving officials in schools and other agencies virtual carte blanche to marginalize and medicate anyone with unapproved opinions, worldviews and attitudes.

The word "incentive" means exactly what you think it means (for once): to spur, motivate and encourage. Federal tax revenues will be used to motivate every state to assess its citizens for perceived mental aberrations, beginning with children in the classroom and extending to teachers, pregnant women, the elderly, prospective employees, and so on. Inasmuch as mental illnesses, as listed in the *Diagnostic and Statistical Manual of Mental Disorders*, rely on subjective observations as opposed to substantial and replicable medical evidence, this bill is bound to morph into a political litmus test of nightmarish proportions that will make the "political correctness" of yesteryear look like a try-out for a high school cheerleading squad.

Another attack on traditional American independence came down from the Supreme Court on June 23, 2005 in a decision allowing state and local governments to take private lands for public use, by force if necessary, with the issues of "fair compensation" and "due process" left to one's tender imagination. In Kelo v. City of New London, Supreme Court Justices Stevens, Kennedy, Breyer, Ginsberg and Souter toppled American notions about private property and individual ownership in the larger interest of enhancing tax revenues. Justice Sandra Day O'Connor, in a dissenting opinion, correctly noted that "[a]ny property may now be taken for the benefit of another private party, but the fallout from this decision will not be random. The beneficiaries are likely to be those citizens with disproportionate influence and power in the political process, including large corporations and development firms."

Guess who will be among the casualties as this decision plays itself out? Those deemed a nuisance because they are "politically incorrect," thereby helping to ensure a leftist conformity. Regardless of the party in power, Republican or Democrat, politically correctness still leans leftward, leaving any politician uttering a non-socialist comment to apologize and run for cover. The left, which dominates the schools and universities, the media, and the courts, has wooed business interests, foundations and professional associations, thereby conferring the "disproportionate influence" to closet Marxists.

Just as the left favored placing political prisoners in psychiatric lockups in the old Soviet Union, it has long been aware of the need to weaken private property rights in targeted countries. William Z. Foster, National Chairman of the Communist Party, USA, wrote in 1932 that "[t]he establishment of an American Soviet government will involve the confiscation of large landed estates in town and country, and also, the whole body of forests, mineral deposits, lakes, rivers and so on." The Soviet Union per se may be gone, but Marxism is still alive and well, even though it has failed to create prosperity for citizens everywhere it has been implemented.

Then there was the ambiguous June 27th Ten Commandments decision (or maybe I should say Ten Commandments "waffle") – another Church-State debate which every year inches closer to a virtual ban on Judeo-Christian concepts about morality and ethics.

In my 1998 book, *Cloning of the American Mind*, in a section subtitled "A Game Called Religion," I describe a typical curriculum that treats religion as a silly diversion.

Children are told to make an altar, and to name an oracle, and then to bring all sorts of questions to this make-believe oracle until, at the end of the "lesson," the children are dissolving in peals of laughter. The message is clear: All religion is just a myth, and your parents' myths are no better or worse than anybody else's, so best not to get too caught up in them.

The new religion is psychology. The tenets of psychology are fickle, of course, and go far beyond a list of "shalts" and "shalt nots." Elementary and secondary curriculums are not set up to teach logic, or philosophy or even chronological history, so the dogma of psychology comes to youngsters in a vacuum. It plays out as diversity training, sexual how-to's masquerading as "education," and dependence on mind-altering drugs instead of developing character and maturity.

As we celebrated the Fourth of July, I was reminded of prophetic words uttered by Benjamin Franklin when, ill and being carried from the Constitutional Convention by his colleagues, he was asked by someone in a crowd what kind of government the Framers have formed. Replied Franklin: "A Republic ... if you can keep it."

If we can keep it.

When the celebrations break out next year over the Nation's Capitol, I can well imagine a very politically incorrect Thomas Jefferson, James Madison, Ben Franklin, and John Adams standing with all the rest of their venerable collaborators, shedding quiet tears among the fireworks.

LOST

Okay. This title is a knock-off of the popular television show of the same name. So sue me.

Being that time of year when people tend to re-evaluate, re-prioritize, or (heaven forbid!) make resolutions, I decided to take a break from writing over the holidays and re-organize the various piles of research materials that had been allowed to accrue. Plopped in the middle of a virtual chronicle covering educational, social and cultural changes that spanned at least three decades, I experienced an epiphany, of sorts. I looked around gloomily at the mounds of paper, and dared to ask a single question: What has the conservative movement got to show for the last 30 years?

The answer came back: Not a whole heck of a lot.

Readers of this column who are not writers or working the lecture circuit should understand that it is first and foremost *passion* that brings our ilk to the word processor. Without passion, writing is flat, speeches are uninspiring, and even the most horrendous or marvelous news is rendered quite forgettable. Talk show hosts have no use for a passionless guest. That is one reason why we who labor among the "chattering classes" are forever amassing documents, tearing out articles and ordering books – to inflame our sensibilities to such an extent that we fall all over ourselves to get to the nearest computer terminal and bang out a pithy article or lecture – maybe even a book, if events prove sufficiently provocative.

Prospective young journalists in college are taught to look for the "Holy Cow factor" (actually, that second word is less, um, refined); something that will make a bored editor levitate out of his (or her) chair and say "Wow!" To such ends, we writers keep pads of paper and a pen on the nightstand, beside the bathtub, and even in our beach gear.

When you're hot, you're hot!

But this day, sorting through the various clippings, I was struck by a dreary sameness. I picked up a column by Brent

Bozell bemoaning, yet again, the liberal bias of "mainstream" news organs. Beside me was a piece by Robert Knight detailing the latest assault on Christian values. To my right, Rich Lowry condemned the "culture of corruption" as exemplified by enormous pork in last year's highway bill, while inches away I found an article by his older counterpart saying virtually the same thing a quarter of a century ago in *National Review*.

Behind me, a news article described how the largest teacher union, the National Education Association, had, once again, defied its tax exempt status by lobbying for ultra-left causes and funding liberal candidates – news that was, in essence, no news. I wrote about that in 1986. In the corner, was a paper outlining further inappropriate excerpts from a sex education course, and right next to it, a recent account concerning a rapist who sexually assaulted, mutilated and murdered a nine-year-old girl.

Then, right in front of me was an excerpt from President George W. Bush's remarks describing how he was going to "reach out" to his Democratic opposition.

How constructive was **that?** I thought ruefully. By 2002, discourse had deteriorated such that if President Bush had said "good morning," the Democrats were demanding a half-hour for rebuttal on national television.

Turning around, I stumbled over a bulging file holding the new federal plan to screen the entire U.S. population for mental illness (under the Marxist-like moniker of "New Freedom Initiative"). It had already passed in the U.S. House of Representatives. Under the plan, schools would become the hub of mandatory psychiatric screening – not only for pupils, but their parents and teachers, with incremental inroads into all categories of individuals. If Democrats had wanted to challenge the President on an issue, this would have been one on which to throw down the gauntlet, inasmuch as it grew out of President Bush's old Texas Medication Algorithm Project (TMAP) in 1995, an alliance between then-Governor Bush, representatives from the pharmaceutical industry, the University of Texas, and the Texas mental health and corrections systems.

Does "Dubya" have any idea he is bequeathing to future generations a legal vehicle for locking up or chemically lobotomizing political opponents? I wondered. *And where were the paragons of the press corps – the investigative reporters on – TMAP? Asleep?*

On the education front, a new *Wall Street Journal* commentary revealed that (gasp!) relaxed standards were compromising substantive learning and, in an upcoming segment of "20/20" ("Stupid In America: How We Are Cheating Our Kids"), ABC's John Stossel was preparing to astound viewers with the disclosure that American high school students fall behind other countries in international comparisons of basic subjects, including even poorer countries like Poland, the Czech Republic and South Korea – a fact I had noted in an article years ago, and it wasn't a shocker even then. We've been on that merry-go-round since about 1956.

Meanwhile, history was being rewritten in a curriculum known as *We the People* – managing, again, to disparage or disregard the Framers of our Constitution and exacerbate what has been a national obsession with race.

We won't even discuss the gay-lesbian issue, which is now in everyone's face 24/7 – despite an exponential rise in AIDS and other sexually transmitted diseases, especially among gay men, who continue to shrug off warnings about "safe sex," according to the Center for Disease Control. Well, never mind, classrooms are steeped in mandated bathroom talk from kindergarten onward, and parents who object are deemed mentally ill ("homophobic," "inhibited"). Even the Parent-Teachers Association has gotten in on the act. Obviously the three to five percent of individuals who are into this sort of thing has trumped all the rest of us who find it repulsive.

The liberal-left, of course, has a cure. It's called "re-education" via gay clubs on campus and draconian hate-speech rules.

Oh, and don't forget the antidepressants. Hah! Now *that's* actually funny. Because most antidepressants, according to studies I've seen, are about 90 percent guaranteed to make you lose your sex drive!

And how about U.S. foreign aid to terror-sponsoring nations in the wake of earthquakes, floods and other natural disasters? Does an American flag adorn every shipped package, and a Christian cross too, if applicable? Do we stem the tide of illegal immigrants, especially from Latin America, where countries increasingly are re-aligning themselves with Marxist dictatorships? No, our citizens serve as cash cows to the world.

Meanwhile, individual Americans practically forfeit their salaries to keep up with escalating health-care costs, high-tech crime-prevention systems, excessive auto-emissions regulations, computer-virus and spam-protection software – all out-of-pocket outlays that would have been unthinkable just 40 years ago, when doctors came to our houses, police actually protected neighborhoods, and people had better things to do than send tons of garbage to every home in America.

What to make of all this? Here is today's Republican leadership sounding more like the liberals of my Baby-Boomer youth, while the self-described liberals are now open socialists, spouting the same twisted logic as Karl Marx. As Wesley Pruden, editor-in-chief of the *Washington Times*, aptly observed in his June 6, 2006, column (See: "Looking for virtue in a wrong place," www.washtimes.com/national/20060106-125033-9458r.htm): "Big government and insensate spending, which were high crimes and misdemeanors when the Democrats did it, suddenly became Republican virtues."

Touché.

Today's 10-year-olds will never know a time when everyone wasn't watched, tracked, monitored, and subject to inspection – all to avoid offending any sponsors of terror in our midst. Youngsters will never experience the thrill of romance or the bittersweet innocence of yearning; instead they will look back on meaningless hook-ups, played to a backdrop of ugly rap lyrics. They will worry more about lost health than lost love.

As for their parents, well, American Life League president Judie Brown may have said it best when she observed in her January 5, 2005, column that motherhood today is about self-satisfaction (read: "trophy kids"), not about the value of an individual child. Indeed, the Commonwealth Education Organization (Pittsburgh, PA) reports a campaign afoot to lower the age for pre-kindergarten schooling, with an eye to making it mandatory after everyone has grown accustomed to getting what would be, essentially, free day-care services for their toddlers.

How ironic that Pope Paul VI warned of all these various outcomes when he outraged the civilized world (including me!) by rejecting birth control in the 1960s. For his foresight, he alone is entitled to laugh all the way to the bank – were he still alive.

I sighed.

That was when an unexpected thought occurred: *You know, you really don't have to do this anymore.*

"Huh?" I said aloud.

You've written scores of articles and three books, two of which were best-sellers. Together with other writers, you provided a thorough accounting of government-sponsored education's legacy on privacy, the family, criminal justice, and the culture. There's really nothing more left to say on these topics that has not been written by someone, somewhere.

That was when reality set in. "So, we *lost,*" I mumbled, suddenly stung by the realization. "We really lost." And come the November elections, we're going to see just how thoroughly, I reflected, more in sadness than anger.

There weren't enough of us who stood up, who insisted, who drew the line, who refused – or who took the time to examine the wildly disparate versions of major news stories.

Which is why I had cuttings from some five newspapers and 14 periodicals staring at me from the floor. Well, that was about to change.

My attention now on more practical matters, I decided the more efficient way to clean out the mess on the floor would be to bring in the large trash cans from the driveway, rather than dragging scores of giant plastic bags out.

I went to collect the trash cans – and maybe fold into retirement.

A pink-orange twilight filtered through the bay window in my office. A swoosh filled the silence as file after file descended into oblivion. *So many outrages, so little time,* I thought. With the advent of instant communications, editors pushed for a 24- to 48-hour turnaround on news commentaries. I couldn't churn out pieces fast enough and still fine-tune them without mistakes, especially on a laptop, with their hard-to-manipulate square "mousepads" in the center. After accidentally deleting an important hyperlink source in penning one article (in part to divert my anxiety while my mother was in surgery), a conservative reporter threatened to sue me, and sent scores of angry e-mails all over creation in an attempt to discredit me for quoting his interview without the hyperlink. After that, I located a mini-mouse for my laptop – but the damage was done, and by a fellow conservative whose huge ego was matched only by his poor timing and his arrogance.

As I went about freeing up countless drawers and boxes, I reflected upon the compulsive sense of urgency I had felt when I was penning my books. Oh, how I agonized over those first speeches and articles! If I got held up in traffic, even for 10 minutes, it was 10 minutes I wouldn't have that night.

Many of my colleagues struggled similarly. Before there was hard evidence of legislation presaging universal mental-health screening, before there were Smart Cards, traffic cameras and computer viruses, many of us recognized that the America we knew was living on borrowed time: an America where topics like rape and sodomy were thankfully spoken in whispers; an America that required prospective immigrants to have a sponsor and a job; an America where Judeo-Christian values were the gold standard, but where other beliefs were respected as long as public safety was not at risk; an America where a person's time was not all but taken up satisfying government *diktats*; an America that rewarded initiative instead of "process"; an America where you could turn on your television and radio without being grossed out.

By the late 1960s, conservative writers were barely make a living, as one by one, magazines, newspapers, publishing houses, and independent radio and television stations were taken over or marginalized by the left. Conservative publications, even the few successful ones, could not afford to place magazines at the corner drug store or give newspapers away free of charge for six months like their liberal counterparts did. This accounted for the fierce turf battles that would eventually ensue over limited funds, fracturing a conservative revival that had started percolating under President Ronald Reagan.

The left, of course, always had access to funds, through second and third parties if necessary, and so their version of events wound up being what most people saw – and what permeated the schools. A gift from George Soros here, a Rockefeller Foundation grant there, an Armand Hammer endowment somewhere else – they could scarcely have spent all their combined assets.

The conservative groups were left to battle it out – for memberships, subscriptions to publications and for professional organizers. This resulted in continual infighting, vicious activists and a revolving door of poorly paid, barely out-of-college gofers, who packed their brief cases the minute they were able to command a decent salary. The few who stayed on to assume higher profile positions (typically thanks to a well-positioned relative) too often exchanged their zeal in digging out the truth for celebrity, however fleating. Swelled-Head Syndrome became a condition commensurate with one's lofty, if precarious, position within the conservative network.

Two examples: A renowned educational analyst wrote in 2001 to the chairman of a conservative non-profit (which shall remain unnamed). The organization had enjoyed some success in challenging universities that discriminated against conservative students and professors. The analyst outlined what he saw as serious missteps in the Republican strategy, especially with regard to academic freedom and free conscience, the organization's primary interests. His letter was three pages long, but thorough. He asked for a meeting and included his e-mail address. The letter was diverted to the vice-Chairman of the organization who, in turn, e-mailed a colleague that the writer was "long-winded but apparently well-connected" and advised a perfunctory response to "keep him happy." *This insulting e-mail was re-transmitted (accidentally?) via e-mail to the analyst in question along with the boilerplate letter that was supposed to "keep him happy."*

Needless to say, the man never made contact with that organization again, even though it could well have benefited from his expertise.

In a personal incident: I was invited to meet with a highly placed conservative leader to discuss the No Child Left Behind Act. This prominent conservative (who shall similarly remain unnamed) "forgot" our first meeting, according to his office manager, and no one ever called to apologize. Upon rescheduling (which I initiated), this same muckety-muck spent our short time together scanning his e-mail, blowing his nose, answering the phone for trivial matters and noisily munching a snack. At length, he asked me to make a three-minute presentation at his organization's weekly meeting of top conservatives – about 100 people, including a couple representatives from the White House. I accepted the offer and took annual leave from work.

The meeting ran out of time and I didn't present. I didn't know whether to reschedule or not. At length, I took the initiative again with a telephone call, thinking perhaps I was simply expected to show up the next week. The office manager confirmed I was on the schedule. *Thanks for telling me*, I thought.

I took off work again. This time, Mr. Big-Shot was on travel, so a 20-something girl from a different organization served as moderator. Armed with handouts that I distributed beforehand (standard operating procedure for presenters), I waited. And waited.

Finally, after nearly half the attendees had left, I was called. I had whittled my talk to under three minutes (a limit nobody else actually bothered about), and began by referencing my handouts. The young lady interrupted, saying that since I had disseminated handouts, I could sit down. I laughed and said thank you, but I'd take my three minutes.

The girl was repeatedly rude – so much so that jaws dropped. Nobody, including me, had a clue what her problem was. The remaining attendees applauded my presentation when I had finished, probably more to compensate for the girl's performance than because of anything I said. (Much later, I discovered that my experience with the young woman had not been unique, and one of the more senior regulars there, a long-time public official, reprimanded her in front of the remaining group for what he called "disrespect.")

Since that time, Mr. Big-Shot began toadying to "conservative" homosexual activists, to the dismay of traditionalists in his camp, and Her Snottyship moved on to other endeavors, in keeping with the ever-revolving door that has become the "mainstream conservative network."

Liberal powerhouses like the Aspen Institute for Humanistic Studies and the Carnegie Foundation do not make such blunders. To the contrary, they turn on the charm. Boorish behavior on the part of so many conservative leaders stands in direct contradiction to Ronald Reagan's quiet confidence and diplomacy. I recall one comment he made about how much could be accomplished when no one cares who gets the credit. Too many today have become drunk on their own importance – which, for all the good it has done, has amounted to their not being very important at all.

Meanwhile, the publishing world has changed, and writers of all political stripes are told that "nobody reads anymore."

By the 1990s, one's work had to be concise to the point of being factually bereft. If it didn't read like Tom Clancy, claimed the syndicates, no one would pick it up. Thus my first book,

Educating for the New World Order: Reviewers and talk show hosts rhapsodized that it read "like a spy novel." Readers snatched it up, then begged for more. So I wrote a second, much longer tome, proving that people really *did* read, after all.

Books by conservatives started hitting the shelves – a good sign, we thought, portending a showdown between parents and government schools, among other things. But it didn't pan out that way. Conscientious parents didn't have an American Civil Liberties Union to pop out of a hat with *pro bono* help. Lawsuits took years and were expensive. Most parent-activist groups eventually burned out. Much like I was now.

Feature writers like me tended to hold alternative "day jobs," often outside our real areas of expertise. A few of us held high positions within government agencies, and decided they didn't like what they were seeing. This was not necessarily an indictment of the Oval Office, but of the bureaucracy, non-governmental organizations (NGOs) and special-interest groups. Such entities were showering legislators under the table with soft support and perks only hinted at in the lobbying scandal starring Jack Abramoff.

Eventually, every serious writer I knew was drowning in a sea of paper and e-mails. They needed researchers to do summaries, clerks to file all the stories, editors, proofreaders, computer specialists to cover the blogs. Scores of my colleagues threw in the towel. The rest of us rationalized that there would be other years to watch a favorite television special, hike in the woods, take a non-business-related trip, or just sit outside and do nothing for awhile.

The liberals, meanwhile, had all the time in the world. Conservative alliances started breaking up as new upstarts and a few old-guard think-tanks went RINO (Republicans in Name Only) like Mr. Big-Shot's organization – the price of legitimacy in the new order.

There are, of course, still millions of folks who revere traditional American values (e.g., the success of films like "The Passion of the Christ" and "The Chronicles of Narnia" and news services like NewsWithViews, NewsMax and WorldNetDaily). But overall, the statistics tell a different story.

To put the matter in perspective, consider the popular TV series, "Star Trek: Enterprise." The show was canceled in 2004 because, according to *TV Guide*, "only" 2.8 million people were watching it. Forget for a moment whether you liked, hated, or even tuned in to the program. Until about 1965, 2.8 million people doing *anything* would have been considered an awesome figure. Today, it doesn't mean diddly. Media executives, like policymakers, are interested in double-digit millions.

Shock-jock Howard Stern got hundreds of millions of dollars from his contract with Sirius Satellite Radio for just this reason. Many more people apparently like drivel, smut and bathroom "humor" than are interested in what used to be called "family entertainment." More sophisticated qualities like subtlety, cleverness, riveting plots and characterization are becoming rarities – thanks in part to 30 years of dumbed-down education and all the things that result from that. Polls, of course, are predominantly liberal and probably skewed to augment figures supporting garbage and claptrap. Even so, the delta between 2.8 million and double-digit millions is hard to fake.

More significantly, every graduating high school class brings a whole new slate of "legal adults" into the fold. These "grownups" don't remember what family entertainment used to look like. As they join the ranks of voters, consumers, and workers, they bring the "new" value system they learned in school with them, and our nation descends further into socialism, welfare, casual sex, narcissism, and political correctness.

As long as the liberal-left faction of government was denying what it was doing, time was on our side. Traditionalists had a chance of winning the larger culture and political war. But when the opposition began bragging about what it was doing instead of denying it, we started losing in earnest. Now we are in a position where people of principle are subject to government harassment at every turn. We are buried in red tape, expensive nuisance-regulations and government-mandated paperwork.

The world has visited this scenario before, under the Nazis and the Soviets, but this time it comes with the dubious benefits of computerized cross-matching and high-tech, long-term tracking. Several news outlets reported, for example, that New York City will track diabetic residents. If you think this project will stop with diabetics or New York City, you're dreaming!

We should have drawn a line in the sand during the hippie movement of the 1970s, a phase that most of us thought would fizzle. Instead it morphed. Had our side quickly bought up media outlets, launched new television and radio stations en masse, funded newspapers in every city, created alternative schools and franchised them, launched class-action lawsuits to stem the dissemination of filth, made pariahs of leftist front-groups like the American Civil Liberties Union, and insisted on laws reigning in the fledgling computer technologies, we might have stemmed the political tsunami. Had we told the environmental extremists where to get off, beginning back when they were first protecting bugs over humans, we might still have trash cans in our parks instead of being forced to carry doggie droppings and dirty paper plates from concession stands in baggies on our belt as we try to enjoy our walks.

But we chose instead to spend the money and energy on election campaigns and Senatorial Committees, even when we had no press to disseminate our message, and no school system to reinforce our values.

Moreover, in 30 years we have succeeded only in filling a few legislative seats with Republican protoplasm, a result which produced only temporary, meager gains. And now, even that is about to disappear with the November elections.

As the eminent columnist Mark Steyn put it in his January 4, 2006, column for the *Wall Street Journal* (See "It's the Demography, Stupid" at www.opinionjournal.com): "...much of what we loosely call the Western world will not survive this century, and much of it will effectively disappear within our lifetimes....[Places like] Italy and the Netherlands will merely be designations for real estate. The challenge for those who reckon Western civilization is on balance better than the alternatives is to figure out a way to save at least some parts of the West."

That pretty much sums up the situation.

As I disposed of the contents in the last file drawer, I couldn't help brooding. How did a fiercely independent, can-do populace turn into a collection of resigned, apathetic and submissive sheep in so short a time?

A little voice whispered: *"Sorry, that's above your pay grade."*

B. K. Eakman

LAST REPUBLICAN STANDING

Congressional Democrats won the mid-term elections for two reasons Republicans would rather not talk about: *education* and *media*.

Conservative pundits and pollsters imagined that because the Democratic Party didn't have a consistent message, or because the class-warfare theme was wearing thin, the left couldn't possibly sweep an election. While the rants of Rep. Jack Murtha (D-Pa.), Al Gore, and Michael Moore have become increasingly wacky, of far more significance is the fact that the old formulas conservative strategists once relied on to win elections no longer apply. The dynamics of the electorate have changed.

Forty years of failure in education policy and media strategy have now come back to bite us.

While Republicans were busy padding the coffers of GOP political action committees, the left spent 40 years infiltrating schools, beefing up publishing outlets and even stripping God from houses of worship. Old-guard Marxists in the United States consolidated their gains, established state and local agents via second and third parties, and either edged out smaller competitors or absorbed them. The National Education Association instituted mandatory memberships on three levels, while left-leaning media powerhouses like the *New York Times* bought hundreds of once-independent publishing outlets. The Big Three networks snapped up most of the cable channels. Religious oversight bodies like the liberal Episcopal Church USA gave local denominations their marching orders while wasting the time and resources of any resisters. And so, by default, closet Marxists won the war of sound-bytes among burgeoning waves of ever-less-educated voters without the verbal and logic skills to defend critical principles of the republic.

270

Unsurprisingly, we are no longer a populace that rationally grapples with philosophical dilemmas. A common store of values no longer serves as a backdrop for earnest discussion. Instead, we're mired in catchphrases, oversimplifications and personality contests—in large part thanks to an education system awash in sports, rewritten history, lax discipline and faddish methodologies.

In failing to secure our schools and media from well-organized, leftist provocateurs beginning in the 1950s, conservatives botched any chance they might have had in preserving values and ideals critical to a constitutional republic. Now it's payback time.

Had conservatives rejected educational psychobabble; had they revamped teacher training in the universities based on what researchers actually know about learning; had they crafted *real* diagnostics for entering schoolchildren, American schooling today would be the best in the world instead of fourth from the bottom. Young adults today would have not only the skills to achieve their own, personal financial independence; we would have a nation with the philosophical and political chops to prevail in a show-down against eighth-century barbarians as well as twenty-first-century socialists.

Had conservative journalists, publishers and media moguls bought up outlets when they were cheap and available, they would have today a credible soapbox instead of being the butt of late-night TV jokes.

Instead, conservatives ignored the electoral consequences of a politicized, increasingly left-leaning curriculum and a psychologized learning environment. Today conservative leaders having more ego than wisdom launch misleading legislation like the No Child Left Behind Act (a sop to Democratic Sen. Ted Kennedy) and initiate psychological profiling nightmares under misleading monikers like "universal mental health screening" (note the Marxist-like ring to the legislation: New Freedom Initiative for Mental Health), knowing full well that such concepts are flawed, bogus, or both.

Even "conservative" think-tanks have treated basic reading and math as if these were rocket science. Only nine things can possibly go awry in learning—spatial and abstract reasoning, visual identification, visual and auditory memory, perceptual speed, mental stamina, hand-eye coordination and thought-expression synchronization. All we ever had to "fix," as it were, was teacher preparation, then pair pupils with instructors trained to handle every child's *weakest* competence on the list. No stigma. No "dummy tracks." Instead, we create ever larger and more bureaucratic "educational" facilities, frustrate thousands of kids to the point of losing their sanity, and stuff powerful, mind-altering drugs down the results of our folly.

On the media front, conservative publications and writers abound. Yet, we continue to shoot ourselves in the foot by hailing as "conservative" every book club, talk show and publication that spouts common sense, even going so far as to publicize lists of "right wing" columnists, when it would have been more correct to characterize the views expressed as "conventional." No wonder the left increasingly marginalizes conservatives with every election cycle, laughing all the way to the bank.

As Texas-based author and educational researcher Donna Garner has pointed out, only some 40 percent of registered voters bothered to vote in the November 2006 election, and no one knows how many Americans are not even registered—probably millions who have simply tuned out. Actually, most elections have even lower voter turn-outs, so accustomed are we to the process of financing candidates (or, more accurately, "personalities") for farcical primaries. Democrats now brag that they have a mandate from the American people to implement leftist policies, but the only mandate that exists was won by default. Garner correctly notes that we are fighting a war on two fronts: one in the Middle East, and an entirely different kind right here.

Arguably, the real "quagmire" exists at home!

Conservative magazines and think tanks complain loudly that their literature is absent from school libraries and magazine stands, and that conservatives always get short shrift in television interviews and on newscasts etc. Well, duh! What did we expect when they leave it to other countries to launch what few conservative newspapers exist (e.g., *The Washington Times*) and play political football with our education system-*cum*-psychological laboratory?

Whenever I go on speaking junkets, I make it a point to get the local newspaper. Smaller towns, in particular, are revealing for where they get their stories. Almost invariably a byline on any topic will read something like "L.A. Times-Washington Post Syndicate" or "Associated Press-New York Times"—meaning, of course, a leftward spin. Add National Public Radio, liberal television interviewers and propagandizing sitcoms, and soon the counterculture becomes *the* culture.

After all that, we try to appease our opponents. For example, Maryland's former Republican Governor, Bob Ehrlich, fired a guy last summer for equating homosexuality to "sexual deviancy." The man didn't say "sinful," or even "unhealthy." Yet, Gov. Ehrlich immediately installed an open homosexual in a prominent post—and of course lost the election anyway. Like George W. Bush talking earlier in his presidency about "reaching across the aisle" and being a "uniter." Exactly what did this strategy buy for him? Can we say "ZERO"?

Why on earth would a conservative Republican try to appease leftist Democrats, anyway? Because we know, in our heart of hearts, that a liberal-*sounding* Republican is the **only** kind— white, black or polka-dot—who's going to survive politically in this day and age.

On August 2, 2007, none other than the Republican National Committee endorsed the liberal rock star icon, Bono, in his scheme to transfer some $30 billion of U.S. taxpayers' money— not his own money, but ours—to fight **global poverty**. That news came right on top of a plan to subsidize poverty right here at home, in the form of health insurance for all so-called poor children—mostly the illegitimate offspring of single mothers who are already being bolstered financially with everything from housing and mortgage breaks to food and easy credit lines. The proposed reauthorization (and augmentation) of the State Children's Health Insurance Program (SCHIP) comes to an estimated $35-50 billion over five years (depending on whose version of the bill you read).

Both of these initiatives—global poverty and SCHIP—reflect an appeasement posture and accommodation of the left. If the initiatives don't pass this time around, or are vetoed, they'll be right back next year, as always, with an even heftier price tag. The American middle class can barely afford to care for elderly parents and send their own kids to decent schools at the same time, and maybe that's the goal here. The middle class is always hurt the most. A family of four making, say, $80,000- $100,000 a year today is no longer able to spend $20,000+ a year for 12 years on private schools for two children *and* support aging parents, mortgages, and other necessities. If Americans are going to have to support not only its own

B. K. Eakman

underclass, but the world's as well, socialism is imminent. Legislators supporting massive giveaways like SCHIP and global poverty programs—think House Speaker Nancy Pelosi, Senators Jay Rockefeller, Olympia Snowe and Ted Kennedy, with their millions in trust funds and "old money"—well, of course, they have no such worries.

Oh, yeah, we still see muddled remnants of traditional American ideals on the Fourth of July, Veterans' Day and Thanksgiving. But the precepts behind the flags and the fireworks are mostly in disrepute, kaput!

The last Republican standing in 2008 will be the one with inexhaustible charisma. Competence would be nice, too, but by 2008 that will be entirely secondary.

POSITION STATEMENT

I support an academic-based education for the Information Age and the Twenty-first Century, undiluted by psycho-behavioral conditioning and psychotherapeutic experimentation. I take issue with teaching methodologies whose primary purpose is to target the emotions rather than to challenge the intellect. My position is that parents, not the state, are typically in the best position to make educational (and other) decisions for their children. When parents are undermined by government agencies, including schools, a message is sent, intentionally or not, that parents are mere "breeders and feeders," and that their input is based in incompetence. This discourages parents from doing their job—precisely the opposite of what our leaders profess to support.

Statistics show that less than one percent of American school-age children have no responsible adult to care for them. The majority of American parents are neither abusive, nor negligent, nor irresponsible. Therefore, state and federal education policy should not proceed on the assumption that only "experts" can raise children.

I oppose the surreptitious use (by both government and special-interest agencies) of psychographic techniques to collect private and traceable information on children and their families for dissemination among non-secure data systems. Federal monies should not be used to fund "prevention" programs and curriculums that rely on psychological snooping under the cover of "mental health" and "socialization" activities. Teachers do not exist to strip away a parent's belief system from children in their classrooms, and to then transmit "new" values. Teachers who teach best are those who back up parental standards and support the uniquely American ideals articulated by the Founding Fathers.

I oppose the creation of non-cognitive curriculums aimed at altering personal and political beliefs, especially when these are passed off as substantive, cognitive learning programs. I reject the use of experimentation on minors without a parent's knowledge and written consent.

Leaders truly committed to reforming education need to begin with the kind of training prospective teachers are getting. Instead of being schooled in real learning diagnostics and remediation, they are immersed in psychobabble. Laws like No Child Left Behind may pretend to focus on the 3 R's, but if teachers do not know how to teach the 3 R's, then there is no sense in testing either reading, writing or arithmetic, even assuming that such tests are something other than psychological profiles.

If government is going to provide funding for education, it needs to be directed toward the university departments of teacher education, not local schools.

What needs to happen first is a complete revamping of teacher preparation, with incentives given to universities that agree to an overhaul. This means educators should have a teaching specialty and a minor in **one** of the following nine make-or-break learning elements, the building blocks of learning: spatial and abstract reasoning, visual identification, visual and auditory memory, perceptual speed, mental stamina, hand-eye coordination and thought-expression synchronization. Children's classrooms then should be reconfigured so that pupils are directed to the teacher *trained* to handle each child's weakest element in those nine make-or-break elements, not his strongest. These elements are not mere learning styles; they are the gateways to learning. We are presently approaching the task of learning exactly backwards.

If the United States, and especially Congress, really expects to reform education here in *America*, then our leaders are going to have to re-think the goals of "school" as a uniquely *American* institution instead of a United Nations construct and a multicultural or social enterprise. Educational priorities should be built around just three things:

- creating a literate citizenry, capable of self-government;
- ensuring financial independence for that free citizenry (because that helps ensure political stability); and
- bolstering moral standards that are consistent with the Founders' unique — and Judeo-Christian — concept of democracy (life, pursuit of happiness, property rights, and free speech).

This means focusing on those nine make-or-break elements cited above, because what we have now, at best, are "normed" tests that are so dumbed down (mostly to conform to UNESCO's concepts about fairness) that anyone can pass.

A second effort, on the part of legislators, would be to remove the red tape from starting a private school. Tuition is high because there are not enough private schools to satisfy the demand; the demand cannot be satisfied so long as bureaucratic red tape and unnecessary regulations complicate the process.

Finally, teaching methodology must focus on tried and true techniques, not fads. Experimental methods are for private, experimental classrooms that parents agree to and pay for. Experimental methods should not be thrust on an unsuspecting populace.

Moreover, I view parents as more than breeders and feeders, children as more than "human capital," and teachers as more than "facilitators of learning"—i.e., glorified entertainers. I feel that schools do youngsters and society a disservice by attempting to teach too much and undertaking too many functions. Schools need to concentrate on their proper academic and literacy functions, which entail quite enough in the way of resources, patience and expertise.

B. K. Eakman

FREQUENTLY ASKED QUESTIONS

1. Can you give a list of viable improvements that states or school districts could implement?

- Return academic soundness to education — i.e., classroom educators and school principals must demonstrate proficiency in a solid academic specialty and learning diagnostics, not merely a bunch of "education" (i.e., social work/psychology) courses.
- Fight all psychologized curriculums, through class action suits if necessary. To be legally viable, lawsuits must show a "pattern or practice" of using behavior modification and other therapeutic strategies (psychodrama, sociograms, etc.).
- Dissolve state education agencies or re-staff them with individuals who will place scholarship over politics and maintain their independence from any federal agency. States should introduce legislation that categorizes schools as captive settings, then move to ban psychographic instruments from educational institutions.
- Expose testing fraud — i.e., purported academic assessments which are 20% or more psychological.
- Protect parents' rights to direct the education and upbringing of their children — i.e., parents' wishes come first and cannot be bypassed by local educators.
- Re-affirm the individual's (student's) constitutional right to freedom of conscience — i.e., there cannot be a scoring mechanism that gives points for "preferred answers" to psychological (worldview-oriented) questions.
- Change the Individuals With Disabilities Education Act (IDEA) so that youngsters who continually disrupt the education process of other pupils can be expelled, not merely suspended.
- Phase out the hiring of school psychologists. Guidance counselors should be academic and career specialists.

- Work to encourage (i.e. remove red tape from) alternative school concepts that provide options for parents within a school district.

2.   Should the public support school vouchers and expulsion for chronic troublemakers?

Expulsion of chronically disruptive students currently involves incredible amounts of documentation, not to mention court costs, simply to get such students removed. Under a voucher system, even if public schools do manage to kick them out, these chronically disruptive pupils end up in private facilities. Parents who have enrolled their children in private settings from the start have generally paid big bucks to avoid the chaos and lax standards of the public school. Suddenly they will face the same mess they paid so much to avoid.

Vouchers, tuition tax credits, and charter schools: All these provide some stop-gap relief for _some_ children. But they don't stop the nation's declining knowledge base, because the flaws in our education system are systemic, especially in teacher preparation. They don't stop, for example, a culture of institutionalized child violence that has been produced due to a focus on psychobabble instead of true cognitive learning.

3.   Should every child have an equal opportunity to a first-rate education?

As things stand today, no, every child does not have that opportunity. One could even say that _no_ public school child has that opportunity, given the chaos and academic environment of today's public school.

Does every child have a "right" to a first-class education? No, again. Every child should have the _privilege_ of _access_ to a first-class education. A "right" in this instance implies something for nothing: a lack of responsibility on the part of the student.

4.   What are the major problems facing school districts?

A more concise appraisal of problems alluded to above are:
- Sincere educators (i.e., scholars) are working in deplorable conditions—an environment of drugs,

misbehavior and crime, with no disciplinary backup by principals and superintendents.

- Kids are permitted to disrespect teachers and the education process itself.
- Sports and sex are given precedence over academics, and schools try to mimic the entertainment industry in a mistaken belief that that will keep kids in school.
- Educators are too busy with paperwork and trivia to teach; they are not prepared to teach, but, rather, to perform social work.
- Teachers labor in a politically correct environment where conscience and principle are given short shrift; politically motivated, forced unionization further alienates the public and American values from the educating process.

5.   Just what beliefs are behaviorist educators trying to instill in today's youth?

The new belief system—i.e., beliefs/values/worldviews—are being modified to reflect the following (Thanks to a faxed handout from teachers in North Carolina who received this list during an in-service workshop in 1991):

- Consensus is more important than principle (thus today's courses in conflict resolution and social science);
- Amenability (i.e., likeability, popularity, being a "team player,") is more important than hard knowledge or expertise;
- Nothing is permanent except change (thus situation ethics courses);
- The collective is more important than the individual (i.e., group lessons instead of individual excellence and the emphasis on free-market socialism over true economic competition);
- There are no perpetrators, only victims (thus lack of personal accountability; it's nobody's fault); and
- Ethics are entirely situational, there are no moral absolutes (or something called "common sense").

6. What is "psychographics"?

Webster's *New World Communication and Media Dictionary* defines *psychographics* as "the study of social class based upon the demographics ... income, race, color, religion, and personality traits."   These are characteristics, says the dictionary, which "can be <u>measured</u> to predict behavior."

The psychological questions and self-reports with which schools today inundate pupils comprise a specialized area known in the world of advertising as "psychographic data-gathering." *Psychographics* is closely related to mass mental health screening, a highly controversial new initiative coming down the pike, as well as to "risk" analysis. Both are turning institutions of learning into a dangerous political weapon.

In schools, personal information is collected from children about themselves and their family, as part of standardized tests or "health" surveys — some of it, right on the covers. These instruments contain self-reports in a true-false format or else what-would-you-do-if,   and   how-do-you-feel-when   queries, usually in a multiple-choice or true-false format. There is a "preferred" answer, which would not typically be a parent-preferred response or a pro-American one, either. These questionnaires, taken together, comprise a concerted effort to snoop into a family's belief system, track the child versus the family's values, and if "necessary," to reconstruct entire curricular programs so that they will subtly indoctrinate pupils into adopting a different (usually socialist) set of values.

Tracking is usually accomplished *en masse* (as for a school district). However, the real "gotcha" here is that a particular student's responses are not anonymous, they are "confidential," which in legal terms means any individual child's responses can be located. It is possible, therefore, for children with a "non-preferred" opinion to be screened out of a university, a job, or any career path that might result in leadership or influence.

This is well on the way toward a police state in which "thoughts" are punished—perhaps not by shooting the victim, but by denying him (or her) status.

The shooting part usually comes a bit later, once the populace becomes accustomed to, and the cultural elite begins benefiting from, the new "rules."

7. Does the Protection of Pupil Rights Amendment (PPRA) apply to mass psychological screening and profiling instruments such as TeenScreen in the schools? Can parents make use of PPRA, or are there too many loopholes in the law for it to be effective?

The key wording in the PPRA legislation is the term "applicable programs." For purposes of the Act, this term is defined as follows: "The term 'applicable program' means any program for which the Secretary [of Education] (or the Department [of Education]) has administrative responsibility, as provided by law or by delegation of authority pursuant to law. The term includes each program for which the Secretary or the Department has administrative responsibility under the Department of Education Organization Act or under Federal law effective after the effective date of that Act." [20 U.S.C. § 1221].

The US Department of Education (DOEd) apparently believes that if it provides funding to a school district, it has administrative responsibility over the program, and therefore it is covered by the PPRA.

In theory, local schools do not get DOEd funding specifically earmarked for particular activities, but some funds *do* become part of their general funds. This could be interpreted to mean that the Department has administrative responsibility over almost any activity of a local school, including any survey it administers. Some DOEd funds *do* go to local schools—most notably in the case of the Educational Quality Assessment (EQA) in Pennsylvania in 1985, where funding for implementation purposes came via salaries when it was piloted in local schools. The EQA carried many psychological assessment questions, and curriculums were brought in to remediate specific viewpoints considered unsatisfactory, the EQA label being right on the covers of the curriculum guides. So, even though the federal funding was discreet, it clinched the case for applicability of PPRA.

In the end, did it matter? Did angry parents get satisfaction? No.

So, technically PPRA applies to any school district that receives federal funding. In practice, districts argue that because the program that resulted in the survey was not federally *administered*, they were not required to comply with the PPRA. Situations like this mean parents are spending money to hire attorneys who must then quibble over "what the definition of 'is' is," to borrow a page out of former President Bill Clinton's impeachment proceedings resulting from his sex scandal.

The position that a survey was not federally administered places the onus on parents to locate every scrap of trickle-down funding emanating from the Department of Education, when in fact many so-called prevention programs are the result of solicitations by the Department to, say, identify at-risk youth, or potentially suicidal or violent children. The winners of such solicitations are the recipients (awardees) of the funding solicitations—for example, a university or a behavioral institute or foundation. It is these awardees, then, who disseminate and administer the offending surveys.

So, are Department funds involved? Of course. But they are indirect, hard to find, and it is even harder to prove whether the local district made the decision *on its own* to adopt the survey, or whether the local district *was responding to* state or federal education *incentives* (i.e., money)—or even to a mandate from the federal government. If it was a mandate, then the district may have, in effect, been *forced* into adopting the survey. If it responded to incentives, then lawyers have to untangle the strands of federal-state dollars which may have gone to pay for *any part of* the screening program.

The only way to clear up precisely what the scope of the PPRA coverage is, probably lies in obtaining a ruling on what "applicable programs" means. But because the PPRA does not grant individuals a right to bring an action in court to enforce its provisions, it may be difficult to ever get such a ruling. To further complicate the issue, the New Freedom Initiative, recently having passed in Congress with a large appropriation for funding, will launch a universal screening mandate which comes from much higher up than the DOEd.

This may have a neutralizing effect on PPRA. Under the new Initiative, universal screening begins with schoolchildren, then their teachers and parents, with the intention to take it to every category of the population (e.g., seniors in nursing homes, pregnant women via the doctor's office, and so on until everyone is covered).

Up until the launching of the New Freedom Initiative, PPRA required at least *annual notice* to parents of the policies adopted by the school pursuant to the PPRA. That means surveys or data collection activities: The school was *supposed* to advise parents at the beginning of the school year of the anticipated approximate date on which such an activity was to take place. Providing notice to parents would not preclude the school from conducting a survey. In practice, "providing notice" generally means that schools give youngsters a slip for parents to sign a week or so before the date of the survey, which is hardly the beginning of the school year and, of course, most kids lose the slip and their parents never see it. Again, the onus is on parents to find out about the survey before it is given and to give consent in writing to the school. Without a mailing from the school district to parents, this clearly is not feasible—and schools know it.

The biggest loophole in PPRA is the lack of a penalty clause if they fail to give proper notice of an impending psychological/mental health survey. Without a penalty clause, PPRA is ineffective, as most parents simply cannot afford the time or the money to press their case. Certainly schools *could* advise parents concerning covered activities—especially in classes prone to such surveys (health, sex education, social studies), but inasmuch as there is no clear indication in the Act that schools may *not* give a survey if it is *not* included in a beginning-of-the-year notice, then for practical purposes, PPRA is not viable.

Another glitch in the writing of PPRA is that there is no statutory definition of the term "notification." Most people *assume* that "notification" means written communication, addressed directly to the parent. PPRA requires that "unemancipated" students not be subjected to surveys "without the prior written consent of the parent," which further lends credibility to this notion. But the provision only *hints*, it does not *state categorically*, that passive consent is not enough. So what has emerged is a system whereby parents are deemed to consent if they do *not* **object**, and this certainly does not fulfill any intent the writers of PPRA may have had to protect parents.

Moreover, the entire issue is so fraught with technicalities and legal sleights of hand (e.g., try sorting out terms like "emancipated" and "unemancipated student"!), that it is nearly impossible for any individual parent to exercise oversight without the help of a qualified attorney, which translates into big bucks. Even if, when things go wrong, a group of parents enlist the help of a like-minded organization to help foot the bill, the case may take years, by which time the pupils have graduated. Also many parents fear, and rightly so, the intimidation of their child by the school, or negative comments about their child placed in the student's electronic (not paper) folder, to be transmitted to an institution of higher learning or to a potential employer at a later date without the parent's or child's knowledge.

But good news may be in the offing. In June 2007 the Parental Consent Act of 2007 (H.R. 2387) was launched in the U.S. House of Representatives. It supports parents against government sponsored and pharmaceutical industry supported universal mental health screening programs.

H.R. 2387 states:

No Federal funds may be used to establish or implement any universal or mandatory mental health, psychiatric, or socio-emotional screening program.

Parental refusal to provide consent to mental health screening for his or her child shall not be used as the basis of a charge of child abuse, child neglect, medical neglect, or education neglect.

If this bill makes it through the House and the Senate, it will protect children from invasive screening that is based on the kinds of vague, subjective, and politically biased criteria which so often results in dubious diagnoses and permanently stigmatizing labels. It will put the brakes on the current trend to drug children with ineffective and potentially lethal medications and bring back some semblance of parental control to the education process. Parents and other taxpayers need to **insist** that a bill like this passes, and be on the lookout for any attempt to water it down—meaning that there absolutely **must** be penalties for noncompliance, should the measure become law.

And there's more good news:

You may have read in July 2007 about the 30-year-old man, Stephen Dunne, who has launched a $9.75 million lawsuit against the Massachusetts Board of Bar Examiners and the Massachusetts Supreme Judicial Court for demanding that students answer, as part of the bar exam, a question about same-sex "marriage." According to news reports, he is claiming that his refusal to respond to the question (because it targeted his religious beliefs and served to legitimize both same-sex parenting and "marriage") caused him to fail the exam, with a score just shy of the required passing grade of 270. He alleged the state government was "purposely advancing" a political agenda.

I have been alleging the same thing about K-12 assessments in educational institutions since 1990—and so have many high-profile organizations. If we all play our cards right, the Dunne lawsuit in Massachusetts represents one the best opportunities I have seen to put the legal brakes on school tests that snoop for political ideologies under the cover of academics. Whichever side wins the case, there will inevitably be an appeal, which means the decision could be precedent-setting at the highest level.

The problem with K-12 "assessment" testing under the cover of academics has always been that:

- To successfully win a case, a parent has to prove "compensable harm," not merely violation of student or parental rights;

- The long time-frame involved in pursuing a case means that a child graduates before the case comes to court or a settlement is reached;

- Individual parents generally have no idea how to proceed, and attorney fees quickly overwhelm them;

- The burden of proof of funding mechanisms always falls to the complainant, and parents end up having to also prove that corrective ("behavioral modification" and "prevention") curricula are being brought in to remediate non-preferred responses (i.e., opinions);

- The burden of proof regarding *individually identifiable* test answers requires a knowledge of surreptitious coding systems on K-12 tests, which requires "discovery" on the part of attorneys, thereby further lengthening the process; and

- Justifiable fears on the part of parents that their child will suffer if they take legal action.

The Dunne lawsuit may just be the "wedge" opening people struggling with PPRA have been waiting for, because it circumvents most, or all, of the problems listed above. A precedent-setting victory on this case would be a Godsend. Mr.

Dunne is representing himself in the case, and while he knows the legal ropes, he is going to need all the help he can get. *We cannot delude ourselves that the various entities funding and creating K-12 assessments, or advocating them, will not recognize the stakes and take action for the State.*

Hopefully, many attorneys will **submit an amicus brief** in the Dunne lawsuit in Massachusetts and get behind this brave fellow, especially in the event it goes on to a higher court, which no doubt it will.

B. K. Eakman

About the author...

Beverly Eakman is an Educator, 9 years: 1968-1974, 1979-1981. Specialties: English and Literature.

Science Editor, Technical Writer, and Editor-in-Chief of the official newspaper of the National Aeronautics and Space Administration's Johnson Space Center, 1976-1979. The technical piece entitled "David, the Bubble Baby" was picked up by the popular press and turned into a movie starring John Travolta.

Chief speech writer, National Council for Better Education, 1984-1986; for the late Chief Justice Warren E. Burger, Commission on the Bicentennial of the US Constitution, 1986-1987; for the Voice of America Director, 1987-1989; and for U.S. Department of Justice, Gerald R. Regier, Director of the Bureau of Justice Assistance, 1991-1993.

Author: 3 books on education and data-trafficking since 1991, including the internationally acclaimed Cloning of the American Mind: Eradicating Morality Through Education. Executive Director, National Education Consortium.

Website: BeverlyE.com
To schedule media interviews
E-Mail: bkeakman@gmail.com

Also by B. K. Eakman

Cloning of the American Mind:
Eradicating Morality Through Education,
Huntington House Publishers

Educating for the New World Order

Microchipped: How the Education
Establishment Took Us Beyond Big Brother
Halcyon House Publishers

How To Counter Group Manipulation Tactics
(Seminar Workbook)
www.lulu.com/midnightwhistler

Except for "How To Counter Group Manipulation Tactics,"
the above books can also be ordered through
Amazon, at Barnes & Noble online bookstores,
as well as by special order at most specialty bookstores.

COMING SOON:
FREEDOM'S FAÇADE:
Professional Agitation for the 21st Century,
the advanced-level, sequel to "How To Counter Group
Manipulation Tactics," divided into issue-specific chapter
(such as religion, elections, education, etc.)